TARDIS Eruditorum:
An Unauthorized Critical
History of Doctor Who
Volume 2: Patrick Troughton

D1565887

Elizabeth Sandifer

ERUDITORUM

P R E S S

ISBN-13: 978-1725513051
ISBN-10: 1725513056

To Anna Wiggins, my dear friend and first fan. Since I gave you no warning I was dedicating a book to you, I imagine that you are blushing a lot while you read this.

TARDIS Eruditorum Volume 2: Patrick Troughton

Acknowledgements

Like a bad analogy, it takes a number of people to make a book happen. This book would not exist were it not for the hard work of my editor, Millie Hadziomerovic. Any words that are spelled correctly are down to her extensive work. The errors, on the other hand, are all me. Thanks are also due to James Taylor for his cover design. Those who are holding paper copies will be reassured to know that there will be a second edition of the Hartnell volume with his art as soon as the found episode of *Galaxy Four* comes out. While we're being thankful, let's also thank Jean Jannon, the sixteenth century printer whose work became the modern font Garamond, in which this book is typeset. But that's just me having a crush on a font.

More broadly, this book is a print collection of a blog of modest success. Its success comes from a fantastic community of readers whose lively discussions of my posts have motivated me through more than one day of not wanting to find another five hundred words to say about a given story. The Troughton era was where that community really started to form, and where I began to reliably get comments on every entry. I look back on many of the entries in this book with delighted fondness.

TARDIS Eruditorum Volume 2: Patrick Troughton

Table of Contents

TARDIS Eruditorum Volume 2: Patrick Troughton

A Madwoman with a Blog (Introduction)

Why hello there! It looks like you bought a copy of the second volume of *TARDIS Eruditorum*, which I, as the writer, thank you for, because that probably means you have given me money. (If you haven't given me money and downloaded this off the Internet, on the other hand, I'm kind of upset with you. Seriously, 80% of this book is already up for free on the web and you're stealing it? I'm an underemployed PhD in English. That was my Ramen money you pirated! On the other hand, I'm kind of pleased to be important enough to pirate. So that's cool. Oh, all right. I forgive you. Just buy the next volume, OK?)

In the event you have no idea what book you're holding, let me explain to you, generally speaking, how this book works. First of all, here's what it isn't: a standard issue guidebook to Doctor Who. Those looking for the nitty gritty facts of Doctor Who can probably get a decent sense of them by inference, but that's not what this book is for. There are no episode descriptions, cast lists, or lengthy discussions of the behind the scenes workings of the show. There are dozens of books that already do that, and a fair number of online sites. Nor is this a book of reviews. For those who want those things, I personally recommend the *Doctor Who Reference Guide*, *Doctor Who Ratings Guide*, and *A Brief History of Time (Travel)* – three superlative websites that were consulted for basically every one of these essays.

What this book *is* is an attempt to tell the story of Doctor Who. Not the story of how it was made, or the overall narrative of the Doctor's life, or anything like that, but the story of the idea that is Doctor Who, in this book from Patrick Troughton's arrival in 1966 to his departure in 1969, but there's more to come. Doctor Who is a rarity in the world – an extremely long-running serialized narrative. Even rarer, it's an extremely long-running serialized narrative that is not in a niche like soap operas or superhero comics – both provinces almost exclusively of die-hard fans. Doctor Who certainly has its die-hard fans (or, as I like to think of you, my target audience), but notably, it's also been, for much of its existence, absolutely mainstream family entertainment for an entire country.

What this means is that the story of Doctor Who is, in one sense, the story of the world from 1963 on. Politics, music, technological and social development, and all manner of other things have crossed paths with Doctor Who over the nearly fifty years of its existence, and by using Doctor Who as a focus, one can tell a story with far wider implications.

The approach I use to do this is one that I've, rather pompously I suppose, dubbed psychochronography. It draws its name from the concept of psychogeography – an artistic movement created by Guy Debord in 1955 and described as "the study of the precise laws and specific effects of the geographical environment, consciously organized or not, on the emotions and behavior of individuals." More contemporarily, the term is associated with writers like Iain Sinclair, who writes books describing lengthy walking tours of London that fuse his experience with the history of the places he walks, weaving them into a narrative that tries to tell the entire story of a place, and Alan Moore, who does the same thing while worshiping a snake.

Psychochronography, then, attempts the same feat by walking through time. Where walking through space involves little more than picking a direction and moving your feet rhythmically, walking through time without the aid of a TARDIS is a dodgier proposition. The easiest way is to take a specific object and trace its development through time, looking, as the psychogeographers do, at history, lived experience, and the odd connections that spring up.

And so this book is the first part of a walk through Doctor Who. The essays within it wear a lot of hats, and switch them rapidly. All involve a measure of critical reading (in the literary theory sense, not in the complaining sense) of Doctor Who stories to figure out what they are about. This generally means trying to peel back the onion skins of fan history that cloud a story with things "everybody knows." But it also involves looking at the legacy of stories, which often means looking at that onion skin and trying to explain how it got there. No effort is made to disguise the fact that the first appearance of the Time Lords is massive for instance, but on the other hand, the book still looks carefully at what their initial impact might have been.

This approach also means looking at how a story would (and could) have been understood by a savvy viewer of the time, and at how the story can be read as responding to the concerns of its time. That means that the essays tend to be long on cultural context. And, in the end, it also means looking at how I personally interact with these stories. This book has no pretense of objectivity. It is about my walking tour of Doctor Who. I try to be accurate, but I also try to be me.

To fully grab the scope of the topic, in addition to the meat of the book – entries covering all of the Doctor Who stories produced with Patrick Troughton as the lead actor – there are four other types of entries. The first are the "Time Can Be Rewritten" entries. One peculiar feature of Doctor Who is that its past is continually revisited. The bulk of these came in the form of novels written in the 90s and early 00s, but there are other examples. At the time of writing, for instance, Big Finish puts out new stories every year featuring the first eight Doctors. These entries cover occasional highlights from these revisitations, using them as clues to how these earlier eras are widely understood.

The second are the "Pop Between Realities, Home in Time for Tea" entries, which look at popular media and culture to build context for understanding Doctor Who. These entries usually crop up prior to the bits of Doctor Who they're most relevant for, and provide background and points of comparison for the show as it wrestles with the issues of its many times.

Third, there are the "You Were Expecting Someone Else" entries, which deal with spinoff material produced concurrently with Doctor Who but that, inevitably, has some significant differences from the approach of the televised material. These exist to give a broader sense of Doctor Who as a cultural object and, perhaps more importantly, because they're kind of fun.

Finally, there are some essays just thrown into the book version as bonuses. These mostly consist of me slogging my way through some established fan debate about Doctor Who and trying, no doubt fruitlessly, to provide the last word on the matter.

It's probably clear by this point that all of these entries began as blog entries on my blog, also called TARDIS Eruditorum. This book version, however, revises and expands every entry, as well as adding several new ones – mostly Time Can Be Rewritten entries, but a few others.

To this end, I should thank the many readers of the blog for their gratifying and edifying comments, which have kept the project going through more than one frustrating stretch. I should also thank the giants upon whose shoulders I stand when analyzing Doctor Who – most obviously Paul Cornell, Martin Day, and Keith Topping for *The Discontinuity Guide*, David J. Howe, Mark Stammers, and Steven James Walker for the Doctor handbooks, Toby Hadoke and Rob Shearman for *Running Through Corridors*, and Lawrence Miles and Tat Wood for the sublimely brilliant *About Time* series, to which this book is a proud footnote. I'd also like to thank my tireless editor, Millie Hadziomerovic, who made this book better.

A final note – although I have expanded and revised the essays in this book from their original online versions, I have not attempted to smooth out the developing style of the entries. Much like the show it follows, this project has evolved and grown since its beginning, and I did not wish to alter that.

But most of all and most importantly, thank you, all of you.

But most of all, thank you, dear reader. I hope you enjoy.

Pop Between Realities, Home in Time for Tea: *Batman,
Adam Adamant Lives!, The Avengers*

If you want to understand 1966 in Great Britain, it is possible that no fact is more immediately relevant than the fact that on Saturdays in 1966, at around 5:15 PM, the latter episodes of Season Three of Doctor Who were airing opposite imports of the 1966 Adam West *Batman* series. (If this does not sufficiently unsettle you, I highly recommend firing up, say, Part Four of *The Celestial Toymaker* or a random bit of *The Ark* and watching it back to back with a Season One episode of *Batman.*)What is unsettling about this is that, with only three channels in existence at the time, ITV viewed *Batman* as the natural competitor to Doctor Who in that media environment. Because other than being adventure stories there's not a lot of obvious similarities. And even that's a fairly new similarity. Up to this point, one of the major characteristics of Doctor Who has been the essential joke of the TARDIS crew being the completely wrong people for this sort of story. In its original form, this is clearest—two schoolteachers, a teenager, and an old Victorian inventor walk into an alien planet. But notably, that motley wasn't put together to appeal to a single "young boys" demographic of the sort normally associated with sci-fi adventure stories. This stock character arrangement belongs to an older view of science fiction as a serious genre with a broad audience as opposed to as a subset of adolescent action serials. It's really not until the third season, in which the dual roles of Barbara and the young female companion were collapsed into one role, that the show went from being about a bunch of people in terrifying circumstances to being about the adventures of a bunch of boys and their girl sidekick.

Even through Season Three and the start of Season Four there was still the Doctor, who was by and large the antithesis of a proper action hero. The whole concept still hinged on the incongruity of the old Victorian inventor and these harshly modern (and increasingly postmodern) settings. As far as the rest of the crew goes, there's nothing too unusual about Ben and Polly as action heroes. Unlike Ian (essentially a middle aged ex-soldier) and Barbara (the charmingly mumsy type) they are attractive young people of the sort who seem to belong in an action serial. But the heart of the show—the main character—was still a conscious and deliberate contrast with what the show had him face. He was a cantankerous old man, not a fun action hero.

In terms of everything we talked about in the first volume of the series, this was a huge contrast with *Batman*. Every element of *Batman* was keyed towards the goal of frenetic and over the top action. Whereas thus far in Doctor Who, the goal has been to explicitly contrast its action/adventure elements with the fact that the protagonist is completely the wrong character for this sort of thing.

It's important to highlight this, because it's the one thing that really separates Doctor Who from all the other action/adventure shows going on at the time. Doctor Who is about the gulf between its concepts and the juxtapositions created by them. Compare that to *Batman*. Even in the most sympathetic readings of *Batman*, where we accept that everyone involved understood that the show was ridiculous, it's hard to be that sympathetic to the show. To grab a random example from the series, there is a plotline in which the Joker uses a van equipped with mirrors on the outside (which can cause it to appear invisible) to kidnap the Maharajah of Nimpah who is actually just the Joker as part of a larger scheme to humiliate Batman into endorsing a ransom check ...

Yes, plotlines of this sort are completely mental and over the top. And this is something we're going to see a lot of in

Doctor Who when, for instance, we get mad scientists trying to drain the ocean, robotic Yeti in the London Underground, or, to start on the other end of the series, the Doctor and Richard Nixon teaming up to fight the Greys. But in *Batman*, the knowing nods about how ridiculous it all is are all there is. The central idea of *Batman*—really its only idea—is to dance around the screen shouting, "Look at me, I'm absolutely ridiculous!" There's something painfully sterile about the entire affair. Whereas the central idea of Doctor Who has always been to put the ridiculous and the everyday on the same screen and have them both steadfastly refuse to acknowledge that the other doesn't belong.

All the same, it's hard to get around the sense that *Batman* just looks cooler. Some of that is a matter of presentation—nowadays we view *Batman* in color, but in 1966 on ITV, it would have been transmitted in the same fuzzy black-and-white as Doctor Who. But for all its facileness, *Batman* is trying to have more fun than Doctor Who is. There's a giddy joy to it that Doctor Who's comparative seriousness has never matched. Even when Doctor Who is in its comic mode (as in *The Romans*) it doesn't have the sort of infectious mania displayed by *Batman*.

One might be tempted to use this as an argument for why Doctor Who made for better action-adventure television than *Batman*. But it's not as though manic fun is in some way hostile to action-adventure television. For proof of that, even ignoring Doctor Who's own future, we can pop over to *Adam Adamant Lives!*, aka "Oh Hey, It's That Verity Lambert Gal Again." Which is to say that while *Adam Adamant Lives!* is notable for a couple of things, including being the source of Adam Ant's name and the most obvious inspiration for Austin Powers ever, one of the things it is most notable for is being the project Verity Lambert and Sydney Newman turned their attention to after Doctor Who. (The show also had Donald Cotton, whom you may remember from one or two past Doctor Who stories.)

Adam Adamant Lives! differed from *Batman* in several key ways, in that it was British, intelligent, and largely a flop. This is in many ways a pity, as it's actually quite good. Its premise is that a classic Victorian adventurer (Gerald Harper) (originally to have been Sexton Blake before everyone remembered about that pesky copyright thing) is frozen and thawed out in 1966 in a plotline that was in no way stolen from Marvel Comics' *The Avengers*. (Look, they respected copyright on *Sexton Blake*, surely you don't expect them to have original ideas twice in a row.) In other words, he gets the obligatory "swinging '60s blonde" female sidekick, and, much as you'd expect, they fight crime.

The show is imperfect, to say the least, suffering somewhat badly from its inability to reconcile the ambitions of its premise with its underlying mandate to provide a generic adventure serial. Harper, its leading actor, did an odd job with the part. Not necessarily a bad job, but he played the part with an impassioned straight-lacedness that was markedly (and willfully) out of place in the larger series. The result on the one hand captures the man-out-of-time feeling perfectly, and on the other hand is at times stultifyingly dull. When, on occasion, he gets a scene with someone who can play off of his demeanor (the episode I watched opened with a lovely scene with an actor named Patrick Troughton, who actually looks a bit like that horrid man who stole the Doctor's face at the end of *The Tenth Planet*) this works. More often, it either makes the show feel wooden or makes it look like everyone was scrambling around desperately to find a show that could actually match up with Harper's acting. (In the end, Sydney Newman ordered Harper to change how he played the part. Harper refused, and Newman cancelled the show.)

On the other hand, when he was on his game, Harper provided a genuinely magnetic leading man performance, often holding the entire show together with little more than charisma and some eye boggling. (Eye boggling turns out to be a fairly fundamental job skill in the world of action-adventure television. See also Tom Baker under Graham Williams.) This gets at one of the key features of this genre which is preserved to the present day in shows like *Bones*, *House*, or *Castle*— charismatic, funny leads. This is another area where *Batman* ultimately falls flat. Short of the endlessly entertaining drinking game of seeing how many times Burt Ward delivers a line in a tone that would not need to be altered at all—if he were seething with rage and plotting Adam West's demise—Robin is generally played totally flat. Because he is seemingly unaware of the absurdity of his world, the audience has no foothold from which to laugh with the show. (Adam West is better at this, but generally prefers to play the joke with a complete straightness that is endearing in a sort of Brechtian sense if, nevertheless, questionable.)

Again, comparing to *Adam Adamant Lives!* is instructive. One thing Harper was unquestionably brilliant at in the show was using the wry smiles of his dandy character to provide an extra-diegetic meta-commentary on the absurdity of the situation. Or, to strip that of literary theory, Harper gives wry smiles that are on one level indicative of something Adam Adamant is actually doing in the story, and on another level commentaries on the story from Harper as an actor (which takes them from diegetic to extra-diegetic—that is, they go beyond merely being diegetic). The impact of this is massive— with one simple piece of gestural acting, Harper adds reams of intelligence to the show because we are suddenly left to constantly navigate the differing narrative levels and genres of the story instead of just getting to take them for granted à la *Batman*.

But for all of Harper's charisma, *Adam Adamant Lives!* fails to hold a candle in the pure charm department to its most obvious influence, Sydney Newman's hit creation for ITV before he headed over to the BBC and made Doctor Who, *The Avengers*. I could have put an entry on *The Avengers* at any point in *TARDIS Eruditorum*, as it predates the show by nearly three years, but the fact of the matter is, when people talk about *The Avengers*, most of the time they're talking about Seasons Four and Five, and most specifically Season Five, which was produced in color and was the version that was actually a hit on US television as well. Series Four and Five, you see, are the Emma Peel years.

It may be necessary to define some key concepts here for those who are not intimately acquainted with the particulars of classic British television of the 1960s. Specifically, and it really is very important that you understand this, Emma Peel is quite literally the sexiest character ever to be put on a television screen. She is the physical embodiment of the ruthlessly classy sex symbol. Indeed, it is a little known fact that when homosexuality was finally legalized in Great Britain, the compromise was that it was legal to be gay just as long as you made an exception for Emma Peel. (Given that Emma Peel gives Lady Gaga a run for her money in the "obviously designed to be a gay icon" sweepstakes, this was not generally taken as an arduous requirement.)

If, for some reason, you are a horribly deluded person that does not recognize the transcendent eroticism of the character the moment you see Diana Rigg in character, well, shame on you. But even that doesn't matter, because it is transparently clear watching *The Avengers* that the show is absolutely convinced of the character's sexiness, and that this truth is held to be more fundamental than piddly details of the universe (such as gravity). Lest you think that I might be overselling the case slightly, I highly recommend sitting down with an episode of *The Avengers*. Because the debt that every other show with a charming double act as its lead characters owes to *The Avengers* cannot possibly be overstated.

As a premise, *The Avengers* is possibly the flabbiest thing we have yet talked about on the blog. Its premise, and I hope you're hanging on tight, is that there's a guy named John Steed, who wears a bowler hat and is very dapper, and he teams up with a woman named Emma Peel, who wears sexy '60s fashions. And they fight crime. That's basically the whole of it. The show is the high-water mark of the subgenre known as spy-fi, in which light espionage and science fiction plotlines are melded to create episodes in which Steed and Peel defend an unending litany of civil servants from various outlandish and poorly explained technological menaces.

That, at least, describes the plot. Watch the opening credits, however, and you'll get a much clearer sense of what the show is about, namely the chemistry between Steed and Peel. Everything else is, at times explicitly, the frame upon which lightly flirtatious banter between a dapper Victorian and a sexy mod is hung. (Watching *The Avengers* for the plot requires a catastrophic lack of active brain cells.) However the show remains delightful because the fact of the matter is, Steed and Peel are absolutely brilliant to watch together. (A particular highlight is the episode "Who's Who," in which they get body-swapped with some thoroughly uninteresting Eastern European agents. The scenes of Patricia Hanes and Freddie Jones trying to emulate the chemistry of Diana Rigg and Patrick Macnee are frankly excruciating, but on the other hand, the scenes where Rigg and Macnee get to let loose and be villains who make out with each other frequently are every bit as wonderful as you would hope. In practice, the entire episode exists to put those scenes in, and everything else is just tiresome plot.)

So why go over all of this, particularly instead of talking about the ostensible topic of the book? Because in practice, one of the things that the Hartnell-Troughton transition was about was getting rid of Hartnell, who never played the part with magnetic charisma (and who by this point was having enough trouble getting through his lines, little yet infusing them with charm) and replacing him with a more charismatic actor. This coincided, admittedly, with a shift towards more straightforward adventure yarns, which we'll talk about as we go. Because, yes—Doctor Who starts being more about monsters, more about action, and more about flashy visual set pieces à la *Batman*. (Though honestly, given that nothing in all three seasons of *Batman* save for Cesar Romano's painted-white mustache comes anywhere close to the barmy spectacle of *The Web Planet*, the degree to which this marks an actual shift in the show is ambiguous.)

All the same, there's a clear attempt to make the Doctor more likable with Troughton. This does not involve going all the way towards the charismatic double act—it's not until the Jon Pertwee/Katy Manning team arrives in 1971 that Doctor Who goes for the full-on Steed/Peel dynamic. Troughton's Doctor instead represents a strange midpoint, combining the overt charisma of the leading men in other action-adventure shows of the time with the unsettling otherness that permeated the Hartnell era. But on the other hand, the shift towards trying to compete directly with *Batman* (which was seen as one of the main reasons for the show's rapidly declining ratings) is clearly a motivating factor in the development of Troughton's character and an almost necessary starting point for any discussion of the show in this era.

An Unknown Power (*The Power of the Daleks*)

It's November 5, 1966. The Four Tops are at number one with "Reach Out I'll Be There." In two weeks, The Beach Boys will take it with "Good Vibrations," and two weeks later it'll be Tom Jones with "Green Green Grass of Home." Lower in the charts are Herman's Hermits, The Troggs, and Bobby Darin.

Meanwhile, in the news, the Rhodesia situation goes worse and worse as thirty-eight African countries issue a demand that the UK use force in resolving it. John Lennon meets Yoko Ono and, along with the rest of his bandmates, begins recording *Sgt. Pepper's Lonely Hearts Club Band* (given that the Troughton era coincides sharply with the psychedelic/Summer of Love culture that this album is emblematic of, this coincidence of their beginnings is deeply apropos). Barbados declares independence from the UK, Ronald Reagan is elected governor of California, and the Binh Hoa Massacre is perpetuated in the rapidly heating up Vietnam War by South Korea, which is, of course, on the same side as the US. Four hundred and thirty unarmed civilians, mostly women, children, and the elderly, are killed.

While on television …

Sometimes Doctor Who is magical. I mean this on several levels, but one of them—and a significant one—is that the show is a clear formative influence on the sci-fi/fantasy culture that will eventually produce writers like Neil Gaiman, Grant Morrison, and, most important for the general philosophical leanings of this project, Alan Moore. As with most of the future, we'll get there in time. For now, the only thing you really need to know is that it's hardly unusual for the show to have something of a spiritual dimension. It reared its head in *The Tenth Planet*, and, as we'll see throughout this volume, it's particularly likely to show up whenever the name David Whitaker is attached to the program.

I mention this because, as *The Power of the Daleks* spins up, it's essential to understanding the only thing that's on anybody's mind—what the heck just happened to the Doctor. Again, this is something that's easy to forget in hindsight; the show has had eight post-regeneration stories in total. We know how these work. But *The Power of the Daleks* isn't written for us. It's written for an audience that has never seen the Doctor regenerate—an audience that has no idea what's going on. And it establishes all of this for the first time. There are no precedents and no basic format for this. It isn't "a regeneration story,"; it's the regeneration story—the first story about what happens when the Doctor changes who he is. Every other story about this topic—arguably everything about the series from now on—is a reaction to this complete re-conceptualization of the show's central character.

Which makes it infuriating that it's so hard to pin down what happens during this transition. The deliberately minimalist exposition of this story and the absence of *The Tenth Planet* Part Four (which begins the second-longest stretch of missing episodes in the series) conspire to make this a maddening thing to piece together. To be perfectly honest, anyone for whom *The Power of the Daleks* Part One is not the episode they'd most like to see recovered is a damn fool. So in the absence of the episode we have to go to the behind the scenes and look at what the people making this thought was going on. For me, the choice quote from Gerry Davis and Innes Lloyd's notes on what they call a "metaphysical change" is this: "It is as if he has had the LSD drug and instead of experiencing the kicks, he has the hell and dank horror which can be its effect."

What does this mean? I probably should have tossed Timothy Leary in back when we did our roundup of 1966 counterculture in Volume One, but suffice it to say that talking about LSD and metaphysical changes ties right in with the existing discussions of spiritual journeys that we've already had. But what, specifically, does the reference LSD evoke (given that it is far from the only psychedelic substance)? Well, let's crack open our Timothy Leary—specifically *The Psychedelic Experience*—and look at his incantations to be used in case of massive acid trip:

That which is called ego-death is coming to you. Remember: this is now the hour of death and rebirth; take advantage of this temporary death to obtain the perfect state— Enlightenment.

So that's kind of familiar.

The other thing we need to take notice of is that this is a David Whitaker story, albeit one with Dennis Spooner doing an uncredited rewrite. Here I'm mostly just summarizing Wood and Miles in *About Time* (primarily Wood in this case, it seems), but it's worth noting. Wood and Miles make an extended argument that Whitaker's writing has a ton of themes from alchemy and classic occultist sources. They demure on the extent of Whitaker's knowledge of these themes, but make a compelling case that they're there. I'll go a bit further— Whitaker said in interviews that "the lure of alchemy" was one of his favorite themes. So reading a sense of metaphysical weight and import into a David Whitaker story is hardly a massive leap. It's been a theme lurking about in his stories throughout Volume One, but in the Troughton era it becomes impossible to look at Whitaker's work, particularly in his two Dalek stories, without that lens playing in.

To recap, in this story we have the Doctor engaging in some sort of metaphysical change brought about by exposure to the rampaging energy of Mondas, which we recognize as a dark mirror of Earth and thus a daemonic power, though not necessarily one that does not lead to enlightenment. (Remember, the Cybermen themselves took a spiritual journey—they just became horrifying monsters as a result of it. But this is the big theme of Grant's Work, and even to a lesser extent Leary's—that the unenlightened are not qualified to judge the enlightened. The Cybermen are horrifying because they are enlightened and we are not.) The tension is simple to start—who is this man who replaced the Doctor? Is he still the Doctor? Is he still a good guy? Or has he been corrupted by Mondas? (And, more distantly, but still utterly present given the opening credits, what are the Daleks doing amidst all of this?)

In practical terms, however, coming right off of a story about existential body horror and daemonic shadows of humanity, we get Ben and Polly bickering. It's worth noting that we've seen Ben and Polly enough now to know how this works. When Ben and Polly disagree, Polly is right and Ben is wrong. In particular, think back to *The Smugglers*, where Ben systematically rubbishes every single premise of the series for comedic purposes while Polly provides the more moderate and credulous perspective. It's a subtle thing, but the fact that Polly believes this strange man to be the Doctor and Ben doesn't is actually a major reassurance that, in fact, he is. The show is still going to have to prove it to us, but we know, from the outset, where this is going.

On the other hand, the road to that proof is, to say the least, a bit rocky. The Doctor awakens from his change screaming, and seems exhausted and relieved to see that it's over. But noticeably, the first thing we see from this new Doctor is weakness—he screams, gurns, flails about, and when he finally laughs, saying that it's over, there is something deeply unsettling about it. It is not a happy laugh but a crazed one. The sense is that the Doctor is shrunken—diminished. (One thing that is not remarked upon nearly enough in reading the regeneration sequence is that Troughton's outfit was intended as a "degraded" version of Hartnell's. The character quite literally looks as though he has fallen apart.)

On the other hand, we do quickly get a reassurance that this is the Doctor. Ben accepts before long that this is the Doctor changed—though he wonders what's changed besides his face—and when Troughton looks in a mirror we see a last flash of Hartnell looking back at him. But this is contrasted with Troughton referring to the Doctor in the third person, and mercurially flitting about before starting to play his recorder madly and obsessively. The episode veers constantly between reassuring the audience that they are in the same show and alarming them with the degree to which the rules have been thrown out of the window.

So what we are left with when the Doctor sallies forth from the TARDIS towards the promised Daleks? Surprisingly little that is sensible. There is someone that might be the Doctor. But he acts wrongly, and seems shrunken and ill-suited to the task. And once he gets to the main action on the Vulcan colony, things get worse—he continues to sulk and play the recorder instead of answering fairly straightforward questions about what happened to him and what's going on. This isn't just a refusal to step into the proper role of the Doctor as investigator; it's a refusal to play with the audience. The Doctor's questions are supposed to be what advances the plot, and Troughton's Doctor flatly refuses to ask them, actively stalling the plot.

Further, when the Doctor finds the Dalek ship, he seems positively giddy, singing "extermination" in an almost taunting voice and actively soliciting the colony to open it despite the fact that he knows full well what's inside. All of this is unsettling. We've been given enough assurance that this man is now the Doctor. But by establishing that, the story brings something bigger into doubt. We know this is the Doctor. What we don't know anymore is who the Doctor is. And we certainly don't know if he's up to the task in front of him.

And in the second episode, at least, he isn't. He seems out of his depth, scared by one or two Daleks when he's previously faced armies of them. He keeps implying that Hartnell's Doctor is the real Doctor, and that he is just a poor impostor. Until finally we get what is, frankly, the key scene of the entire six-parter. The Doctor and Lesterton face off, and Lesterton unveils the Daleks. One glides past the Doctor and turns to look at him, clearly recognizing him and acknowledging who he is. This, finally, nearly two episodes into Troughton's tenure, is the firmest assurance we have that the Doctor is the Doctor, and that he is a hero. He must be: the Daleks fear him. It's a single visual moment that packs everything that the later "Oncoming Storm" image reaches for, and while "the Oncoming Storm" may be a better catchphrase, Whitaker's image surpasses it in raw and chilling power.

And then the Daleks win. They get everybody on the colony to turn against the Doctor, shouting him down with their repeated cries of "I AM YOUR SERVANT" as he insists, louder and more pointlessly, that they are evil terrors. And this sets up what *The Power of the Daleks* is actually about. The Doctor, having confronted the ultimate cosmic darkness in Mondas and having engaged in a terrifying metaphysical battle with it, has to rebuild who he is in light of that revelation. He has to make his return to Earth and turn his enlightenment into a material being. And he has to do it in time to stop the Daleks, threats that can call into question the very nature of who he is and how heroic he is.

To be clear, this is not a narrative collapse story. This is something altogether stranger—a story in which the narrative has already collapsed by the time the Doctor enters it. The moment at which the Dalek recognizes the Doctor is also the point where it's already far too late for the Doctor to stop the Daleks. The Doctor has been reduced to nothing and has to rebuild his entire character, and the Daleks, the usual engines of narrative collapse, have already taken over the story. This isn't about the Doctor trying to maintain the integrity of what a Doctor Who story is against an onslaught of Daleks. It's a story about the Doctor trying to create a Doctor Who story in a story where the Daleks have already won.

And so it's striking that in the third episode all of the uncertainty over whether Troughton is the Doctor is gone. Instead, the uncertainty is whether he's good enough at being the Doctor. And what we see over the next few episodes is a magnificent slow burn. Rather than continuing to heap on dramatic moments like the "I AM YOUR SERVANT" confrontation, Whitaker, with astonishing confidence, trusts that the cliffhanger in the second episode worked as intended and that its impact means that he can spend the next two weeks ratcheting up the tension with agonizing and meticulous slowness. The Daleks get closer and closer to the point where they are completely in charge while the Doctor continues to fail to get a toehold into the plot. This could be taken as a disappointment—certainly, rereading that paragraph, it sounds like I'm saying the story delays for three episodes. It doesn't. I can't say that enough—this is grippingly plotted, and it is absolutely worth it to track down a reconstruction. This is, simply put, the best Doctor Who story we've seen yet and one of the absolute high points of the series. The slow burn here is a beautiful and unceasing building of tension.

Until finally, in the fifth episode, it boils over magnificently. The fourth episode ends with the revelation of a massive assembly line of Daleks. One thing, in fact, that this story does extremely well is make the Daleks scary again. After their massive universe-threatening antics in *The Daleks' Master Plan*, Whitaker makes them an intimate threat and takes care to repeatedly stress the contrast between their robotic exterior and their fleshy interior, playing up the essential strangeness of the concept to make the Daleks seem unusual. This is brilliant work on Whitaker's part, and gives the Daleks a new lease on life—previously they had to be in bigger and bigger adventures to satisfy us. Now, having expanded them so far, Whitaker puts them in a story that is almost too small for them so that they can occupy an outsized and terrifying place in the narrative.

Following this sudden revelation that there are a vast number of Daleks in the story (as opposed to the three we'd seen to date) we also get Lesterton—previously the Daleks' stooge—having a complete nervous breakdown at the horror of what he's done. And it's like nothing we've ever seen, it's clearly an extended scene of mental agony. Lesterton rants, eventually declaring that humanity is doomed and the Daleks are now the supreme species. And again, what Whitaker is doing here is taking where the Daleks were in *The Daleks' Master Plan* and tweaking it—re-using battle-tested Dalek tricks and simply streamlining them. This is the exact same scene we have encountered when Mavic Chen went from top dog to extermination fodder at the end of that story. It's just done far better now because there's a second source of tension; if only Lesterton could pull himself together, he might save the day. But, of course, he can't pull himself together. And now there is an army of Daleks. The Doctor has failed. The Daleks have won.

There's a side point to make here about the fact that there are two revolutions going on in this episode. Firstly, the Daleks are trying to overthrow humanity. Secondly, a bunch of rebels attempt to use the Daleks to overthrow the colonial government. There's an intimate link between these two phenomena—one that is highlighted when a Dalek asks, in all seriousness, why humans kill humans. This is another brilliant touch—this line challenges the notion that humans are morally superior to Daleks because it is asked from one Dalek to another instead of to the Doctor or Lesterton. The Daleks, here, come to represent the same horrific darkness that Mondas does—a complete challenge to the very nature of humanity (a theme reinforced by Lesterton's mad rant). The same one that destroyed the Doctor. (Ironically, then, it's this story that actually establishes that the Cybermen are on the same level of villainy as the Daleks.) Seeing as the Daleks are running rampant and slaughtering everybody by this point, Ben and Polly believe it might be best to run for their lives. There appears to be no hope. Even the main characters have given up. And only here, after it's gotten apocalyptically bad, does the Doctor step up and intervene. What is most striking is how he intervenes. Throughout this story we see the great difference between Troughton and Hartnell. Troughton has the magnetic charisma of a leading man in the John Steed tradition—he's charming, witty, and energetic. So when he finally gets to work on the task, there's an electricity to it—especially given that the previous three episodes are all about him failing to get a toehold into the plot and being relegated to the sidelines to sulk on his recorder.

What he does, however, is far darker and more chilling than anything normally associated with the fun and charismatic leading man. First he sacrifices a ton of guards in order to distract the Daleks, seemingly unworried about the ethics of sending Bragens guards to certain death. The Doctor is going to play this his way, and woe befall those who get in the way. The Daleks declare that the law of the Daleks is in force—a fact terribly demonstrated when the Daleks, after Lesterton begs for them to spare him by saying that he gave them life, simply respond "Yes. You gave us life," and then shoot him dead.

In response, the Doctor demonstrates his own law. Except that this law is calamitous: the Daleks are destroyed in explosions of horrific viscera. And the Doctor is knocked out for it, coming to and reacting with glee when he's told the extent of the destruction he wrought. ("Did I do all of that?" he asks energetically as he finds out the extent of what's been done.) And then, when confronted by the colonists with how much damage he did, the Doctor laughs it off and sneaks away. And, more troublingly, when Ben asks him if he had a plan all along he returns to sulkily tooting on his recorder.

And so, even if this episode ends with Ben, Polly, and the audience putting their trust in the new Doctor, this trust is granted warily. The Doctor is dangerous in a way he wasn't before; Hartnell was alien simply because he was a temperamental old man. Troughton, on the other hand, is scary because he is a force of pure chaos willing to bring the world down around people's ears. Even if we've been reassured of our initial concern—that the Doctor has somehow become possessed by Mondas— now we have a whole new one. This impish, chaotic Doctor, while he is clearly capable of stopping any monsters, might take the rest of us down with him. And while this was always a part of the Doctor and his identity—the anarchic spirit and slight revelry in chaos—those aspects of him now seem wholly unchecked. The fear at this point is not that this isn't the Doctor. It's that maybe we never really knew who the Doctor was.

Time Can Be Rewritten: *Wonderland*

The Second Doctor and psychedelia are, as I've noted before, a natural fit. The Patrick Troughton era overlaps the parts of the 1960s we think of when we talk about the 1960s, encompassing the 1967 "Summer of Love," the point where the wave broke and rolled back in 1968, and, indeed, bringing us right to the brink of the Moon landing in 1969. But Troughton got out along with the decade, and the question of cleaning up in the aftermath of the 1960s was largely left to other actors.

In a sense, then, *Wonderland*, one of the Telos novellas that attempted more literary takes on Doctor Who in the latter days of the so-called wilderness years, is a necessary bit of catching up. Having failed to grapple with the end of the 1960s on television, Troughton's Doctor is given the chance to look at it from a position of historicization instead of as a part of it. So we get the TARDIS at Haight-Ashbury a few months before the Summer of Love, leading up to the January 14, 1967 "Human Be-In."

Mark Chadbourn opts to line the story up almost exactly with the Doctor's era, having the Doctor arrive in what is essentially his present – the Human Be-In took place the same day that the first episode of *The Underwater Menace* aired, and Chadbourn goes only a hair earlier in the timeline, setting this between *Power of the Daleks* and *The Highlanders*, with Ben and Polly as the companions. This is, in and of itself, an interesting decision. Chadbourn is, on the whole, honest to the period within the Troughton era he pulls from; the Doctor flits about the edges of this story, remaining at a distance from the plot at times. It's very much drawn from the Doctor in *Power of the Daleks* – the one we can't quite trust, although the warmer and more playful take on him that eventually became standard is constantly peeking out.

Chadbourn makes no bones about the Doctor's cultural allegiances here. He's shown in a head shop admiring the bongs, giving advice to Timothy Leary, and waxing poetic about the historical role of psychedelic drugs. Which, while there are surely people who would object, is largely keeping with Troughton's Doctor. It's off-putting only inasmuch as there's a materialism to the setting that is largely lacking in Troughton's stories. His only historical was *The Highlanders*, and that story was largely unmoored from history itself in favor of a genre pastiche. To see his Doctor engaged with the material residue of history to this extent is strange. But it is that, not the fact that he's largely sympathetic to psychedelic drug use, that is odd.

But there are limits to the degree to which the book can simply embrace the 1960s counterculture. In the 1960s itself, of course, it would have been impossible for the Doctor to directly embrace the counterculture – the BBC would never have allowed it. So instead we get a countercultural Doctor whose allegiances are slightly veiled. He may mix up a bunch of acid to foment a youth revolution in *The Krotons*, but it's actually acid in the conventional sense, designed to attack their evil alien overlords. Indeed, this sort of explicit embrace of psychedelia could only happen in the wilderness years. It's just as impossible to imagine David Tennant affectionately handling a bong on television.

But equally, the sort of historical detail this book musters is only possible because it's not really a case of the Troughton era engaging its present. It is a historical, albeit one with aliens. The characters fretting that the Summer of Love is going to bring it all crashing down are poignant in part because, historically, we know how it plays out and we know they're right. One cannot write in 2003 about the 1960s as though they're going to go on forever and as though the forces of the countercultural left are going to triumph.

And so the book's narrator, Summer, finds out that her boyfriend has sold out and gone corporate, getting in ahead of the trend. But, of course, it is the trend. It's how the 1960s really did end. People abandoned the utopianism and returned to the status quo. And in many ways it was worse than what came before. It was one thing not to aspire towards the utopian. It was quite another to consider it and then reject it – to decide that utopianism was a nice aesthetic, but unfit for actual political use. And so *Wonderland*'s picture of the 1960s comes crashing down, as the real thing did.

More broadly, there's a lurking paranoia through it all. The major threat for most of the book is the prospect of bad acid that makes people disappear being distributed, and it becomes clear that this is a conspiracy on the part of powerful forces looking to undermine the 1960s. The novel ends in a haze of paranoia, with Summer spending her life on the run from agents who occasionally decide it's time to clean up a loose end, living, in essence, in a perpetual conspiracy thriller.

Curiously, but fittingly, it is not Troughton's Doctor who is left to confront this. He solves the problem in 1967 and then drops out of the plot just as much as he drops out of the world. This does not, however, mean that the Doctor himself is absent – instead the Fourth Doctor shows up, some thirty years later (i.e. roughly in the present day) and rescues Summer, whisking her away as a companion while talking romantically of the good the hippies did and telling her that the conspiracy will eventually be revealed.

Which is also fitting. Troughton's Doctor never confronted the end of the 1960s. And it would be strange, in the end, for him to. It would necessitate forcing the character into a confrontation he was never designed for, and one that he cannot help but lose. Part of the appeal of Doctor Who is that it gets to reinvent itself, and Troughton's Doctor was, in the end, a figure of the late 1960s. When those petered out, the show reinvented itself to address a new era. To pit any era of Doctor Who against its own future is necessarily an unfair fight.

And so instead we get an intervention from the future from a portion of Doctor Who in which the ideals and aesthetics of the 1960s remained influential, but where they were allowed to change and grow. Much has been made of the similarities between Troughton and Baker's Doctors, and quite reasonably. But Baker's Doctor does exist well into the 1970s, in a more paranoid and jaded world. His subversive optimism is not a perfect match for his times, but a carefully gauged reaction to them. He captures, in other words, the way in which the 1960s did survive: as a form of rebellion and protest.

It would be reductivist to treat the Troughton era as co-extensive with psychedelia. Nevertheless, the two intersected repeatedly. And *Wonderland* serves, accordingly, as a necessary encapsulation of the era. The best stories set in past eras are the ones that fill holes and gaps in those eras, telling stories that the eras themselves couldn't have, but that are nevertheless clearly based on that era's concerns. *Wonderland* is a prime example. The Troughton era wouldn't be complete without it. And wonderfully, like its vision of psychedelia, it's not complete with it either.

Fry Something (*The Highlanders*)

It's December 16, 1966, and time for us to ring in 1967. Almost everything you need to know about music in 1966 can be explained by the fact that Tom Jones is at number one with "The Green Green Grass of Home," while The Kinks are at number seven with "Dead End Street," a song about inescapable economic despair with a chorus of "We are strictly second class / We don't understand / Why we should be on dead end street / People are living on dead end street / Gonna die on dead end street," while a background shout of "dead end!" repeats. To be fair, after two verses of maudlin sentimentality, "The Green Green Grass of Home" turns out to be about waiting on death row, but the degree to which this feels like a pale imitation of Simon and Garfunkel's "Silent Night/7 O'Clock News," (which does the smash fade from sentimentality to harsh materialism with far greater aplomb and was released in the US, at least, two months earlier) ultimately reminds us that this is still Tom Jones we are talking about. Jones will hold the number one spot for the entirety of this story, while The Supremes, Donovan, Elvis Presley, and The Who join The Kinks in the lower reaches.

In actual news, meanwhile, you've got a nice illustration of how '60s news works in hindsight. There's basically three categories of events. The first is of significance only to people who think that the '60s are about youth-cultural revolution. For instance, The Doors releasing their self-titled debut on January 4. The second is of significance only to people who think the

'60s are about an obnoxious assault on traditional culture. For instance, the theft of millions of dollars of art from the Dulwich Art Gallery in England. And then there is the news that is significant to both groups, and thus reveals, through the fault lines, what was actually going on at the time. For instance: Prime Minister Harold Wilson withdraws all offered settlements with Rhodesia and insists that the UK will only recognize a majority-black Rhodesian government.

This paradigm is not entirely unhelpful in understanding Doctor Who in its fourth season. On the one hand, you have the stuff that's chum for fans of the more recent Doctor Who eras: The Doctor is funny! Lots of contemporary Earth stuff! On the other hand, you have the stuff that feeds the Troughton era—backlash over the loss of things that were around in the Hartnell era: No historicals! Endless bases under endless sieges! And on the third hand, because this is British science fiction and we have Zaphod Beeblebrox handy whenever we want him, you have stuff that turns to Marmite: Monsters! And ... um ... more monsters, really.

The underlying issue is this. In its first season, Doctor Who flailed around in the attempt to figure out what it was. In its second season, though, Doctor Who was ruthlessly confident about its identity. This confidence was arguably misplaced at times, but it was unquestionably there. But just over the course of Season Three, that confidence progressively waned until Innes Lloyd decided to reboot the entire show. But the reboot is not entirely straightforward, and now, in Season Four, we're flailing about again trying to make a new show. As it happens, we're going to get there, and Doctor Who is going to turn out to be a massively influential and utterly fascinating television program.

But we're not there yet. So instead we get things like this— a story so weird that virtually nobody comes close to even describing it accurately. The spotter's guide version of *The Highlanders* is "last pure historical story and first appearance of Jamie," but neither of these statements are quite true.

The fact that so many fans understand this story so poorly is not actually surprising. After all, we're reeling about in territory that (as Doctor Who fans) we're spectacularly ill-suited to understand. I've been knocking on about this for a while now, but it really cannot be stressed enough: watching this stretch of the show from the viewpoint of someone who knows how Doctor Who changes its lead actors is the wrong way to go about it. The entire point of everything that is going on in these early Troughton stories is that the audience doesn't know what to make of them. The fact that this purposeful disruption of audience comprehension was so memorable means that we now understand these episodes, or at least, we understand the many repetitions of them that have been made. But understanding the repetitions only takes us further and further away from understanding the main purpose of the stories themselves.

I mention this because the second story is normally the one where we get a preview of the new status quo. *The Silurians* tells us that the show is going to be about the Doctor butting heads with UNIT even as he helps them. *The Ark in Space* tells us that we're going to see a lot of gothic horror. Even *Paradise Towers*, for all its faults, shows us that we're going to return to a more materialist and grounded sense of the series. But if you try to apply that framework to *The Highlanders*, you will end up, more or less, on a completely different planet. The one thing this story is absolutely, and unequivocally not about is revealing the show's aspirations.

There are several reasons for this. First of all, it would be extremely difficult for the series to confidently step up and show us what it's going to be like with Troughton because nobody working on it actually has the foggiest idea. This story was slapped together in a desperate hurry, and the next one was initially deemed too bad to use (it was only brought back onto the schedule when it became obvious that every other story was even worse). It's not until *The Moonbase* that Doctor Who starts to look like it was written by people who had a clue what they were doing again. At this point, however, the sense that the audience doesn't know what's going on is fully and completely shared by the production team.

Beyond these issues, the show just can't do the confident switchover at this stage because what it's trying to do is too strange to just pull off and hope nobody notices. It would be like The Beatles releasing *Sergeant Pepper* immediately after *Help!* instead of going through *Rubber Soul* and *Revolver* first. So instead, the show hits on the frankly brilliant idea of having the Doctor go through a horrifying metaphysical change that destabilizes the basic core of his identity and forces him to rebuild who he is on the fly. Unable to take its next step decisively, it instead enters phase two of "what happens if we recast the Doctor," in which the show flails about for eight weeks uncertain of what to do after the main character attains enlightenment and becomes a trickster figure.

The result is *The Highlanders*, an episode that is considerably more about establishing the ways in which the show is not like what it was under Hartnell than it is about establishing what it is like under Troughton. At its core, this story is an unstructured romp across some famous historical events in which, in lieu of following any discernible plot, the Doctor runs around playing dress-up for four episodes. Taken on its own terms, it is easily the single most baffling Doctor Who story to date, making *The Web Planet* look perfectly normal and routine. Taken in context, it seems considerably stranger, in that it offers the bewildering spectacle of Doctor Who refusing visibly and loudly to be the show we've known it to be.

Let's first clear up the easy part of the spotter's guide fallacy. Yes, Jamie McCrimmon appears in all four episodes and departs with the TARDIS crew at the end. But he's a completely minor character with very little to do in this story, elevated to companion status out of nowhere except for the realization that Frazier Hines has some star power. His sticking around at the end of the story is only slightly more probable than Dodo sticking around at the end of *The Massacre*, and that's down purely to the fact that at least Jamie appears during all four episodes of his debut story. No, the story that introduces Jamie is actually *The Underwater Menace*.

But the real misconception is the idea that this is the last historical. It's not. And not in the sense that there are more historicals before *Black Orchid* gets attempted as a throwaway in the 1980s. No, the issue is that this isn't a historical in any sense that we've previously understood the term.

This is clear from the opening moments, really. The TARDIS arrives just after the Battle of Culloden, and it looks like we're in for a standard historical in which we learn the basic shape of the battle. It also gives us the sense that Doctor Who is doing a genre pastiche—the BBC had done a very high profile docudrama on Culloden in 1964, and once the story starts up it gestures towards being a Robert Louis Stephenson imitation. However, upon arriving the Doctor does something very unusual. As soon as he sees that the TARDIS has landed in a battlefield with cannons, he tries to turn tail and run, responding to Polly's quite reasonable question "You don't want people to think you're afraid, do you" with "Why not?" It's only Ben and Polly's insistence that they appear to be back in England that convinces him to stay.

From there, almost immediately, the story becomes a compilation of "stuff we couldn't get Hartnell to do." Prance about in a German accent and do intense and oddly violent comedy scenes while humorously torturing people? Check. Cross-dress? Check. Be abnormally obsessed with stealing people's hats? Check. Basically, liberated by his metaphysical change from the tedious requirement that he be remotely sane, the Doctor goes completely nuts here—hamming for the camera, firing off one-liners to nobody in particular, and generally having a good time, while, distantly in the background, some kidnappings and rescues go on.

This is where the spotter's guide approach falls short, then. Because nothing about this even faintly resembles the historicals we've seen before. This is only a historical if we define that genre as the absence of overt science fiction elements. To be fair, this is how fans in the post-historical eras of the show have defined the historical, but it's manifestly not how it was defined when they were actually making the things. In terms of televised Doctor Who, *The Smugglers* was the last historical, and this is just a parody of the genre. Just to reiterate for anyone who didn't get the memo from *The Power of the Daleks* that the entire rulebook has been chucked out the window. We'll deal with the issue of the historical being abandoned as a genre in the "Time Can Be Rewritten" essay on Mark Gatiss's *The Roundheads*, so for now, let's just look at how unlike a historical this sort of mad romp is.

To be fair, there are two distinct strands of historical that we could be talking about. These two styles split very sensibly on the lines of who wrote the first four historicals. The first two historicals—*Marco Polo* and *The Aztecs*—were written by John Lucarotti, and are essentially stories about being trapped in a hostile past. *Marco Polo* is a hugely extended epic of the TARDIS crew being trapped in the Himalayas. *The Aztecs* is a shorter epic of the TARDIS crew being trapped in ancient Mexico while Barbara tries and fails to make the most of it. In both cases, the main point is that history is a scary, chaotic place.

Compare to the second style—the Dennis Spooner approach—as displayed in *The Reign of Terror* and *The Romans*. Both of those stories can be fairly described as "romps" in which the major, iconic bits of history are thrown into a blender to produce a sort of highlight tour of the historical time period, or, more accurately, of modern views on the time periods. Where the Lucarotti historicals are about giving the past a richly detailed texture and forcing the TARDIS crew to survive it, the Spooner historicals are a sort of history tribute band, playing through a greatest hits album of "Roman stuff" or "French Revolution stuff" where the primary pleasure is the recognition of the key elements. So in *Marco Polo*, Kublai Khan's palace is a hard-earned resolution of six episodes of freezing death. When he shows up, there's a sense of relief and a sense that the danger of the past six episodes has partially passed as we head towards some sort of ending for the story.

Whereas when Nero shows up in *The Romans*, it means we've finally gotten to the good bits that we've been teased with. It's not a sense of relief; it's a sense of delayed gratification.

From those first four historicals (or, really, four of the first five, with *100,000 BC* basically being a Lucarotti-style historical), we get pretty much all of the rest. *The Crusade*, *The Myth Makers*, and *The Gunfighters* all belong to the Spooner tradition (though *The Crusade*, as one would expect from Whitaker, is in many ways its own thing). *The Massacre*, on the other hand, belongs to the Lucarotti tradition. (It is perhaps worth remarking, albeit somewhat sadly, that the Lucarotti tradition is maddeningly restricted to stories written by Lucarotti, although Steve Lyons' novel *The Witch Hunters*, covered in the Hartnell volume, is firmly a Lucarotti-style historical, and many though not all of the modern efforts to restore the genre, mostly in audio form from Big Finish, have gone for the Lucarotti approach. That said, the Spooner approach is closest to how the pseudo-historicals of the new series are done—*The Unquiet Dead* or *The Unicorn and the Wasp*, for instance.)

That's not to say that the genre didn't evolve—*The Gunfighters* is far smarter, more complex, and better than Spooner's amateurish go at *The Reign of Terror* (indeed, Donald Cotton went and spruced up *The Romans* hilariously when he did the novelization), and *The Massacre* works in ways that *The Aztecs* and *Marco Polo* never did. But for the most part, these are the two approaches to historicals for the first three years of the series.

With *The Smugglers*, however, things started to break down a bit. On the one hand, it's clearly a Spooner-style romp through the highlights of the pirate genre. But all of the previous Spooner-style stories had basically been comedies, with the possible exception of *The Crusade*, and even that spent an awful lot of time on Shakespeare parodies. In terms of its plot, it feels Lucarotti-style—the characters are stuck in a hostile past. The key clue that it's not a historical? Not since *The Aztecs* had Doctor Who done a historical without famous people in it.

Seen in hindsight, though, *The Smugglers* seems like a natural evolution of what came before simply because it meets the modern definition of "no aliens." Put in context, *The Smugglers* establishes a third sort of historical and looks like a model for how historical stories could have worked under Troughton, with the leading man providing the comedy instead of the situations. This freed the writers up to explore non-comedic bits of history.

Put simply, there's absolutely a way to do a historical with Patrick Troughton in it. That is not the reason the historicals died. But what is striking, then, is that this is nothing like either the Spooner or Lucarotti traditions. Figuring out why *The Highlanders* isn't a Lucarotti historical should just be a matter of watching a few minutes while Troughton is in drag. But why isn't it a Spooner-style historical? Well, fundamentally, the Spooner-style historical is about the regulars playing stock roles in a defined type of adventure and laughing about their being cast in those roles. This is part of why *The Crusade* is a Spooner-style historical despite the many interesting things Whitaker does with it—because the sections where Ian is Sir Ian of Jaffa are ultimately about the idea of a 1960s science teacher having to be a knight in the Crusades, not about Ian's terror at being put in the situation.

So what's wrong with watching the Doctor be cast as Doctor Von Wer, the Hannoverian Doctor? The thing is, the entire point of this casting is that the Doctor can put on a funny voice and play at being someone else. The Spooner-style historical is about the TARDIS crew being miscast but having to play their roles anyway. *The Highlanders* is about the way in which the Doctor can put on a disguise and, most importantly, parody the very role he's supposed to be playing. The Doctor, when he is playing at being Doctor Von Wer, acts neither like himself nor like a Hannoverian physician in 1746. Instead, he acts like the Doctor parodying a Hannoverian physician.

In this sense *The Highlanders* is a complete mockery of the Spooner historical. The TARDIS crew puts on costumes and romps about laughing at the genre they're ostensibly in. This is not just "a bit different" from Hartnell historicals—this is an overt mockery of the entire Hartnell era, with Troughton's Doctor repeatedly refusing to play the role of the Doctor (and in fact spending the bulk of the story playing any other role he can find). "I should like a hat like that," indeed.

This is actually quite a high-wire act, because it's an absolute assault on the good will of the audience. If *The Highlanders* at any point tips into a mean-spirited dig at the stupidity of historicals, the entire thing comes crashing down. Remember, most of the audience at this point has not made up their mind on this whole "new Doctor" thing, and if they've been watching Doctor Who thus far it is safe to assume that they like Hartnell-style adventures, historicals and all. In hindsight we all love Troughton and so automatically forgive his excesses here, but that was in no way a sure bet in 1966/1967. So putting on a mockery of the previous three years of the show is not the safest move.

Thankfully for the show, Troughton is up to the task, and even though this is miles from where his characterization of the Doctor is going to settle, he is a good enough actor to charmingly hold this together. But watching *The Highlanders*, by far the most important thing to remember is that there is absolutely no reason why this had to work. The Doctor enters and exits this story as an unrestrained force of anarchy (as he was at the end of *The Power of the Daleks*). No effort has been made to establish to the audience what Doctor Who is like now that Hartnell has left.

But on the other hand, we have gotten four weeks that are essentially about how much fun Patrick Troughton is. And they worked. *The Highlanders*, in the end, is a story about convincing Doctor Who fans that they didn't really like Hartnell all that much and that Troughton is going to be much more fun. And, astonishingly, given that Hartnell's Doctor Who was really quite good, the show more or less pulls it off.

But the consequence is a story that is by necessity nobody's favorite. Troughton fans don't get their version of Troughton in it, and Hartnell fans get a slap in the face. Taken as a story, this is an abject failure. Taken as a step in making the transition from one era to the other, it's a success, made all the more satisfying by how improbable it is that it worked in the first place.

Another Rotten, Gloomy Old Tunnel (*The Underwater Menace*)

It's January 14, 1967. Tom Jones has yet to give up number one, though he will in a week when The Monkees take number one with "I'm a Believer." It is worth remarking on the nature of The Monkees as a band—an American band manufactured for popular success in an attempt to reverse-engineer The Beatles at the exact same time that The Beatles were busy exploding their own formula recording *Sergeant Pepper*. In fact, the top three singles when the second episode of *The Underwater Menace* aired are an instruction manual to 1967—corporate pseudo-mods, Tom Jones, and The Who with "Happy Jack," (complete with psychedelic cover). The Monkees retain number one for the duration of *The Underwater Menace*, with numbers two and three switching to Cat Stevens in his first really big single and The Move, a Birmingham rock band, with "Night of Fear," a song that is very obviously about a bad acid trip.

Meanwhile, in news that does not sing, the US is found out for experimenting with germ warfare, the opening strains of the Summer of Love happen in San Francisco with the Human Be-In, which also introduces psychedelic culture to the masses (never mind that Doctor Who did it two months earlier; in a few chapters we'll watch, astonished, as Doctor Who invents steampunk in 1967 and gets no credit for that either). The UK begins negotiating to enter the European Economic Community, pre-human fossils are discovered in Kenya ... So far we're two days into the four weeks this story ran.

Thankfully things slow down, and over the rest of it the major news consists of the UK nationalizing ninety percent of the steel industry, the Apollo 1 disaster, and the US, USSR, and UK (who were apparently still expected to make it to space in 1967—a fact that may be relevant in 1970 for our purposes) signing the Outer Space Treaty to demilitarize space.

If you have the sense that the 1960s are kicking into high gear very suddenly, you're not far off. So I am deeply amused to bring you *The Underwater Menace*, long considered one of the worst Doctor Who stories of all time. Back in *Doctor Who Magazine's* definitive "Mighty 200" fan poll, it came in as the seventh worst story of all time, and five years later when they did another poll for the 50th anniversary it climbed all the way to eighteenth worst on the back of an additional episode being recovered (though admittedly not yet officially released).

Although an eleven-place jump is modest, though, the recovery of the second episode clearly still helped this episode's reputation. Given how long it took for the episode to see official release (although it hit torrent sites well before that), one suspects that this was mostly on the basis of the clip they released when the find was announced, which was the bit of the story everyone who'd listened to the audio already knew was great, and which we'll talk about it later.

But the truth is that the case against this story is fairly easy to make: the script makes no sense, the villain is ludicrous, and the whole thing is an effects-driven wreck of a story assembled under pressure. Wood and Miles take it to task in *About Time* for the fact that "it displays utter contempt for the audience. It's not so much that it isn't trying, it's that it doesn't think we care that it isn't trying." Shearman and Hadoke are kinder in *Running Through Corridors*, both admitting that they love the story's barminess, but there's a general consensus that this is crap.

But the truth is that few of the usual reasons for writing off this story hold up to scrutiny, and scrutiny has become considerably easier now that it's out on DVD. Yes, the plot revolves around drilling a hole in the bottom of the ocean to drain it into the Earth's core and explode the planet. Need I remind you, however, that one of the most acclaimed and "classic" Doctor Who stories of all time features hollowing out the Earth's core to drive the planet around as a spaceship? Yes, the madman wants to blow up the planet because he can. But how can we, as a fandom, praise Davros's monologue in *Genesis of the Daleks* contemplating unleashing a deadly plague on the universe and then complain about Zaroff? They are, after all, the same scene, complete with a scenery-devouring villain.

So we're left with the fact that the third episode ends with the mad-scientist villain shouting "Nothing in ze world can stop me now!" Which actually comes very close to identifying the main problem with this story—its third episode was for ages all we had. As an orphan episode, its airings would have been at fan conventions for a long time. Nothing with so absurd a cliffhanger would have a chance of being anything other than a "so bad it's good" experience in such a setting. But that cliffhanger isn't meant to be approached in isolation from the episodes spent building up Zaroff as a scenery-chewing madman. It's over the top, yes, but it's earned, the culmination of a steady escalation of stakes that Joseph Furst actually does quite a lot to sell. As Toby Hadoke wisely argues, Furst makes a deliberate choice to play the role as a pastiche, and hits his target with magnificent skill. When Zaroff is a comedic figure, which is often, the audience is laughing with the actor, not at him.

And this gets at the truth about this story, which is that on the whole it's quite fun. To quote Shearman, "Is it entertaining? Just about, if you hold on tight, and don't resist where it takes you." Failing to have a good time watching *The Underwater Menace* requires something of a conscious choice not to enjoy it—to decide that ridiculousness is a problem as opposed to a mode of fun that's well-matched to what ITV was airing at the same time.

Certainly I'm more sympathetic to the "just go with it and it's fun" position than Miles and Wood's frankly bizarre assertion that the story isn't trying. Although the behind the scenes information lets us know that this was not a story beloved by parts of the production team, the flipside is that they had a hole in their schedule and opted to fill it with this despite the fact that it was obviously going to shatter their budget. Miles and Wood argue that this suggests that means that the show valued spectacle or its own sake, sneering that "Lloyd seriously thought this was all Doctor Who was capable of being, all the license payers were entitled to expect from the series." But this doesn't entirely follow. Or at least, the show has traded on spectacle before and had it be interesting—Miles and Wood even cite *The Web Planet* as a point of contrast.

But the better move would be to cite it as a point of comparison. *The Web Planet* is one of the great Marmite stories, but as I insisted when I wrote about it, almost everybody who dislikes it does so for the wrong reasons. The entire point of *The Web Planet* was to put something on the television screen that was unlike anything viewers had ever seen before. It's neither realistic nor entirely sensible—as I argued in Volume One, *The Web Planet* is shooting for a Georges Méliès look—but rather that had a texture unlike anything the viewer had seen on television. It was a theater of spectacle—something that is interesting because it is so unlike everything else. In this regard, *The Web Planet* succeeded, providing us with four beloved characters stumbling around a strange and terrifying landscape.

And this is very much what's going on here. Tremendous effort has been made making Atlantis look strange and alien. There's an effort put in to building a fascinating setting that we do not always see the show make. The lengthy fish people dance sequences get stick for how bizarre they look, but that's an effort the show is soon going to stop making in favor of an endless parade of monsters and bases. Similarly, the opening, in which the TARDIS crew wanders around trying to figure out where they are, is a Hartnell-era standard that's soon to find itself de-emphasized. Unlike, say, *The Tenth Planet*, where the nature of Snowcap Base is squared away in minutes and we just do a runaround for the rest of the stories, here we keep learning new things about Atlantean culture for three of the four episodes. Effort is made to show us how strange Atlantis is throughout the story.

And so calling this a demonstration of Lloyd's worst tendencies is profoundly misleading. Since taking over the program, Lloyd has mostly tried to do two things. First, he's focused heavily on making the series more exciting. Second, he's worked on making the TARDIS land in more accessible places. The latter may well be grounds for criticism, although doing so means that you're also offering an indictment of Russell T Davies's oft-stated distaste for stories without a human element. (This is fine, but as with the difficulties in identifying any difference between Zaroff and Davros, if you complain about Lloyd here, you have to extend the criticism to the more beloved figure. Although one suspects the pro-Davies/anti-Lloyd lobby is limited in scope.) The former, on the other hand, seems difficult to complain about unless you want to dismiss virtually every post-Hartnell era of Doctor Who. (And again, there is nothing wrong with doing so. The fact of the matter is, the Hartnell era was different from what we're looking at now, and the show never went back to most of what was lost in the Hartnell transition.)

We should also remember that Troughton is still in the trial phase. This is the first time we've seen him have a "normal" story, inasmuch as Doctor Who's norm is science fiction. (And the Delia Derbyshire theme, which plays over historicals and monster stories alike, is a pretty strong clue in that direction.) For all the reports that Troughton (and the rest of the cast) were at war with the director throughout this story, his performance is fantastic, and you can see him rapidly learning to rein in the more overtly comedic elements of his performance and to play scenes through understatement. In particular, his episode two scene with Zaroff where he clearly recognizes that Furst is going to completely blow him off the screen in terms of charisma and over-the-top antics, and so instead reins it in massively, asking in a very hushed, polite tone why Zaroff wants to destroy the Earth, is a thing of splendor.

This is a tactic Troughton will make much of for the next three years—emphasizing things by dialing back his performance. It's pretty clearly the first moment where Troughton finally and firmly becomes the Doctor that fans of this era remember. (Whereas the sequence at the start, where we get to hear what each character hopes they'll find when they open the doors and Troughton giddily says "Prehistoric monsters!" is, in many ways, the moment when he becomes the Doctor that more casual fans of his era remember.)

But this is far from the only highlight served up by the recovered second episode. The scenes in which Polly is about to be surgically transformed into a fish person are breathtakingly distressing, and while it's hard to get too excited about high-quality torture porn, it speaks to the fact that this story isn't all dancing and scenery chewing. This story also serves as the real introduction to Jamie, who was a minor character in his actual debut, but who here gets to start actually doing things. (Also he's in a wetsuit, a fact exciting enough to make it into famed playwright Joe Orton's diary.)

So what we have on the whole is a deeply transitional story, setting up much of what we're going to see over the next three years while retaining many of the trappings of things it's going to rapidly stop doing. In many ways, as we noted, the thing it most resembles is *The Web Planet*, only stripped down to four episodes and given a proper villain in a real and genuine attempt to wed the Hartnell-style of exploration to the more contemporary-thriller style the show has been developing. On top of that, we have a story that tries to bring strangeness to Earth. It's not often commented on, but by all appearances *The Underwater Menace* is set in 1970. In other words, on top of everything else, this is part of the five-minutes-in-the-future vibe of *The War Machines* and *The Tenth Planet*.

It's here that the cracks begin to show in this story. Juggling Hartnell-esque worldbuilding, suspenseful action, and a near future setting is a bridge too far, and does make the storyfeel messy. Any two of those is an interesting exploration of the series' potential. All three together, though, raises the question of whether this is actually a brilliant leap forward for the series or if it's just the product of a bunch of people with no clear ideas of what to do gluing bits together. Certainly many of the people involved in it thought it was the latter, and not every steaming mess of contradictory influences is secretly a work of postmodern genius.

But on the other hand, it is impossible to overstate how necessary it was to do a story like this. After two stories that are primarily about breaking from the Hartnell era and doing something completely different, a story that makes an effort to combine the Hartnell era with the emerging Troughton era is welcome—especially after a not entirely friendly parody of the Hartnell era. Yes, it fails, but even that points forward, demonstrating how necessary the changes taking place really are. And in any case, its failure is greatly exaggerated by years of only having the third episode. This is far from one of the highlights of the Troughton era, but we're going to hit a point in this book where it gets very hard to say anything interesting about stories that are very much like the ones on either side of them. This is interesting and weird, two words that should always be central to what Doctor Who is.

Every Single One of Them, at Some Point in Their Lives, Will Look Back at This Man (*The Moonbase*)

It's February 11, 1967. The Monkees top the charts with "I'm a Believer," holding it for one week before ceding to Petula Clark's "This is My Song." Two weeks later Englebert Humperdinck unseats her with "Release Me." The Rolling Stones, Jimi Hendrix, Cat Stevens, and The Beatles also chart.

In other news, Suharto takes power in Indonesia, maintaining control of the country for the next thirty years. The USSR moves troops near the Chinese border—a sign of the continuing deterioration in the relationship between the two main Communist countries in the world. Queen Elizabeth Hall opens in South London, and Joseph Stalin's daughter defects to the US.

And on television Doctor Who offers us *The Moonbase*. Which is a story that gives us a lot to talk about. Eventually we're going to get to the bit where we conclude that this story marks the completion of the Troughton transition and conclusively establishes a new paradigm for what Doctor Who is. But before we get to all of that we have to start with the reason why it was inevitable that this story was going to be made in the first place and what that says about where Doctor Who is going.

On one level this is fairly obvious and has been covered elsewhere. Of course Doctor Who was going to do a lunar story in 1967. Equally, it's fairly obvious how this marks a transition from the exoticism of the Hartnell stories towards what's often called the "base under siege" model that dominates the Troughton years. What's not usually remarked upon is the fact that these two facts are two sides of the same coin.

Since I am apparently possessed with a strange and obsessive need to reference *The Web Planet* in every essay (mostly because it embodies the explorer spirit of the Hartnell era better than anything else), it is worth contrasting this story with that one, especially given that *The Web Planet*'s most obvious visual inspiration was Méliès's *A Trip to the Moon*, meaning that it's the previous closest thing Doctor Who ever did to a moon story. And, more to the point, it aired exactly two years before this story.

The thing is, there's a huge division in science fiction that can be drawn in July of 1965. Before that, you get things like, on the paranoid side, Quatermass, which assumes that space is teeming with awful threats, and on the more optimistic side, *The Web Planet*, which, even though it's set in a different galaxy (but see Miles and Wood for several discussions of the extremely sloppy way in which the word "galaxy" is used throughout Doctor Who), tells us that space is teeming with fascinating and theatrical worlds. The default assumption was that planets were full of interesting stuff, and when you went to them, you'd encounter it.

Then came July of 1965, and, more importantly, the Mariner 4 probe. This, perhaps more than anything, explains the stark change over the third season of Doctor Who; more or less concurrently with the end of *The Time Meddler*, Mariner 4 flew by Mars and determined that there was almost certainly not life on Mars, nor had there probably ever been ancient civilizations there. Space, in point of fact, was more or less empty.

As you can imagine, this sparked a major change in science fiction. It wasn't an overnight shift in the same way that the moon landing seemed to be, but it was fundamentally a change in what was considered the normal expectation of the future. When we explore space, we now knew, it will not primarily be about encountering the strange and alien civilizations that flit about Vortis: It will be about building the means to survive. That's why the base under siege format arose—because of the realization that space was mostly going to be a matter of building bases and colonies on barren and inhospitible worlds (not about tripping over the Zarbi, or, more often, being tripped over by them).

This is not a problem for most science fiction. A cold and empty universe hostile to life still lends itself quite well to Quatermass-style paranoia, even if the meteorites need to originate from further away than Mars. (Indeed, looking at *The Quatermass Experiment* itself, one of the striking things is that it's just assumed that horrible fungus monsters might be just sitting around the solar system. They are not fungus monsters from Mars or Jupiter, but rather a threat of space itself.) However, there is one way in which it does profoundly change science fiction: stories like *The Web Planet* become much less interesting compared to stories like *The Moonbase*. If our exploration of space is going to be more about our survival than about the amazing things we see, a rich and textured world like Vortis is appreciably less interesting than something real and material like the moon.

So a lunar story was necessary not just because it was a current event, but because the nature of science fiction has been changing out from under Doctor Who. And a story about humans exploring space was a better reflection of where the relationship between science and humanity was going than *The Web Planet*.

But none of this explains the strangely iconic power of this story. Though to be fair, this is a case, unlike the several stories in a row I've referred to as little-known (due to the fact that they are missing and weren't novelized until the late '80s) this story has the opposite fate. It was novelized extremely early, with the title *Doctor Who and the Cybermen*. The title is important—it actively positions this as the iconic Cybermen story—the equivalent to *Doctor Who and the Daleks*. On top of that, when we talk about the "base under siege" subgenre, we should probably acknowledge that the story that is explicitly called *The Moonbase*—in which the base commander actively refers to them as being under siege—necessarily marks a major turning point in the genre even if it's not the first story to use the structure.

On top of that, the story actually has two whole episodes intact, which meant that, prior to the discovery of Part Two of *The Underwater Menace,* it was the first Troughton story that we had a majority of, and it was the second most complete story of Season Four. (This season is actually Doctor Who's most decimated season.) So we have a story with a particularly good novelization, released early, that we can see two parts of. Of course it's going to be influential. If anything, this is setup for an entry in which we take a look at a supposed classic and discover that it's not nearly as good as we'd been led to believe.

Except the old maxim that there is such a thing as an undeservedly forgotten story, but no such thing as an undeservedly remembered one, applies well here. *The Moonbase* has some gaping flaws, but watching it in sequence makes it easy to see how it would have established itself as a memorable story from the day it aired. The biggest problem watching it today is, as usual, that we treat it as a movie instead of as four parts of an almost-always-running serial. As a movie it's solid, if unremarkable. As a serial taken in context with what's been happening over the previous months, it has a different effect.

Remember, it's been just fourteen weeks since Hartnell left—three months, basically. We're only just now shaking off the jitters and starting to settle in to an idea of what the heck this show is actually like now. And this story—which Innes Lloyd, a savvier producer than anyone likes to give him credit for being, decided to hype as the big relaunch story—is very much the story in which the transition we've been in the midst of settles out. In many ways, the show has been up in the air since *The Massacre,* if not since *Mission to the Unknown.* The Wiles era issued a fundamental challenge to what the show was, and the tail end of the Hartnell era never really found an answer to that challenge. After this story, it stops being up in the air.

When the TARDIS crew steps out at the start of *The Macra Terror* the question of what Doctor Who is will be settled, at least for the time being.

But it's not quite there yet. In fact, this story begins with a Hartnell-esque exploration sequence, taking a good six minutes to get to where there's any sense of danger or adventure. Before that, it's vamping about on the moon doing moonbounces and stuff. Yes, at this point we're far enough from Hartnell that this sort of vamping and the Doctor's propensity for reciting fun space facts feels fairly unlike what we would have gotten from Hartnell, especially in the last year or so of his tenure. But it's still a program that is in the Hartnell exploration mode, where the central question of a new story is "where are we this time and what is it like?"

But that quickly changes. We're quickly thrust back into a setting that is an active retread of *The Tenth Planet*—a military installation. But where Hartnell felt like an out of place and marginal character there, Troughton ingratiates himself with the base at a staggering speed. Even when he comes under suspicion in Part Two he never comes anywhere close to the sort of marginalization that Hartnell saw three months prior. This is a marked change and one where both halves are well within the viewer's memory—all the more so when the Cybermen show up and we actually hear *The Tenth Planet* mentioned, and are told that "every child" knows about it. So the viewer is invited to contrast Troughton with Hartnell in order to see that Troughton is much better suited to this sort of situation.

Similarly, the fast confidence with which Troughton strides into the plot reinforces the sense that this is normal. The first episode has, other than its six minutes of moonvamping, a breathtakingly fast start. This is gutsy and confident, just like throwing the new Doctor in with some Daleks was, and it pays off almost as well. Despite the fact that this type of story is still quite new, and despite the fact that the last time we did one its entire point was to disorient the audience, the viewer quickly acclimates to the surroundings.

But the flip side of this is that the Cybermen are back. This is a big deal. It's the first time that monsters have returned since the Daleks came back. And more to the point, these are the monsters that killed the Doctor. Their return has to go down as a terrifying prospect—terrifying in a way that we haven't seen since, well, a Dalek rose out of the Thames. And even then, the Daleks needed to show up in London in order to have their return be truly terrifying. The Cybermen can just be epic as soon as they strut onto the screen.

Though, of course, the Cybermen have seen a massive revamp—enough of one that I'm not actually a hundred percent sure the cliffhanger to the first episode would have worked to a non-*Radio Times* reading viewer, because the monster that's revealed looks nothing like its previous incarnation. The entire previous concept of the Cybermen—dark mirrors of humanity who went on a spiritual journey and achieved a terrible and inhuman enlightenment in the Kenneth Grant sense of it—is ignored here. Mondas gets a few token mentions, but nothing that resembles an explanation. The connections to the past are so muddied here that when Gerry Davis novelized it, he switched the Cybermen to being from Telos, a planet we won't even encounter until *Tomb of the Cybermen*, and had Mondas be their spaceship planet used to attack the Earth. (Which actually is a hell of a lot more sensible than the Cybermen origin is ever going to look again.)

No. These Cybermen are far simpler—they're robots. Yes, they still prattle on about how they've upgraded themselves and have no emotions, but at the end of the day, these Cybermen are just robots who like mocking people. (And they do so very much like mocking people, referring to "stupid earth brains" and, after Hobson figures out where they were hiding on the base, taunting him by sarcastically saying "clever, clever, clever" like a giant robot Jóse Mourinho.) Polly even refers to them as metal, despite the fact that their previous appearance made it obvious that they were plastic.

The flipside, from a modern perspective, is that this story is the first appearance of the Cybermen in the form we actually recognize. It is perhaps a stretch to imagine that this was part of a deliberate transition and that Lloyd, knowing he was going to lose the rights to the Daleks shortly, oversaw a transitional story that would nod to the Cybermen that were the one-off villains of *The Tenth Planet* while simultaneously changing them into viable Dalek replacements. On the other hand, coming up with a better explanation is a stretch as well.

Because, see, the thing is that the story does rely on the Cybermen from *The Tenth Planet*. And on the building of the Doctor's character that we've seen to date. Remember how in *The Underwater Menace* the key moment for the Doctor's character is when he quietly, fearfully asks why Zaroff wants to blow up the Earth? Here we have an even more significant one—the single, definitive moment when the Doctor settles down out of his post-regeneration chaos and becomes the Doctor in his fully mythologized, heroic role.

The line is one of the better known moments of Troughton's tenure, actually—certainly one of the ones most often included in clip shows and documentaries. In it, Ben suggests that, given that they're being treated with extreme suspicion by the base, they just go back to the TARDIS. And the Doctor refuses. This, at least, we've seen before—the Doctor has refused Ben's suggestion to go back to the TARDIS in both *The Smugglers* and *The Power of the Daleks* on the grounds of moral obligation. But here he goes further, and delivers the key line: "There are some corners of the universe which have bred the most terrible things. Things which act against everything we believe in ... They must be fought."

The important thing about this is Troughton's delivery, which is often misrepresented. The line is not a triumphant, rousing call to arms. Rather, he delivers the first part of the line in a quiet, almost scared tone, before concluding, after a pause, that they must be fought. The declaration that these terrible things must be fought is not triumphant, but rather the weary acceptance of a duty—a point that is reinforced when the Cybermen inform the Doctor that he is known to them, to which he calmly answers, "And you to me." (This again echoes his debut in *The Power of the Daleks* where he is similarly recognized and legitimized by the monster.)

Remember that the Doctor's regeneration was seemingly caused by exposure to the Cybermen and their energy drain, and that his regeneration is paralleled consciously with the Cybermen's own terrible spiritual journey. This, then, is the moment when the Doctor accepts the knowledge he gained through his metaphysical change—the knowledge that there are terrible things in the universe that must be fought against.

Yes, this episode is the point where the show transitions to a show about monsters. But what's crucial is that this transition is not just a lazy shift of tone as the show sells out exploration and buys into action-packed materialism. This is a story about a Doctor who is finally accepting the consequences of his regeneration. It's one where all of the clowning around we've seen is revealed for what it is—a cover for the fact that a man who had previously been defined primarily by his desire to escape now knows that he has a duty in the universe.

We should also talk about the companions, who, Ben's lapse aside, are unusually committed to trying to save the world this week. Again, this is a transition—back in *Planet of Giants* it was remarkable that Barbara risked her life out of a general moral duty. Here the companions, when separated from the Doctor, are the ones who figure out how to drive the Cybermen out of the base, at least temporarily. The Doctor is not the only one who has changed from an explorer to a world-saver. The entire nature of the cast has made the transition.

Perhaps more importantly, however, it is Polly out of all of the companions who figures out how to stop the Cybermen. Much is made of the other big clip from this episode—the Doctor asking Polly to make some coffee. But usually this clip is trotted out to illustrate the sexism of the episode. Never mind that the Doctor's asking Polly to make some coffee is a strategic decision in the context of the story, nor that Polly spends the rest of that episode being the Doctor's main interlocutor in figuring out what's going on, nor even that her coffee is the key to figuring out what the Cybermen are doing.

Never mind also that, as I said, it is Polly who figures out the plan to stop the Cybermen. (Admittedly, her plan to mix large quantities of random solvents together is a terrible plan that, in reality, would have gotten everyone killed. It still, within the story, works.) And though Ben and Jamie steal the credit from her, we as viewers are meant to find that uncomfortable and awkward. Which is to say that while that clip is trotted out to illustrate the supposed sexism of the era, in context it's one of the best moments that female companions get in the 1960s.

By and large, this story is about finishing the transition to Troughton and establishing what the show is about—something we haven't really known for over a year. Yes, this story will be copied at least four times in the next two years. Yes, this story marks the point where the show fully turns away from the goals of the Hartnell era and becomes a show about monsters. But none of this is done out of laziness. It's unambiguously, in the context of the time, a move forward. The fact that it's virtually the last real move forward for two years is not this story's fault. This is a deliberate and conscious change. No, more than that, it's a necessary one.

Pop Between Realities, Home in Time for Tea: *Cathy Come Home*

It's November 16, 1966. We've been here before, actually, and so I'll refer you there for the standard litany of pop songs and news events. But we're going to need to flash back, because what we didn't deal with in amongst everything else going on in *The Power of the Daleks* was the fact that the BBC aired *Cathy Come Home*, a TV movie about homelessness that has been recognized, apparently, as the second best British TV program of all time. So since it's one of apparently two things in the history of British television supposed to be better than Doctor Who, we should talk about it on those grounds alone.

At a glance, mind you, it's not easy to see what *Cathy Come Home* possibly has to say about Doctor Who. One is a fairly theatrical science fiction show. The other is a pseudo-documentary about homelessness and urban poverty that makes heavy use of techniques from social realism (and indeed is a seminal text in defining that genre). The similarities are in no way obvious. And unlike with *Z Cars* and *Dixon of Dock Green* (covered in Volume One), which also had little enough to do with Doctor Who, *Cathy Come Home* was strikingly atypical for its time and so can't be used to provide a baseline of comparison for Doctor Who. No, the interest in *Cathy Come Home* is more esoteric.

It should come as a surprise to nobody that the 1960s, particularly the late 1960s, were a time of some social upheaval. And *Cathy Come Home* is overtly a program about social change and social conditions. It is worth looking at, in other words, in order to get a sense of how television related concretely to the social changes afoot. As I suggested, the most immediately obvious thing about *Cathy Come Home* is that it uses a pseudo-documentary style and hand-held cameras to tell its story. This was certainly one of the big things noticed at the time, and *Cathy Come Home* became something of a flashpoint in a debate about the line between news and entertainment (a debate that has yet to resolve, but hey). In essence, it was criticized for looking so real that it risked confusing the audience and making them think that it was, in fact, a depiction of real events instead of a fictional play. So in the (increasingly usual) spirit of my blowing a perfectly publishable academic paper topic on a self-published book about Doctor Who (though to be fair, more people read this than will ever see one of my academic articles) ...

The usual account of *Cathy Come Home's* use of documentary techniques describes them as a major change in how television was presented. To some extent it is—Ken Loach, the director of *Cathy Come Home*, went on to become an extremely acclaimed filmmaker and unsurprisingly his camerawork was thus ahead of the game for television. But treating *Cathy Come Home* primarily in terms of the extremity of its innovation misses the fact that it worked for a large number of viewers at the time. Yes, it was undoubtedly an advance in terms of camera technique and storytelling, and perhaps it even confused some viewers, but at the end of the day we are talking about a piece of television that succeeded. It couldn't work if it were too far afield from the viewer's expectations. In other words, *Cathy Come Home* works not because it attempts to fool the viewer into believing they are watching a documentary. It works because it trusts that the viewer has a sufficiently good intuitive understanding of televisual storytelling that it can import documentary narrative techniques into ordinary television.

The idea that *Cathy Come Home* might have confused viewers tends to obscure the fact that it was aired as part of the

Wednesday Play anthology series, a known quantity that provided considerable context to its viewing. A negligible number of viewers would have come to it thinking that they were getting a documentary, and the opening credits (giving it a writer) are a pretty unambiguous sign that it's not a documentary. So the idea that its documentary techniques were ever deceptive requires that you assume camera movements are a bigger signifier of the genre of a piece of television than the opening credits and explicit presentation of the show. (The concern that viewers might have tuned in midway is somewhat valid, but it is important to remember that channel flipping was an invention of the 1980s. Television sets in the 1960s were slow to warm up and had no remote controls, and the BBC was designed with an "always on" rhythm that assumed viewers who turned it on and watched for a prolonged period of time. Discussions of this approach appear throughout Volume One.)

Put another way, the people who complained that *Cathy Come Home* was misleading in its use of documentary techniques (people, we should note, who have definitively lost that debate, what with the piece being recognized as the best-ever piece of British television) are assuming an audience of people who are very bad at watching TV, whereas the makers of *Cathy Come Home* are assuming an audience that is very good at it. Specifically, they assume an audience who recognizes that documentaries and news programs are still engaged in storytelling, and that their narrative techniques can be applied to fictional storytelling. On these grounds alone the arguments against should be treated with skepticism. In general arguments about how a text can be misread are difficult to take seriously unless there's actually some evidence that the misreading is solicited by the text.

If these terms, then, it is worth pointing out that the same technique had been being employed in prose in the nineteenth century. The use of documentary techniques for a fictional story is just the television equivalent of the Victorian convention of representing fictional characters with names like "Mr. D——" as if a name had been removed to protect a real person's identity, or the epistolary techniques of, for instance, *Dracula*. We would recognize any critic, even one writing contemporaneously with Stoker, who accused Stoker of trying to fool the audience into believing in vampires to be incompetent.

But this doesn't answer the real question—what is the point of the documentary techniques if not to provide a convincing illusion of reality? The answer to this question helps us understand Doctor Who in the 1960s tremendously. While it's not going to be until *The Ambassadors of Death* in 1970 that documentary-style techniques make any sort of serious appearance on Doctor Who, the show repeatedly uses other techniques to achieve what *Cathy Come Home* achieves through the mixture of documentary elements and fiction. We'll see this starting with our discussion of *The Macra Terror* in the next chapter, but first ...

I said earlier that *Cathy Come Home* is a seminal text in social realism. It is worth explaining what that means. The point of social realism is simple. It's out and out politicized art. You do social realism because you want to get people to change something about how they live their lives—often in terms of political views, occasionally in terms of direct and immediate action. There's not a lot of subtlety to *Cathy Come Home* in this regard. It's flat-out about trying to get people angry about homelessness so they force politicians to take action and fix it.

It's worth making one of our periodic side comments for Americans here. In this unfortunate country, the idea of a social safety net is controversial. This is because the more right-wing party of our two-party system would, in any other country in the civilized world, be a preposterously extremist fringe party. In civilized countries such as the United Kingdom, the debate is not "should we have a broad social safety net" but rather a debate about fine-tuning it. And so a piece like *Cathy Come Home* is not, as it would be in America, about people being homeless with no one to turn to, but rather a piece about inefficient and uncaring bureaucracy that is doing an insufficient job of dealing with the problem. The terms of the debate are not, in other words, "should the government do something about the homeless problem?" but rather "is what the government is doing sufficient?" And if you watch it without realizing this it's very easy to miss what's actually going on in it.

I mention this because it's actually somewhat important to understanding what social realism is about. Or, perhaps more accurately, what it's not about. Even though *Cathy Come Home* is full of intense emotional moments, including a justifiably well-regarded final scene in which Cathy has her children taken away from her, it is fundamentally not about Cathy as an individual. This is evidenced by the fact that Cathy actually has very little characterization beyond her family life and financial state (and even there her children are completely uncharacterized). What we are supposed to see is not Cathy's suffering specifically, but rather the way her suffering is generic—the fact that there is nothing remotely special or unusual about her story. *Cathy Come Home* spends, in fact, a tremendous amount of time looking at the world around Cathy and at how everyone else is in just as bad a situation as she is. Cathy is there to provide a strong and immediate emotional core for the story, but she's not what the story is about as such.

This gets at the real point of the documentary style as well. *Cathy Come Home* is engaged in a fundamentally different project than character-centric narrative. Instead of being a story about Cathy, it is a story about her surroundings—her larger world. That's what the documentary style does—it's a technique designed to show what an aspect of the world is like. This is why *Cathy Come Home* is social realism, as opposed to just regular realism. Its purpose is to show how the entire society that it is set in works.

And here we reach a point where it is helpful to look at the term "social realism" once more and to realize that it actually means two things at once. *Cathy Come Home* is socially realist in both senses of the term, but it doesn't have to do both. See, the word "realism" in the term "social realism" is doing double duty. That is, it means both "realism that is social in focus" and "a work that takes a realist approach to society." The latter means that effort is made to portray a society that works in the manner of real societies. The former means that the story is set on present-day, non-sci-fi Earth. To be clear, neither of these two senses of realism implies the existence of the other. To pick an example from contemporary television, *Glee* is realist only in the sense of being set on Earth. It in no way is about depicting a functional society that works along realistic lines.

Doctor Who, by its nature, can do the former form of realism—treat how societies work in a realistic manner—but not the latter. Thus far, of course, it hasn't really done either. The handful of exceptions are basically the Lucarotti historicals—*Marco Polo*, *The Aztecs*, and *The Massacre*. A case might be made for *The Ark* also being mostly about real society, at least before it becomes a piece of neo-colonialist trash. But even when the show returns to contemporary Earth in *The War Machines*, it hasn't put much effort into portraying the world as a society, instead of as a backdrop over which the set pieces of an adventure story can happen.

But there's no reason Doctor Who has to be like that. The few examples to the contrary suggest this, in fact. And we're going to see, over the next two and a half years of Doctor Who, more stories like this—stories that are to a significant degree about showing what a particular society is like. Ironically, this happens after the series departs its "exploration" mode. But that it happens is unsurprising. If we take the Doctor's regeneration as being primarily about the moral position unveiled in *The Moonbase*—the knowledge that there are monsters in the world—then a focus on actual people living actual lives is a straightforward corollary of the premise. If there are monsters, and if this fact matters, the reason why it matters is that the monsters threaten real people within that world. The claim that there are monsters who "act against everything we believe" and the claim for a need to pursue a social justice agenda in the end obtain their moral force from the existence of a material community. There must be a "we" to believe and a society to have justice within.

But more broadly, this reflects a basic shift in the way in which the world is being thought about. The late 1960s are the high-water mark of the youth counterculture that has been bubbling about Doctor Who since day one (where Susan's "unearthly" status marked her as an image of the future). Thinking about how society works—and perhaps more importantly, aggressively questioning why society works in the ways it does—is a fundamental part of the culture here. And a science fiction program like Doctor Who is still going to follow that, putting the Doctor in situations where he confronts the structure of society.

The Scourge of This Galaxy (*The Macra Terror*)

It's March 11, 1967. In the charts, Engelbert Humperdinck's "Release Me" is edging out The Beatles' first single from the *Sergeant Pepper* sessions, "Penny Lane/Strawberry Fields Forever." Improbably, he will do so for the entire run of this story, and The Beatles will fail to make number one with that single. Also not making number one are ... well, every piece of music ever made that is not Engelbert Humperdinck's "Release Me," but among the ones that come close are The Hollies, Donovan, Herman's Hermits, Tom Jones, and Nancy and Frank Sinatra.

In the real news, the psychedelic movement spreads from San Francisco when a copy of the Human Be-In takes place in Central Park, and Pope Paul VI releases his encyclical *Populorum Progressio*, affirming the Catholic Church's commitment to social justice—a striking commitment to make in the larger context of the 1960s. A military coup takes place in Sierra Leone, the Torrey Canyon wrecks off the coast of Cornwall and is sunk by the British military, and there's a diplomatic kerfuffle as a UN delegation to Aden in advance of Yemen's impending independence arrives and then leaves, declaring that the UK had been unhelpful. For their part, the UK says the delegation never actually contacted them.

While on television, we get *The Macra Terror*. As with a lot of Season Four, this is a story that is misleading when approached with hindsight. The problem is the same problem we ran into with *The War Machines*—which, as it happens, was also by Ian Stuart Black. Namely, it's that this looks a lot like stuff that came after it, and so we view it as a "normal" story on the grounds that it fits into the well-trod "monster" subgenre of Doctor Who. The trouble is that the bulk of this subgenre was built upon what *The Macra Terror* did, and while it looks perfectly normal to a modern Doctor Who fan, it was miles from normal when it aired.

This may seem like a surprising statement. After all, at its heart *The Macra Terror* looks like a pretty standard entrant into the base under siege subgenre that was mostly established with *The Moonbase*. The Doctor shows up somewhere where monsters are doing bad things and stops the monsters. In terms of that basic plot summary, it's the fourth version this season, and that's discounting the subtle variation of this summary in which we often get a mad scientist doing bad things instead of a monster. On paper, this is a straightforward development of the standard theme of the show lately.

But even when we keep historical context in mind, there's something a bit odd here. Seven monsters make their debut over the Troughton era—the Macra, the Chameleons, the Ice Warriors, the Yeti, the Weed Creature, the Quarks, and the Krotons. Of those, two—the Ice Warriors and the Yeti—appear again in the classic series. But only one of the seven appears in the new series: the Macra. There is surely something worth remarking on when a monster is brought back after forty years—not just as a name check, but as an actual on-screen appearance as a story's primary monster (albeit not its primary antagonist—the Macra in *Gridlock* fill the "obligatory monster" role, but the story is hardly about them).

Admittedly part of it is pure whimsy on Russell T Davies's part—he's said that he really just wanted to bring back an obscure and abandoned monster. And another part of it comes down to the fact that *Gridlock* is actually, in terms of its themes, very close to this story, making it a more sensible shout-out than if it had been, say, the Chumblies. But there is something about *The Macra Terror* that made its titular creations the pick of the litter of long-abandoned monsters.

The reason for their return is often lost on people who come at the story from the novelization era of fandom, where it was "that Patrick Troughton story with the crabs" (and little more, since it wasn't novelized until 1987). A 1992 release of the audio turned it around a bit; it was one of the first two missing stories to make it out on audio, and Loose Cannon opened the bidding on the reconstructions in 1998. And so the importance of this story roughly comes down to when in Doctor Who history you formed your impressions of the old stories. To those who learned about them from the books it's just another Troughton monster story, albeit a seemingly well-regarded one.

But for those who have encountered the story on television, what stands out is how unlike business as usual it is. For one thing, it is the story where the new credit sequence debuts. This may sound like a minor, fannish detail, but credit sequences are important. They're what tells you what sort of show you're watching. We stressed the bizarre, mysterious tone of Delia Derbyshire's theme music and the initial opening credits when we first saw them, and how ahead of their time they appeared. So what has changed? Two things. Where the original opening credits started with a single bright white line slowly creeping around the screen, the new credits begin with a full screen design of shimmering lines of light that dissolve not into the logo as the old credits did, but into Patrick Troughton's face, then the logo. This indicates two things. First, it indicates a greater level of comfort with the basic visual imagery of the credits. The old credits started with a basically recognizable shape and distorted it. The new ones start with full psychedelia. Here the basic visual iconography of the show is confirming the turn away from an aesthetic of strangeness that we've been seeing for several stories now. Second, it confirms what we've seen over the last few essays—this is a star-driven show now in which Troughton's charisma is one of the big selling points. First and foremost, this is now a show about Patrick Troughton.

But even more telling than the new credits is the bizarrely chirpy musical number the episode opens with. This sort of music (happy, cheery numbers about working away in the mines) continues throughout the story. It's like nothing seen on Doctor Who before. And watching it in 2011, it's easy not to know what it is. Especially because, in 2011, the more traditional parts of this episode are the visible ones—and not just the Macra. In particular, the episode features an oppressive regime that uses brainwashing to crush all dissent. This is such a standard trope of '60s television, and of Doctor Who, for that matter, that seeing it, it's easy to ignore the weird, chirpy singing and latch on to the intelligible bits that look like what came after.

Indeed, at a first glance, the music seems to be a part of the story's general introduction of its slightly humorous bits. Case in point? The Doctor's comedic sequences in which he figures out the formula for the gas, and then jokes around as he erases it (now try comparing this to any of the exposition in the Hartnell era). For those of you who enjoy this sort of thing, there's another delightful sequence in the first episode where the TARDIS crew are cleaned up by machines in the colony, and the Doctor, in protest, jumps into a "rough and tumble" machine to get nice and disheveled again—a sequence whose absence is easily one of the most painful holes in the archive. (The idea of a spick-and-span Troughton is too good to pass up.)

But this comedic distraction obscures the fact that there's a real darkness to the story as well. One of its major plot points is that Ben is brainwashed by the colony into obedience, and betrays the Doctor. The Doctor has had companions mind controlled before—most obviously in Ian Stuart Black's previous offering, *The War Machines*. In *The War Machines* mind control was a straightforward affair. When Dodo and Polly were brainwashed you could tell by just looking at them—they acted wrongly. What is striking about Ben's brainwashing is that he remains in character even as he betrays the Doctor. There's no flat monotone of obedience here. Instead, Ben lays into the Doctor, accusing him of thinking he knows best all the time.

What's particularly striking about this is that Ben isn't just criticizing the Doctor, he's twisting the Doctor's best attributes into a criticism. As Shearman and Hadoke point out, it ties in nicely with the refocused credit sequence. Ben is reacting against Troughton's know-it-all attitude at the exact moment where Troughton takes on an outsized role in the production that Hartnell never had. The Doctor really is more of a take charge know-it-all now, prancing about the universe with cold moral certainty that he's one of the good guys.

This make's Ben's turn far more gripping; it means that the audience is never quite certain what to make of it. Take, for instance, the sequence where Ben saves Polly from danger, misleading the audience into believing that he's overcome his brainwashing. But his brainwashing isn't superficially obvious and stems from his character traits. Because of this, the plot allows for a crushing reversal shortly thereafter when he suddenly denies the evidence of his senses and turns on his friends again.

What's more interesting than Ben's turn, however, is how Troughton treats Ben for it—with a sort of paternal tut-tutting that mostly sounds like the Doctor is disappointed in him for succumbing. Notably, Jamie and Polly both avoid the brainwashing, despite being exposed, and so this does suggest a level of failure on Ben's part. But the Doctor tips into overt condescension towards Ben, warning him that Jamie will be less forgiving than he is, and seemingly, in doing so, tacitly approving of whatever Jamie might do to Ben if left alone with him (and one gets the sense it will be rather violent). And it's here that the nature of the chirpy singing becomes crucial. Because there is, in the story, a reason why Ben is the one who succumbs to the brainwashing. The brainwashing is, in fact, expressly tailored to Ben more than the rest of the TARDIS crew. Why? Because Ben is explicitly working class.

Ah, I've lost you, haven't I? Here's the thing. The chirpy singing? It would have been immediately recognizable to anyone watching in 1967. The colony, you see, is obviously a holiday camp. What? That doesn't make it completely clear? You don't know what a holiday camp is? Do you people learn nothing about 1950s British working class culture anymore? Oy.

OK. So holiday camps. Basically, take a stretch of land, perhaps near a beach, and set up a bunch of housing there. Then take people there for week long stays, provide room and board, and give them a sort of slightly grown-up summer camp experience. There's lots of extreme cheeriness, random singing, mandatory fun, communal meals, and, of course, legendary anti-snogging patrols with vaguely fascistic undertones. In a somewhat struggling post-war economy, these were the holidays that were available to people. Once air travel and package tours became available the holiday camp vacation model declined to where there's now something vaguely sad and pathetically dated about it. But for a significant time, they were the mainstream British vacation—pile a bunch of families into a colorful resort town and start line dancing and holding strange competitions. Everybody laughs, social norms are overturned, and then it's back to work after a week. (Holiday camps also make an appearance in the Sylvester McCoy era with *Delta and the Bannermen*, for anyone particularly interested in this topic.)

So when it's Ben that succumbs to the brainwashing, it's because the brainwashing closely parallels his own working class background. He's the only one of the four regulars who has probably actually been to a holiday camp. (Polly might have, but is mostly a bit too posh for it. If she did, she didn't enjoy it. Ben would have.) So it's not surprising that he's the one that succumbs to the brainwashing.

But wait a second. Now this story has gone weird on us. When it was just about a fascistic, futuristic, brainwashing state run by crab monsters, it was a typical Doctor Who story. We expect that. But now it's a fascistic and futuristic holiday camp run by crab monsters. Suddenly we've gone from science fiction as political commentary to science fiction as direct social commentary, with the social norms of the present day pastiched into a futuristic society.

In other words, this story has suddenly imported social realism into Doctor Who, or at least, the mode of social realism in which it focuses on the nature and texture of a society. *The Macra Terror* is miles from the intense social realism of *Cathy Come Home*. But it's still doing the same basic thing—trying to get us to see this colony not as a bunch of oppressive lunatics, but as something that is recognizably part of the social order as we understand it—something that we can understand as a coherent world, instead of as a sketch of a political ideology. Unlike in *The Savages*, where the future civilization is obviously a stand-in for colonialist ideology, *The Macra Terror*'s future is modeled off of ordinary lived experience from the audience's lives. That is a massive shift in what Doctor Who does. Even when Doctor Who visited contemporary London, it sketched it in general iconic images. Here Doctor Who is firmly intruding not into the mythology of British life but into the day-to-day minutia of it.

What this means is that *The Macra Terror* is not a generic story about the dangers of conformity. The major sin of the colonists is not their conformity but the superficial nature of their society—the fact that they're governed by a holiday camp. Look at the scene where the controller reiterates to the colonists that they should all be good little colonists, and there are no such things as Macra. The controller is not working as a fascistic authority figure. He sounds terrified by the idea of Macra. The failure is not conformity here—it's the ludicrous, superficial stiff upper lip attitude—the tendency to, if you will, keep calm and carry on. That's what the Doctor is resisting, and the sorts of bad laws he insists should be broken. This isn't some generalized parable about non-conformity, it's a focused attack on a specific aspect of British culture.

What's significant is that the Doctor's resistance in this story makes him even more of an anarchical figure. He's not just a force for chaos who subverts the norms. He has, in both this story and the one before it, a very clear idea of what evil looks like. He knows monster from man, and knows good government from bad. He is not the chaotic sort of anarchist. He's the far more compellingly scary sort—the one who knows exactly what he's doing, and exactly what it is he wants to tear down.

There is one gaping problem with this story, though. Well, two. The first is, of course, the sheer condescension implicit in having Ben's working class origin make him more susceptible to brainwashing. But the second is that, from the script, it sounds like the Macra are the native species of the planet, making the Doctor's casual genocide of them a jarring bit of ethics on his part. That said, there's some ambiguity here. The Macra are repeatedly described as insect-like parasites. And, as Miles and Wood point out, it is hardly like the crucial gas controls were designed for creatures with gigantic claws in place of hands. This leads them to suspect that the original intent of the script was that the Macra are not actually entirely sentient, but are mental parasites that only come up with this scheme in reaction to the humans settling on their planet. A different retcon is offered in *Gridlock*—there the Macra are viewed as infiltrating the colony, not the other way around.

One might expect me to end up pretty sour on this, given my sharp criticism of *The Ark* for its treatment of colonial ethics. But I can't quite. The Macra are not portrayed as doing anything besides lurking in caves, killing people, and controlling minds. Everything says they're "parasites" and "germs." And, crucially, they're completely inhuman, unlike the Monoids who had distinct culture and even individual personalities. So I'm largely inclined—especially given that Ian Stuart Black is the writer of *The Savages*, a pretty expressly anti-colonialist tale—to give the script the benefit of the doubt here and believe that Black had something like one of the two retcons in mind, but it didn't quite make it to screen. Especially because the story, broadly speaking, seems so progressive and socially engaged—considering the nature of the Doctor's rebelliousness. There is a school of thought about Doctor Who (one I'm quite sympathetic to) that says that the show is, at its heart, fairly liberal, and at its best when this liberalism is engaged with. This story, more than perhaps any previous one (save maybe *The Savages*) is where that tendency really begins to crystallize. That alone, really, justifies the interest, even forty plus years on.

Time Can Be Rewritten: *The Roundheads* (Mark Gatiss, BBC Books, 1997)

I try not to jump too far ahead of the time I'm actually talking about in these books, but to understand *The Roundheads* it's necessary to understand where Doctor Who was in late 1997. It's tough, in 2011, to express quite how depressing it was to be a Doctor Who fan in 1997. I gather it was bleak for most of the '90s, and for a fair share of the '80s, but since I only became a fan in the early '90s I don't really have the ability to compare those periods to the heyday. In any case, 1997 was a stunningly bad year even by the standards of the period where the show was off the air. By then it was quite clear that the Paul McGann TV movie was as big a bust commercially as it had been aesthetically. Worse than that, the TV movie had been used as the excuse for bringing Virgin Books' license to produce original Doctor Who fiction to an end, and to move the license in-house to BBC Books. This was a perfectly sound financial decision—the BBC was understandably not thrilled with another company making money doing something they could do perfectly well themselves.

Aesthetically, unfortunately, it was a train wreck, as we'll see when we get to *The Eight Doctors*. Never mind that the second BBC Book—*Vampire Science*—was quite good. By then the Paul McGann years had suffered the same problem the Colin Baker years had just over a decade earlier—two staggeringly bad opening stories that eviscerated the possibility of long-term success. Then, five months in, the coup de grâce came. The one advantage the BBC Books plan maybe had over the Virgin plan was that BBC Books proudly maintained that they had the rights to the Daleks. And so the fifth book of the BBC Books range—John Peel's *War of the Daleks*—was a big deal.

Unfortunately, it was an abomination, one of the most legendarily hated Doctor Who books ever. If you're keeping track, this means that within five months BBC Books (following the epic turkey that was the TV movie) had managed to release two epic turkeys of its own. Add that to the fact that the series now had seemingly no feasible way back to television, and that nobody could actually tell you what the Eighth Doctor was like in a meaningful sense, and you have yourself some bleak times. And not just bleak in the way that every year had been since the show was cancelled. These were bleak in a new way. There was an intractable sense that a fundamental opportunity had been wasted—that we had just suffered an appalling false dawn. It was impossible, in 1997, not to have the sense that Doctor Who had actually been in much better shape before it made a try at coming back—that it had done cancellation better the first time.

Which makes the events of November of 1997 all the more intriguing. In the main line of Eighth Doctor novels, just one month after the John Peel trainwreck, something called *Alien Bodies* by Lawrence Miles happened. For those of you who are going to learn a huge amount about the world of Doctor Who novels when this project actually gets to 1997 proper, *Alien Bodies* is a landmark book. There are a couple moments in the novels where everything changes—landmark novels that are as important as landmark stories such as *The Tenth Planet* in terms of the development of the series. And if you're listing those moments, the first two you write down are basically Paul Cornell's *Timewyrm: Revelation*, and Lawrence Miles's *Alien Bodies*. *The Roundheads*, on the other hand, is the other book that came out that month. And rather than making it an uninteresting footnote, this was perhaps the most appropriate time for a book like *The Roundheads*.

One of the things about those landmark moments—and we've just finished seeing the impact of one of them—is that we tend to think of them from the perspective of what's created but not what's destroyed. Of course, it is equal parts each. Our first regeneration story is the perfect example. You don't just get the start of a new era. You get, as I said in the essay on *The Tenth Planet*, to see the show you loved get cancelled. Every time someone's favorite era of Doctor Who begins—and every era, even the Colin Baker or Paul McGann years, is someone's favorite—the show someone loved dies to make it happen. Intrinsic to being a Doctor Who fan is accepting this. And more to the point, intrinsic to being a Doctor Who fan is learning to love this, and learning to see why it is necessary for a great show to end. The answer is that, over time, every great show becomes a merely good show. Doctor Who doesn't have to. Never mind that it sometimes does become merely good, and occasionally strays into not-actually-very-good. Doctor Who has a license that no other show has—the right, and indeed the obligation, to throw everything out while the show is still great and start over to try again.

But none of this minimizes the importance of the elegy to Doctor Who. And that's why it's strangely nice to see *The Roundheads* come out right when Doctor Who is busily getting itself cancelled again. Because *The Roundheads*, at its heart, is an elegy for William Hartnell set in the Patrick Troughton era and published thirty years later.

The most obvious reason to describe it as such is that it is one of the relatively few pure historicals done after *The Highlanders*. These are not a massively uncommon phenomenon—the TV series did one in 1982 with *Black Orchid*, and virtually every spin-off line has done at least a couple, with the Big Finish audios having several quite nice ones. Even among these, however, *The Roundheads* is a curiosity. Most of the subsequent historicals are returns to the form—historicals featuring Doctor/companion teams who never got a historical. Alternatively, they're ones that are firmly in the age where historicals happened like Gareth Roberts's *The Plotters*. This is something else—a historical adventure set after the historical had ended, but not so far after that it is inconceivable that a historical could have been shown. It's after *The Highlanders*— and thus after the end of the genre—but all of the regulars in it have appeared in at least one televised historical. It is, in other words, an attempt to do a new "last historical." Which is reasonable, given how far *The Highlanders* was from a normal historical.

But it's important to be very precise about what's happening here. This is not a defense of the historical as a genre. A defense would be a Third Doctor/Jo historical, or, if you really want to challenge yourself, finding a way to make a Fourth Doctor/Romana II historical work. That would show that the historicals never needed to end and could have continued functioning in any era of the show.

No, *The Roundheads* is written with the knowledge that it is part of a doomed genre. It is written to say goodbye to the historical at the last point at which a historical could remotely, plausibly have appeared on the schedule of the actual television show—after the next story the TARDIS crew changes to include the first companion never to get a historical. (No, we're not counting Sara Kingdom today.) It is an elegy—consciously and deliberately a celebration of a mode of Doctor Who that evaporated just one story later.

It's worth remembering that the first Doctor Who story was a historical. Because fundamentally, in its original conception, Doctor Who was about taking Ian and Barbara— two ordinary people—and putting them in extraordinary circumstances. And to stave off having the show appear to be "Ian the schoolteacher goes and has fantastic adventures with his friends Barbara, Susan, and the Doctor," the show puts them all in a prehistoric setting where the concern isn't "saving the galaxy" or anything like that, but rather the delightfully prosaic "try not to get your skull bashed in." This communicates—in a way that *The Daleks* never could—that

Doctor Who is not a show about fantastic adventures, it's a show about scary places.

Obviously the show has moved away from that. But the degree to which it has moved away is nothing compared to what happens when Ben and Polly leave next story. It's not the first time that the show has had no representatives of contemporary Earth—that's true from *The Time Meddler* through *The Daleks' Master Plan*. But notably that stretch of the show is a massive transition in which the TARDIS crew changes practically every story. After *The Faceless Ones* the lack of anyone from contemporary Earth is the status quo. This, more than anything, is what kills the historical. If you imagine the next companion team having a historical adventure, there seems very little point. Why have a sixteenth century Scotsman and a Victorian woman appear in history? That's where they belong. It would be like shoving Ian and Barbara into a contemporary London adventure.

Gatiss takes full advantage of this, splitting the TARDIS crew into three plots. Polly gets a political intrigue plot in which she's used as a pawn by the Cavaliers, Ben gets a big naval adventure plot, and the Doctor and Jamie share a plot that, if you look closely, actually basically amounts to them marking time while waiting for Ben and Polly to get back with their plot resolutions. In other words, the bulk of this book is about shoving people from contemporary Earth into historical danger—just like the show itself originally was. This is a striking departure from the stories it's set between, in which Ben is increasingly marginalized in favor of Jamie (and indeed, next story, shown the door).

But none of this is enough to paper over the other reason the historical died. Back in *The Highlanders* entry, I talked about two basic flavors of historical—Lucarotti style and Spoonerstyle. The Lucarotti style—*Marco Polo*, *The Aztecs*, and *The Massacre* most notably—are basically survival stories about the cultural differences between the past and the present. Their central tension is getting the TARDIS crew back to the TARDIS given that history is both unchangeable and dangerous. The Spooner style—and basically every other historical save for *100,000 BC* itself—is what we apparently have started calling a "romp" where the story is just a tour of the major tropes of a genre.

Here's the problem, then. Spooner killed his own style of historical off with *The Time Meddler*. Yes, there were four historicals in his style after that, but he still delivered a mortal blow to the subgenre by showing that the romps are even more fun when you give the Doctor an antagonist who's in on the joke. The reason *The Time Meddler* is such a delight is that the Monk and the Doctor both get the fact that the Middle Ages are a strange and backward place. And so begins a train of thought that ends up, at the time of writing, right around *The Curse of the Black Spot* (which was part of a swap designed to move Mark Gatiss's episode for this season to the fall, just in case you forgot why we cared about this book).

See, *The Curse of the Black Spot* is actually basically a remake of *The Smugglers*—it even sets itself up subtly as a prequel to it. But where *The Smugglers* was a tour of major tropes of the pirate genre, *Curse of the Black Spot* was a tour of even more major tropes of the pirate genre. It has all the stock characters *The Smugglers* has, all the iconic piratey bits, plus a ghost ship and a siren—two bonus bits of piratey goodness that *The Smugglers*, being a pure historical, had to pass up. Similarly, look at how *The Fires of Pompeii* hits almost all the same jokes as *The Romans* (including a nod to "the ants in honey joke") and then adds a bunch more because it can have giant fire monsters in it. Heck, look at Gatiss's own televised Doctor Who—three of the four are Spooner-style historicals with monsters. If you want to do a tour of genre tropes, there's no compelling reason to limit yourself to "realist" ones.

That leaves the Lucarotti-style historicals, which, let's face it, are the ones that tend to be the picks of would-be "sophisticated" fans. Here the problem is more subtle, and relates to the overall shift in Doctor Who. It's worth noting that two of the three Lucarotti-style historicals come before *The Sensorites*, and the third requires the Doctor to be marginalized heavily. Why is this important? Because *The Sensorites*, as Miles and Wood point out in *About Time*, is the first story in which the Doctor agrees to help because it's the right thing to do. Previous stories relied on the TARDIS being disabled for their plot. *The Sensorites* starts with that, but midway through there is a point where the Doctor could leave if he wanted to, but chooses not to out of a desire to help.

This is the first step towards the tendency that we're seeing explode now with things like *The Macra Terror*. It's the first time the show starts to turn towards treating the Doctor as a star, and, equally, it's the first time the show starts concerning itself with social justice questions (like how to improve society). The Doctor, between *The Aztecs* and *The Roundheads*, has become a character who does not travel the universe just because he's an exile, but rather one who travels the universe to make it a better place. That's what the entire Troughton regeneration was about, and why I went to such lengths to stress the bizarre nature of the Cybermen in *The Tenth Planet*.

But it's a death knell to the historical. If the Doctor is a sympathetic and likable character in part because of his commitment to fighting evil then we run into a huge problem when we put him in a historical setting. *The Massacre* is, for all its genius, the story where we can see this problem actually killing the genre before our eyes. I described the heart of the problem in that essay—which, actually, is in the back of this book because I'm an idiot and somehow left it out of the print edition of Volume I, so you can go read it. But in short, in *The Massacre*, Steven is right and the Doctor is wrong. It is clearly and unambiguously the case that slaughtering the Huguenots is wrong. Having the Doctor simply walk away from it saying that it happened so there's nothing he can do about it is only possible in that story because the Doctor has been so spectacularly diminished by the stories immediately preceding it. Under normal circumstances, watching the Doctor shrug his shoulders and walk away from vicious wrongdoing is … well … wrong.

Nowhere is this clearer than the mercifully aborted Brian Hayles script "The Nazis," which would have featured the Doctor, well, meeting up with the Nazis. Try to wrap your head around that one. Try to figure out a way to put the Doctor face to face with people who slaughtered six million people in a mechanized and industrialized way that is the closest humanity has ever come to Dalekdom, and then remember that he's not allowed to stop them. It's horrifyingly crass. Sufficiently so that Paul Cornell observed that the reason Sylvester McCoy is his favorite Doctor is that he was the first Doctor you could imagine walking through a concentration camp without it ending up as a moral travesty, because finally the Doctor had ethics complex enough to handle it. (Whether you agree with Cornell is, of course, another matter.) The problem, in other words, is that there's something fundamentally unsatisfying about a crusader for good who will stop any travesty unless it happened on Earth prior to the year 1967.

And so once the show actually settled on the Doctor being a hero, the historical rapidly withered. And this is the problem Gatiss can't quite get around. He tries, giving the Doctor a good speech about needing to maintain history. But his explanation is … well, let's look at it:

> Have I seen them? Yes, I've seen them. Or heard of them. Englands with a third, fourth, or fifth Civil War. A resurgent monarch who ruthlessly oppresses all democracy. Or a triumphalist, hereditary Puritan Protectorate that rules the country until the twentieth century. Or an invading Catholic army which takes advantage of England's crisis to take over most of the known world. Oh yes, they're all out there. All kinds of futures. Some great, some truly terrible.

What's wrong here, of course, is that the same could be said of overthrowing the Macra, or stopping humanity from being converted to Cybermen, or any other time the Doctor has intervened to save people. The Doctor—Troughton's

Doctor in particular—is infamous for sneaking out instead of sticking around to help clean up his own mess. The Doctor has never cared how civilization will rebuild itself when he's thrown a spanner in the works. Except for when he does this arbitrarily—when the civilization is Earth prior to the date of transmission.

Gatiss manages to get away with it mostly because the appeal of putting Charles I back on the throne and avoiding Oliver Cromwell is limited. As much of a git as Cromwell is, it's not like Charles I was winning "Monarch of the Month" awards or anything. It's pretty easy to write around the moral problems with this setting because nobody has a moral investment in the alternative. But that's a weak justification that itself indicates a mortal wound to the subgenre— we can only do historicals when nobody is going to care about the history.

But none of that erases the fact that, generally speaking, Gatiss is working in the increasingly shrinking margins of the transition from Hartnell to Troughton. Here, in the last days of Hartnell's last companions, it is still just possible to reach across that gap and tell a story like they used to be told. But from here on out, looking back is going to be much harder. This marks the point, in other words, where Doctor Who grows too large to be treated straightforwardly as a singular concept. For the first time, one vision for the show has been cancelled and does not look like it is ever coming back.

Smaller on the Inside (*The Faceless Ones*)

It's April 8, 1967, and Englebert Humperdinck will not die. Actually, this is his last week at number one. Next week it's Nancy and Frank Sinatra with "Somethin' Stupid." Once again we're just seeing the pendulum in action here. It's just that the pendulum is unusually swung at the moment—nothing all that interesting in the entire top ten (though number eleven, Jimi Hendrix's "Purple Haze," reminds us that there is a counterculture out there). It peaks at number three, and The Who, The Mamas and the Papas, and Cat Stevens all break the top ten in the next few weeks as well, bolstered by a population who, having listened to Humperdinck for a month and a half, finally intuitively get what this "youth revolution" is all about. The flip side is that Sandie Shaw wins the Eurovision song contest for the UK with "Puppet on a String," bringing this touching song about complete physical and emotional submission to your man to number one. ("If you say you love me madly, I'll gladly be there like a puppet on a string." Stay classy, British pop music.) Oh, and Pink Floyd charts, but nowhere near the top ten.

Whereas in the world of things that don't sing, the Tories win the Greater London Council elections which is never a good sign for Labour. (Indeed, Harold Wilson's government will go down in the next election.) Mass protests against the Vietnam War take place in the US, while Surveyor 3 lands on the Moon. Greece falls to a military dictatorship, like you do, and Vladimir Komarov, a Soviet astronaut, is the first to die in their space program due to a parachute malfunction. Most interestingly, however, Prime Minister Harold Wilson announces that the UK will be applying to join the EEC.

Most of these can be slotted into standard '60s fare, but the last one might be lost on you, which probably also means that Mark Gatiss's great joke about Euroskeptics in *The Roundheads* was lost on you too. So sad. Basically, the EEC is an earlier version of the European Union. It's one of several "communities" to crop up after World War II—the first of them being the ECSC, European Coal and Steel Community, which sought to establish control over the basic supplies needed for war. A few more stabs in the dark in this general area eventually led to the EEC, which quickly became fairly powerful in that it made intra-European commerce more efficient, allowing Europe as a whole to remain a major force even as few of its component states retained the superpower status they had prior to the World Wars.

The thing is, the EEC and the UK kind of have a ... history. Because shortly after the EEC was founded, Charles DeGaulle shut down the process for countries to join because he didn't want the UK to join, fearing that it would basically serve as a US puppet state. Given that the UK rarely required reasons to be ambivalent about its status in the European community, the re-opening of applications and the UK's decision to apply in 1967 is, by any standard, a major shift in the general tone of European cooperation. Or, if you're the sort of person who is extremely anxious about the loss of national identity implied by greater integration of the United Kingdom with the rest of Europe ... Well then, you might just see the entire thing as being vaguely similar to an airport full of aliens who steal people's identities and threaten to eliminate the entire youthful population of Britain.

Speaking of which, on television we have *The Faceless Ones*. And lest you think the show can't respond that fast to current events, keep in mind that applying for EEC membership was a continual issue in 1967, and that the show was, at this point, running with virtually no buffer (the overspend on *The*

Underwater Menace having left them with only a one week lead time between filming an episode and airing it). *The Faceless Ones* was, in other words, filming the week that the final episode of *The Macra Terror* aired. While this still doesn't line up with the timeline so that this story can be read as a direct allegory about the EEC, it does push them close enough that it's more than possible to read the story as responding to general concerns about the shifting nature of Britain and Europe.

There are two ways to look at *The Faceless Ones*. On the one hand, it's a tour de force. For one thing, it has the most effective use of location filming in the series to date. In the past, locations have been used for exterior shots. At its most cliché, this means some running around in a rock quarry before you get to running around some space station corridors. Occasionally it's livelier—the location work in Cornwall for *The Smugglers*, for instance. But here we have something altogether stranger—indoor location work. And it's impossible to overstress how fascinating this is. Flip back to *Cathy Come Home* to get a sense of why. The use of cameras moving around large indoor spaces—and "large" does not really get at the full difference between Gatwick airport and any other modern building—again serves to establish these events as things that are happening in a world as opposed to on a televisual stage. This accelerates Doctor Who's shift towards a social realist mode in which the show was set, whether directly or indirectly, in the same world it was transmitted in.

On the other hand, plotwise, this is the same story as *The Macra Terror*, *The Moonbase*, *The Tenth Planet*, and *The War Machines*. You can create these stories with Mad Libs. Take a noun that is something people have, a verb ending in -ing, a creature, and a location with people and you too can write a story in which Noun-Verbing Creatures attack a Location. Last time the arrangement was Mind, Controlling, Crabs, and Holiday Camp. Today we get Identity, Stealing, Humanoids, and Airport.

All of which said, this isn't so bad. Or if it is, it's probably time to skip ahead a decade or so in Doctor Who and try again, because it's not like the "find a Mad Lib and plug it for all it's worth" approach is going away. And why should it? The approach works. The fact of the matter is, in terms of sheer watchability, the show is doing far better than it used to. Yes, it's playing it safe, but the consequence of that is that it manages to hit its mark with reliability. This increasingly frees it up to try being experimental—not in the sense of *The Underwater Menace* (the closest thing to a disaster the show has had since *The Celestial Toymaker*) but in the sense of *The Macra Terror* in which the show starts to have something to say instead of just trying to be inventive for its own sake (and in the process manages to be incredibly inventive).

The problem isn't even that *The Faceless Ones* forgets to be interesting. It does a ton of interesting things, which we'll get back to. The problem is that *The Faceless Ones* took one for the team and expanded to six episodes to make up for the cost overruns on *The Underwater Menace*. The mechanics of this are simple—the highest cost for any story is its first episode, for which most of the costumes and sets need to be constructed. The remaining episodes mostly just re-use the stuff from the first episode. So if you need to save money, you make stories longer so you have to make costumes and sets less often. That's why there are eight four-parters in Season Three, six in Season Four, and then one each in Seasons Five, Six, and Seven and two in Seasons Eight through Eleven—because budgets got increasingly tight and multipart stories were turned to in desperation.

The problem is that this decision was rarely made on the basis of what stories should be longer. Previously this was decided sensibly: you expanded the Dalek stories, because those were your bigger hits. So Dalek stories could be plotted for six episodes, and inasmuch as Terry Nation was capable of thinking that way he did so. Except now we end up in a period where everything gets expanded, whether or not there's actually a reason beyond the financials. So we get six episodes of *The Faceless Ones*. And, worse, we get six episodes where no individual episode is that bad. At least in the next story everyone knows, or, rather, thinks they know, which episode is padding. Here, though, what we have is actually a three-episode structure in which each episode should be about thirty to thirty-five minutes, but is instead fifty minutes split up into two episodes each. The first two episodes are the TARDIS crew sneaking around an airport; the second two are half of the TARDIS crew doing *Quatermass*, and the final two are a trip to a spaceship to liven things up. It's a fine structure, but there's not actually enough story for it. Every episode is about twenty-five percent too long.

And, crucially, this isn't because of the cliché that television pacing has sped up over time. It has, due largely to the fact that editing is now easy and you can tell your story with camera movement and cuts instead of dialogue. But this feels slow compared to *The Macra Terror*, never mind slow compared to a Steven Moffat episode. And it's unfortunate, because this is a good story—considerably better than some of the supposed classics in Season Five. But it's the point where the changes in the show we talked about really start to show their dark side. *The Faceless Ones* would have just seemed a bit slow in the past. But as a formulaic story that comes after a raft of other stories done on the same formula, and then stretched out to be fifty percent longer, it's just a bit too much, and the strain becomes a bit too visible.

And this is really unfair, because the fact of the matter is that Malcolm Hulke is—as he'll show in Seasons Six through Eleven, a damned good writer. I can't speak for David Ellis, his co-writer on this story, simply because he doesn't return to the show, but Hulke is enormously sharp. The fact of the matter is that switching from a standard four-episode structure to a three-act structure of two-episode parts is sharp, and it's a better way of handling the onerous requirement of having two extra episodes tacked onto your story than most writers manage. It's not their fault—it's one imposed on them. But it still wrecks an otherwise good story.

But look, in the end, these are problems which stem from the reception of the show and the way in which it is viewed, not from the writing. And we should be a little suspicious of them. We're still in a period that's mostly reconstructions. The reconstructions are for the most part very good. But they're still static images with a soundtrack. They're not as good as the real thing. And the show is designed to be watched an episode a week, not at the two or three a day rate I do in researching these pieces, and certainly not at the "as a movie" pace that fans tend to prefer. So we're dealing with not-quite-as-good reconstructions of episodes at over seven times the pace designed. This doesn't erase the problems with pacing, but it does mean that we're a lot more sensitive to them than the intended audience of the show is. Our "unbelievably tedious" is the actual audience's "not quite as pacy as last time."

Which is to say that, yes, this is too long and too formulaic. But that's not all there is to say about it. So let's get back to the good. Those shots of Gatwick! They're amazing! They're the clearest example of social realist techniques in Doctor Who to date. But that's a bit of a trap. When we say Doctor Who and social realism, we start to stray towards Jon Pertwee's oft-repeated comment that Doctor Who is at its scariest when it's a Yeti in your loo in Tooting Bec. This comment, however, is problematic in several regards. We'll deal with the urological tendencies of Yeti more when those are actually monsters that have appeared in Doctor Who, but the thing to stress here is that Gatwick Airport was in no way familiar ground for the audience. It's part of their world, certainly, but not part of their experience.

In fact, having this story come right after a story about the 1950s vacation mainstay of the Holiday Camp is oddly fitting timing. If that story was about the receding past of working class vacations, this was about the new future offered by economic and technological development. The package tour—which is what this story ultimately centers on—basically served to take the holiday camp concept and instead flit about Europe having scheduled tourist experiences instead of sitting about having mandatory fun. And in their main innovation, the package tour offered something the holiday camp never could—an experience designed for a single young traveler.

The impact of this is significant, and ties in with what we were talking about earlier with the EEC. Previously, for most people, the only reason you'd go to mainland Europe was if you had to fight a war or perform some other form of public service. Now the UK was connected to Europe in a way it never had been before. For a working class household, this was every bit as much a new frontier as space was. And in the rhetoric around the EEC—the twin sense of anxiety and opportunity—you can see a reaction that is nearly identical to the issues surrounding space exploration.

But this also gets at one of the most important things about *The Faceless Ones*: it's scary. This is the most committed the series has been to suspense up to this point. The music is droning bass, everyone is sneaking around, and one of the dominant themes of the story is surveillance, with a tremendous amount of action taking place as characters watch other events on television screens. (This leads to one of the most peculiar cliffhangers in Doctor Who, in which the cliffhanger is actually a character watching TV in horror as something unexpected happens.) This is a story about how this weird "commercial air travel" thing is scary, and might steal our children. (This is not, as is often claimed, about immigration. It makes no sense as a story about immigration.)

But, equally impressive, it doesn't end up there. This is the debut of Malcolm Hulke, and for those of you who love it when Doctor Who borders on leftist propaganda, this is a big day. So we're not going to end up on some xenophobic point about how these European stand-ins really are nefarious. Instead we get a scene that is actually, in its own right, as iconic as the line, "corners of the universe that have bred the most terrible things." The Doctor opens "negotiations" with the Chameleons instead of making them explode. And it works. The Chameleons slink on home, and all is well. This is arguably anti-climactic (though with the pacing issues, I'd suggest it's hardly the story's biggest problem with climax), but is, more accurately, something we'll see repeatedly in Hulke's Doctor Who work—a serious ambivalence about the idea that "alien" and "monster" are in any way related concepts.

Oh, and then there's the companions. As I alluded in the post on *The Roundheads*, this is where we say goodbye to Ben and Polly. They basically vanish with no trace in the second episode, showing up in the last scene in a pre-filmed insert, a write-off that is only slightly better than Dodo's in that they remember to bring them back to say goodbye. They even remember to have the Doctor make reference to their existence in the sixth episode before they show up again! So things are improving since the days of Dodo!

But not by much. This is another crass companion write-off of the sort we've become maddeningly accustomed to. And it's a pity. Ben and Polly were a good pair of characters. But they were, in the end, caught between two extremes. On one level they were supposed to be companions in the Ian and Barbara mode—reluctant travelers who wanted to go home. On the other, they were supposed to be young companions representing Britain's future. The trouble is, by this point, when traveling with the Doctor seemed so fun and exciting, that disparity doesn't work. Another consequence of the decision to make the Doctor fun and charismatic is that the reluctant traveler model falters. And, more to the point, in a period where youth and the Doctor's anarchism are increasingly allied, two representatives of Britain's youth culture are never going to be the reluctant travelers, just as two squares like Ian and Barbara aren't the appropriate companions for someone like Troughton's Doctor. Ben and Polly are, in this sense, victims of the cultural shifts that Doctor Who is finding itself caught up in.

Still, even if Ben and Polly kind of fall into the crack between two approaches, it's tough not to find their departure irritating. Yes, more of an effort is made than with Dodo, but that's kind of like saying that euthanasia is more medical attention than leaving someone to die. And while I've restrained myself on the accusations of Polly being portrayed in a sexist manner—not that she isn't, just that I think she's by and large in better shape than female characters of the era usually got—holy crap is her send-off one of the most appalling pieces of sexist drek I have ever seen. The Doctor tells Ben to go off and become an admiral ... then seconds later tells Polly to go and look after Ben. Ouch.

The problem here is that investing in the '60s companions is a bit of an uphill battle sometimes. With no emotional plotlines serialized across the stories, or even, usually, within a single story, the characters spend much more time fulfilling plot functions than acting like characters. They're stock characters, expected to be drawn out in broad strokes, and then thrown into situations where the stock characters don't belong. Occasionally they transcend this—Barbara being the one with the most examples of scenes in which she works as more than a stock character. But for the most part, they do not.

Another way to think about this is that we care about the characters when the show cares about them. We care about Ian and Barbara because the show finds space to give us scenes of them marveling at their circumstances even quite late in their tenure, after we've gotten used to the characters. When, as is the case with Ben and Polly, we never get those scenes, and are forced to read in any depth we add to the characters, and then are treated to perfunctory departure scenes like this, it is difficult to muster up any real emotion at the event. Why should we care about Ben and Polly when it's obvious that the show doesn't? There are answers to that question, but ultimately most of them are tautological—we care because we are Doctor Who fans and are committed to the history of the show. But in the end, there is more to say about Anneke Wills, who is still a wonderful presence on the convention circuit— and Michael Craze, who died far too young, than there is about either of their characters.

While talking about the companions in this story it's also necessary to mention Samantha, played by Pauline Collins, who was apparently offered a role as a companion, and thought to be completely mad for passing it up. She's got an OBE, a

BAFTA, and an Oscar nomination, which is more than can be said for anyone who did take a role as a companion, and, frankly, her character is insufferable here, so really, let's leave it at that.

Everything You Were, Everything You Stood For (*The Evil of the Daleks*)

It's May 20, 1967. The Tremeloes, best known as the band Decca signed instead of The Beatles, are at number one. The Tremeloes, like The Beatles, came from the Merseybeat scene we've talked about some already (the name Merseybeat is also why The Beatles are spelled the way they are), and unlike The Beatles of 1967, were still churning out generic, doo-wop inflected rock numbers such as "Silence is Golden," which held number one for three weeks before Procul Harum takes number one with a nice, sweeping prog/psychedelic rock epic "A Whiter Shade of Pale," which holds the number one for the remaining four weeks of this story. Elsewhere in the charts are The Mamas and the Papas, The Supremes, The Monkees, The Beach Boys, The Who, Jimi Hendrix, and The Kinks. But let's face it, the real news is this: *Sergeant Pepper's Lonely Hearts Club Band* is released, and becomes the soundtrack to the so-called Summer of Love, which we'll discuss more in the next chapter.

In news that anchors who don't sing won't take, Celtic beat Inter Milan to win the European Cup, making them the first British team to win that competition. On one level, this continues the brief and shining moment of British domination of the sport. On another level, you have to understand Glaswegian sports fandom, the Old Firm rivalry, and sectarian violence to even start to understand what the phrase "Celtic won" means, and since none of those things are remotely relevant to *The Evil of the Daleks*, hey look, we've moved on.

(Though I'm sure it made Frazer Hines, a complete football nut, followed it avidly.) The Soviet Union, the US, and the UK agree not to put nuclear weapons in space, which is very nice of them.

In other news, let's take a deep breath. First Israeli/Egyptian tensions flare up mightily as the Six Day War breaks out and ends, which is the sort of thing that happens when you schedule a six-day war in the midst of a seven-week Dalek serial. Biafra begins its futile attempt at independence, while a Marxist rebellion begins in India. Loving v. Virginia is decided in the US, legalizing interracial marriage, and, on a related note, Thurgood Marshall is nominated to the Supreme Court. Also on the subject of race in America, race riots break out in Tampa and Buffalo. While back in Europe the EEC is merged with the ECSC and EAC to form the European Communities, and, three days after this story finishes, homosexuality is finally decriminalized in the UK, a move that most immediately impacts the artistic community, where numerous quasi-out homosexuals worked, including Max Adrian and Waris Hussein, both of whom worked on Doctor Who in the Hartnell era.

While on television, we have *The Evil of the Daleks*. Which is as hard a story to see straight as exists in Doctor Who, so let's just dust off the old-fashioned tricks and go through the thing linearly to see how it works, then sort out the rest.

There's a fine and at times difficult to pin down line between a methodical, suspenseful pace and a slow one, and this story walks it. Coming into it, the first and most important thing, then, is the title card: *The Evil of the Daleks*, by David Whitaker. By this point in the show's run, those words mean things. We know that Dalek stories are the event stories—and note that major cast changes happened in every return the Daleks have made. But, equally important, by this point anyone who watches the show closely knows what some names mean. David Whitaker has had credits on both Dalek movies, two novelizations (including *Doctor Who in an Exciting Adventure with the Daleks*), the previous Dalek story, and three stories prior, plus he was the script editor for the first year and change. He is the most known quantity writer at this point—one who we, by this point, recognize as the writer of Important Stories.

I say all of this because it's essential to understanding the first twenty-five minutes of this story. Whitaker starts with astonishing confidence—much as he did in *Power of the Daleks*. He clearly trusts that the word "Daleks" and, to a lesser extent, his writing credit buys him some patience. And so the most interesting thing about the first episode of *Evil of the Daleks* is that so little happens. The Doctor is stuck playing Sherlock Holmes, doing a nice little pointless runaround chasing the stolen TARDIS while the actual plot goes on with Waterfield in his antique shop. This requires some real faith—both in Troughton and Hines and their ability to vamp out a double act for their screentime and in the viewer for being able to accept that this story is going to take twenty-five minutes of screentime to get all the pieces on the board.

Thankfully, the pieces are fascinating—'60s mod coffee bars, a Victorian man in 1966 (this is, again, one of the most important things about this story and *The Faceless Ones*—they were set in the recent past), a stolen TARDIS, evil and mysterious overlords, etc. So when a Dalek makes his obligatory end-of-the-first-episode cliffhanger appearance here, it's become juxtaposition. Ironically, by taking twenty-five minutes to set up the plot on the promise that there are Daleks coming and it'll be worth it, Whitaker manages to make the appearance of the Daleks—the entire reason the audience doesn't give up before the end, and thus the only thing we go into the minutes actively expecting—into a genuine surprise again simply because he spends the first twenty-five minutes of this story building up the non-Dalek elements of the story so well that there barely seems to be room for the Daleks. Then he drops the Daleks in, and for once there's a genuine sense of mystery to them again—a question of "well what does this mean" for the story as opposed to a giddy conviction that a lot of things are going to explode soon.

When this is followed fairly early on with the Doctor and Jamie being transported to Victorian England in the second episode—where there are still Daleks—we get to a point where this story has gone, for lack of a better phrase, completely mental. To be clear, we have Victorian time travelers selling brand new antiques in 1966 and luring the Doctor into a trap so that he can be transported back to 1866 as part of a plot by the Daleks. In 2011, this sounds very much like Doctor Who. But other than *The Chase* and *The Daleks' Master Plan* we've never even had a story that jumped between two timeframes, and in those cases it was a matter of the TARDIS and a Dalek craft traveling in parallel. The idea of events in 1866 affecting those in 1966 directly and of the Doctor traveling through time via something other than the TARDIS is wholly new. So is the idea of Daleks in Victorian England. Not Daleks just dropping in on Victorian England as they chase the Doctor around, but Daleks who have already integrated themselves into Victorian England—who have a plan already in progress.

And so the first thing Whitaker does is spend an episode playing with the tension of this, throwing two scenes that, in 1967, were bizarre. First, we get Victoria Waterfield (hereafter Victoria), Edward Waterfield's (hereafter Waterfield) daughter, captured by the Daleks. The initial shot is practically fairytale—she feeds birds like she's Snow White. Then a Dalek comes in and menaces her. And, crucially, it's two things that absolutely do not belong in a shot together. Which is, as you may recall, the whole original purpose of this series back when David Whitaker basically invented it.

The second scene is even stranger. Waterfield and Maxtible explain how they invented a time machine. Let's take a quick look at the script here, because this is an incredibly weird section.

> MAXTIBLE: I have always been fascinated by the concept of travelling through time. Waterfield here is an expert in certain technical matters and I have the money to indulge my

whims. Everything you see about you here was constructed by us two.

DOCTOR: To try to find a way of exploring time?

MAXTIBLE: Yes, now this is my theory. A mirror reflects an image, does it not?

DOCTOR: Yes.

MAXTIBLE: So, you may be standing there, yet appear to be standing fifty feet away. Well, following the new investigations twelve years ago by J. Clark Maxwell into electromagnetism and the experiments by Faraday into static electricity …

DOCTOR (*suspicious*): Static?

MAXTIBLE: Correct! Waterfield and I first attempted to refine the image in the mirror, and then to project it. In here, Doctor, are one hundred and forty-four separate mirrors.

WATERFIELD: And each is of polished metal. Each is subjected to electric charges, all positive.

MAXTIBLE: Like repels like in electricity, Doctor, and so next, Waterfield and I attempted to repel the image in the mirror, wherever we directed.

First of all, this makes no sense whatsoever in any context that can be recognized as reality. Well. OK. In almost any context. There is one context where it makes perfect sense: alchemy. There are several clues here—the fact that a mirror's reflection is treated as equivalent to the image itself (the image of a time traveler becomes a time traveler), the fact that electricity is used because "like repels like," and the fact that the number of mirrors is exactly 144, i.e. twelve squared. We'll pick this point up later.

More significant is the fact that an alchemical Victorian time machine has apparently summoned the Daleks. Which, aside from being a bewildering juxtaposition, also means that

Doctor Who quietly invented steampunk—in 1967. This is significant, in no small part because it's wholly true. If you take as a fair definition of steampunk—"a subgenre of science fiction concerned with juxtaposing the structure and imagery of Victorian adventure stories from which science fiction developed with concepts from contemporary science fiction," which is, I think reasonable, then *Evil of the Daleks* is steampunk through and through, ages before it was cool, or, for that matter, existent. (The obvious refutation is that Victorian science fiction invented steampunk, but this is preposterous. Steampunk depends specifically on the nostalgia for Victorian culture and adventure stories mixed with an existent love of tropes that postdate the Victorian. H.G. Wells is just Victorian. *Evil of the Daleks* is steampunk, right down to the Doctor's anarchic and destructive tendencies.)

From here, having methodically laid out its basic premises, *Evil of the Daleks* goes into three episodes that are, by any standard, a bit rough. There are reasons for this—Troughton took a vacation during the filming of the fourth episode and appeared in prefilmed inserts, and the story got an added episode that was used to pad out the middle section. So we get three episodes of Jamie running around in a Victorian mansion full of mashy spike plates with a black Turk whose "mind is undeveloped," or so we are told. Hooray for scientific racism! Which is to say, five points off for David Whitaker. That said, let's be fair, his scrip identifies the character as a Turk, while the scientific racism about some races having inherently inferior intelligences was usually focused on Africans. So a lot of this came from whatever idiot decided that "black" and "Turkish" were synonyms. Were I to take a guess, I'd observe that the script editor for the first three episodes of this story was the same guy who rewrote *The Celestial Toymaker* and co-authored the next story we're going to talk about.

But we do get some important thematic setup over these which we should deal with. Maxtible becomes steadily unhinged in his quest for the knowledge of how to transmute base metals into gold (a secret the Daleks apparently have) over the course of these episodes. At the same time, you get the Daleks' primary concern—isolating and identifying "the Human Factor," which is apparently what makes humans the way they are as well as an injectable liquid. So that's probably news to the Human Genome Project. The story also features Dalek mind control plates, making this now the fourth consecutive story that discusses mind control. These episodes are not, in other words, incidental to the plot of the story—they're just nowhere near as interesting as the first or last two. (They're also where the padding takes place.)

What's significant, and we see this over the course of the final two episodes, is that all three of these are different facets of the same theme. Maxtible's quest for the philosopher's stone is explicitly paralleled with the Daleks' quest for the Human Factor (and by extension the Dalek Factor, which turns out to only be understandable in contrast to the Human Factor), and the fact that the Daleks can control people's minds is paralleled with the fact that the Human Factor can be synthesized and given to Daleks. In both cases, scenes dealing with the issues are presented one after another so that the viewer sees how these concepts are equivalent or related. So at some point we're going to need to sit down and figure out what to make of these big symbols and their parallels.

But first we have to get to the end of the major concepts. After wasting three episodes by making Jamie compete in a Victorian version of a Japanese game show where he dodges mashy spike plates and has emotions that the Doctor can identify so they get included in the Human Factor, Whitaker discovers that the weirdness dial has three settings. And so, in a glorious upgrading of his "I AM YOUR SERVANT" cliffhanger on *Power of the Daleks*, Whitaker writes a plot in which Daleks who have been given the Human Factor give the Doctor rides around Maxtible's study as he proudly shouts "They're playing a game!"

(It is very easy, if you are only reading this description, to believe that this sounds like the stupidest thing ever. I know because I spent most of my life completely mystified as to how a story with game-playing Daleks and something as stupid as "the Human Factor" could possibly be a classic and a contender for one of the best Doctor Who stories ever. Then I listened to the audio for the first time. No explanation of this story prepares you for how completely and utterly bonkers the human Daleks sound. You really just have to, unless you've seen or heard the thing, take on faith that this scene is as completely and utterly mindblowing as it is. For a vague sense, imagine getting a Dalek drunk, feeding it helium, and getting it to shout "Dizzy Dalek" before giggling. Then play that scene completely straight instead of as a comedy.)

From there it's all over save for the action sequences as the Doctor sparks a civil war among the Daleks by making more Human Factor Daleks, shortly after meeting the Dalek Emperor (a character who merits a brief digression). The idea of the Dalek Emperor is not original to *Evil of the Daleks*, but is instead straight out of the comics—the same ones that provided so much of the tonal background for *The Daleks' Masterplan*. But like fleets of Daleks swooping around the skies, the Dalek Emperor is something that viewers, while familiar with, would have assumed existed only in the comics. To suddenly see it was a genuine shock (a "wait, can they do that?" moment), and one that was intensified by coming alongside the plot twist of revealing that the point of synthesizing the Human Factor was really to develop the Dalek Factor and use the TARDIS to spread it. At which point the Doctor mutters that this may be the final end of the Daleks, and then we see amidst the wreckage that one Dalek is still alive.

Actually, let's start there, now that we've at least got a firm idea of what all the moving parts of this story are. Yes, this story is Doctor Who's farewell to the Daleks, who will not appear in the show again for the next five years. It was intended to be their last Doctor Who story so that Terry Nation could launch a Dalek TV show in America. This plan eventually ran aground when Terry Nation ran into the fairly obvious problem—that nobody in America had heard about the

Daleks—and "So there are these really cool, evil robotic saltshakers" is the worst start to a pitch ever.

Somehow, the fact that this story was meant to be the end of the Daleks in Doctor Who has, over the years, turned into the assumption that it's meant to be the end of the Daleks in general. It's obviously not. The final episode bookends the Doctor's claim that it's "the final end" with both Maxtible talking about how the Daleks will never die and with clear evidence of a lone survivor. The Daleks obviously survive this story. Which makes sense, since killing them off is probably not the right thing to do before launching your spin-off. It's enough for Doctor Who to wave goodbye to the Daleks, yes, but it's manifestly not the end of the concept.

I mention this mostly because John Peel has published entire books devoted to the sole task of re-establishing this story as the true end of the Daleks, and has opted to inanely retcon huge swaths of the television series in pursuit of this task. This would be stupid and unnecessary even if this were actually intended to be the final end of the Daleks. The reversal of that would barely merit as one of the great retcons of Doctor Who. But to go to such lengths to preserve a supposed point, which self-evidently isn't actually in the episode, is downright staggering and makes *War of the Daleks* even dumber than it had originally appeared.

The second thing we should deal with is the obvious admissions. There are some real problems with this story. Not just the lengthy middle, although this is a much larger problem than people give it credit for. The usual refrain is that the story is fine but has one extra episode in the middle. But that's too simple of an explanation. The story depends, as I said earlier, on the fact that it moves methodically towards a known conclusion. Every step of the way we know we're getting closer to a big Dalek epic, and we accept each step because it changes the game interestingly. But when this progression of interesting developments seizes up for three weeks, the whole story goes limp. It's not one extra episode—it's the same problem that *The Faceless Ones* had where every episode is slowed due to the padding. For three solid weeks this story is in "extra episode" mode even though, by any measure, two of those weeks were needed for the development of the story. The story would have been better if there were one clear padding episode. Yes, the story is good enough in its sixth and seventh episodes to win the audience back, but it has to start from near zero. Unnecessary padding in a story that has already opted for the "slow and deliberate" approach to its plotting is a genuine disaster, and is reason enough to prefer *Power of the Daleks* to this when ranking your classic stories. (This one, frankly, is valued more than *Power of the Daleks* because it has bigger Dalek battles and a Dalek emperor rather than because it's better—a consequence of fandom's monster fetishism. But that's a tendency we'll talk about over most of the next season.)

But the real problem isn't just that the plotting is slow. It's the fact that the Doctor and Jamie are really just hanging around until they get to Skaro. They have no actual function to the plot, and are actually in the way. For the third through fifth episode, the real problem is that the Doctor does not seem to have a plan and is just doing what the Daleks say. For all the impact of Jamie getting angry at the Doctor for his manipulations, the larger problem here is that it's not at all clear that the Doctor is doing anything other than marking time. Arguably his insistence on stressing the positive parts of human behavior while deriving the Human Factor indicates some plan, but the fact of the matter is that even the Doctor spends three episodes seemingly twiddling his thumbs and waiting for the Daleks to begin with their real plan. This is understandable— Whitaker is very, very good at these sorts of slow burns, and it's clear that he's trying to dangle the eventual confrontation in front of us before setting it off in the finale. But that requires meticulous pacing, and Whitaker isn't afforded that with the extra episode.

But more to the point, it's very obvious that Whitaker is writing the same Doctor he was writing in *Power of the Daleks*. Which is only a problem when you consider that the character has developed considerably since then. So the characterization is continually just a bit off. This too isn't a crushing problem, because Troughton plays it well and the characterization Whitaker picks is a fascinating midpoint between Troughton and Hartnell that has the happy accident of coming off very close to, say, Sylvester McCoy or David Tennant. In particular, the scene where the Doctor bluntly informs his companions that he will let them die if it means stopping the Daleks is a tour de force that makes a mockery of every stupid scene where the Cybermen get the Doctor to back down by threatening his companion and then chortle about how his emotions make him weak. Heck, it makes a mockery of "The Parting of the Ways," an episode that tries desperately to be a sequel to this episode, but that presents the Doctor with this exact choice, with the emperor forcing the Doctor to choose between being a coward or a killer and the Doctor choosing "coward, every time." Clearly not every time. (Though if you read that, as I do, as the Ninth Doctor's tragic flaw and moment of failure, it spruces things up considerably.) As is the case with bewildering frequency for Whitaker, he is astonishingly capable of screwing up in ways that end up being way ahead of their time. It's like magic.

Also like magic is Whitaker's entire sense of science, as mentioned. Much of why *Evil of the Daleks* manages to be steampunk seven years before punk was invented comes down to the fact that Whitaker is writing a science fiction story in which the Daleks explicitly work according to an alchemical logic. We should start by nailing down some particulars. Miles and Wood, in *About Time*, have an essay in which they make a compelling argument for how alchemical themes run throughout Whitaker's work (an argument which is an expansion, in many ways, of an earlier essay by Tat Wood on the subject). But at the end of the essay they kind of cop out and suggest that these ideas were common to children's literature and that Whitaker was likely just picking up on them and was not a wacky occultist.

I'm going to go ahead and say that, no, actually, probably David Whitaker was a wacky occultist, or at least that he was very much familiar with how occultism worked. First of all, let's make it clear that the alchemical themes are not in the least bit accidental. That's easy enough. There's an interview with Whitaker (one of only a few) in which he says that the "lure of alchemy" is one of his favorite themes to deal with. Clearly the presence of alchemical themes in *Evil of the Daleks* is not just a technobabbly piece of window dressing. Alchemy was explicitly intended as a major theme of the piece. So whatever we find by pulling on this particular thread is something that was intended to be there.

The next obvious question is "what is alchemy anyway?" The answer would be massively long, so let's instead offer three very important points about how alchemy works and leave it to the reader to explore the issue more broadly and to see if they can be as much of a weird occultist as one of the most important writers in Doctor Who history is! It's like a rainy-day activity book, only with more magick.

First of all, a basic definition. Alchemy is a mode of human inquiry in which symbols and objects are treated interchangeably so that action on one affects the other (a viewpoint summarized by the maxim "as above, so below"). In other words, for instance, a reflected image of a person can be viewed as equivalent to the person itself. Similarly, because in electricity like repels like, electricity can be used to separate two images of a person (which are alike, and thus, with electricity, repel each other) and thus attain time travel by putting one person in a different place. See now how that's supposed to work?

Second, and equally importantly, alchemy is primarily a spiritual pursuit. The major alchemist's quest—the ability to turn lead into gold—is not about profit margins. Maxtible is already insanely wealthy, and his "sell antiques one hundred years in the future" racket is as good as any metal transmutation racket he might be able to cook up. His alchemical goals are about a different sort of power—a form of spiritual enlightenment. Lead, you see, is just gold that's gone wrong—that is more base and worldly than the pure solar brilliance of gold. So transmuting it into gold means that you have the ability to purify and perfect base materials into holy ones. If you can turn lead into gold, you can also turn yourself into a holy and sacred being.

Third, there's a bunch of astrological symbolism that's really important to alchemy. We don't care about most of it, although rest assured that if you know it and go through Whitaker's stories it proves remarkably useful over and over again. Most interestingly, consider that Saturn is the planet most associated with time, but is a very stodgy, cold, obsessive force very much unlike the Doctor. In fact, it is almost as though the Doctor's temperament might be fundamentally different from those of his people, who are probably a more conservative, hoarding, slightly power-mad sort who are, like, lords of time or something. The Doctor, on the other hand, is very clearly associated with Mercury. To ridiculously simplify thousands of years of occult traditions into a few sentences, Mercury is the planet (and element) associated with smart trickster figures who work as guides to humanity. Suddenly the fact that the Daleks were paralyzed by being shoved into a mercury swamp in *Power of the Daleks* makes sense—the Daleks are enemies of the (mercurial) Doctor, and so mercury is lethal to them. Along with gold, in fact, mercury is largely the most important and beloved element to alchemists and occultists, which is why the most important occult organization of the late nineteenth/twentieth century is the Hermetic Order of the Golden Dawn.

OK. So with all of that in mind, what do we have here? We have the Daleks' quest for the Dalek Factor explicitly paralleled with Maxtible's quest for the ability to transmute base metals into gold. So we have to understand what the Daleks are doing in this story as a form of alchemy. Which makes sense. The Human Factor is, in the end, a material symbol that represents humanity. Humans and Daleks are diametrically opposed (hence the repetition of the idea that the Daleks are our superior replacements—an alternative to humanity in the same sense that the Cybermen are—in both of Whitaker's Dalek stories). Because of this, understanding one allows you to understand the other. The Daleks, being Daleks, cannot see themselves—they must understand themselves through the metaphor of the Human Factor—through a reflection into the symbolic realm. So the factors are alchemical concepts—symbols that have real power.

The biggest clue to this is the fact that the Daleks demonstrate the ability to transmute base metals into gold. In other words, they have alchemical spiritual enlightenment down, and what they're doing is a "higher form" of it—another symbolic reflection. The implication, then, is that Whitaker is condemning alchemy because it's associated with Maxtible and the Daleks. Following this logic, alchemy has rendered Maxtible irredeemable, turning him into a mad servant of the Daleks at the end.

But this isn't quite right either. We have to remember that the Doctor is every bit as alchemical as the rest of them. Consider his claim when he concludes that the Daleks have presented him with a fake copy of one of the Daleks he named—"You think I don't recognize my own mark?" It is the fact that Troughton has named the Dalek—given it a symbolic mark (a Greek letter, tellingly)—that identifies it. Troughton has engaged in an alchemical symbolic manipulation to create the Human Factor Daleks, and it is his magickal mark that he recognizes—not the Dalek itself. Alchemy, then, is not purely the province of the bad guys. Rather, there are two competing senses of alchemy going on.

Furthermore, the Doctor beats the Daleks by using their own alchemy against them. He submits to their efforts to infect him with the Dalek Factor, but he is immune to it because he is superhuman. Then (after a great sequence in which he plays the Doctor as a Dalek—a scene that Hartnell could frankly never have done) he turns the Dalek machinery around on them and applies his alchemy to infect the Daleks with the Human Factor. In other words, the Doctor here is a sorcerer. One who can outdo the crass and false spirituality of human alchemy and replace it with his own higher magicks. He has, in other words, attained a true enlightenment (which we knew already from Whitaker's previous story). This is very different from the Daleks' false enlightenment in which they only focus on the material transmutation of lead to gold.

What is this enlightenment? The clue is in the Daleks' plan. Even though they can synthesize the Dalek Factor, their plan requires the Doctor's involvement because they need the TARDIS to spread the Dalek Factor across the universe. So whatever level of (false) enlightenment the Daleks have, the TARDIS is something more powerful than it. And as we know from *The Daleks* (script-edited by Whitaker), a vital component of the TARDIS is … mercury.

So there we have it. The Doctor can triumph over the Daleks because his enlightenment is the TARDIS and its mercurial, shifting anarchism—his magical box that wanted to see the universe, and so stole him so she could, and who took him where he needed to go until, finally, she made him into the hero he should be. Yes, it was Neil Gaiman who codified all of this, but Gaiman is open about his debt to the early Whitaker conceptions of the show. Indeed, he's said that the mercury fluid links were mentioned explicitly in an early draft of "The Doctor's Wife." Gaiman, it should be noted, wrote the introduction for the newest edition of Whitaker's *Doctor Who in an Exciting Adventure with the Daleks*, where he talks about making a point of searching for books by Whitaker whenever he visited a bookshop as a child. And it was, after all, Whitaker who edited the script that started us off with a long pan through a junkyard to a magical, blue box. It was Whitaker who wrote *The Edge of Destruction* and turned the box from a mere spaceship into a thinking, conscious being. And it was Whitaker who wrote this story, where the thing that makes the Doctor better than the Daleks is his magical box.

Without David Whitaker, the Doctor would just have a time machine. Instead, he has a TARDIS. Whitaker is undoubtedly a strange man. A madman, really. You have to be to write alchemical science fiction in 1967. Which is, of course, why he's the most important writer the show has ever seen—

the one who, more than anyone else, can be said to have created Doctor Who. Not the one who came up with the idea, nor the one who wrote the first story, but the one who oversaw the creation of what Doctor Who is—the one who created its soul. David Whitaker: a madman with a box.

Pop Between Realities, Home in Time for Tea: The Summer of Love

We have to start, I suppose, with Sergeant Pepper and his Lonely Hearts Club Band. There's a monolithically long essay in *About Time*, after all, called "Did Sergeant Pepper Know the Doctor" that tackles this directly, although if we're being honest, it mentions both Sergeant Pepper and the Doctor somewhat less than its title might suggest and thus may not be quite as great of a jumping on point as it first seems. So let's start instead with the album itself. The first thing to point out about it is that it is ostensibly the first ever "concept album." The phrase "concept album," of course, is one of the most degraded phrases in pop music. Very few supposed concept albums actually are, and *Sgt. Pepper's Lonely Hearts Club Band* is no exception. In practice, hardly any concept albums are, and it's difficult to quite figure out what the concept of the album is or how it impacts most of the songs.

So when we call it a concept album, what do we mean? Generally what we mean is this—past Beatles albums were simply collections of songs with no unifying factor beyond having all been written and recorded around the same time in the same set of sessions. Indeed, past albums from most bands were like this. What the Beatles did with *Sergeant Pepper* was add a continual soundscape between the songs so that they flowed into each other and the album basically never faded to silence from start to finish. Indeed, in the original UK vinyl pressings, it never faded to silence at all, the record being manufactured so that it would just play a continual noise loop at the end.

What was so significant about this was that it made the album one coherent experience instead of a set of short, separate experiences. Even though there wasn't really a unifying concept to the album, it felt unquestionably different from albums before it—bigger and stranger. Listening to it meant spending time in a weird new place—in real, substantial time. The term "concept album" here is really just an overstatement of the idea that the unit of music production is not the individual song but rather the album as a whole.

What's important to note about this shift is that it is immediately compatible with the logic of the acid trip—itself a brief sojourn into a strange and new place. This is the big connection between the album and psychedelia. Not the fact that "Lucy in the Sky with Diamonds" was obviously about LSD, but rather the fact that the album was a concentrated effort to create a strange and different mental space. Which is actually what psychedelia is supposed to be all about. That's what the word actually means—soul manifesting, essentially. Psychedelia is supposed to be about the revealing of the essence of the self.

Or, at least, that's the noble version of psychedelia. There is, unfortunately, a rather darker one lurking beneath the debauched patina of the Summer of Love. The description of it all as "sex, drugs, and rock and roll" turns the experience into an unchecked hedonism. Which, to be fair, in the classic Summer of Love—the Haight-Ashbury scene of San Francisco—it was. San Francisco in 1967 managed to be positioned, partially through actual events and partially through a gigantic self-feeding media story, as the cool place to be. And so San Francisco filled to the choking point with youth on break from school looking for what they were told was the coolest place on Earth. And in doing so, they almost incidentally killed the entire thing.

The problem with a large wave of people coming because they wanted to experience the scene is that it effectively rendered psychedelia a brand. For something that is ostensibly about internal spiritual experience, this cannot possibly be a good thing. And so within the Summer of Love you had a focus on the superficial—the clothes, drugs, and, of course, the sex. For the bulk of the crowd coming in, these were the points of the experience. In other words, it was a mess ripe for exploitation. The San Francisco government had no plan in place to deal with the influx, and a bunch of doped-up college kids looking for adventure were easy prey for criminals. By October, the whole thing had crashed to the ground, setting the stage for the long post-revolutionary hangover that characterized American culture from about 1968 to ... oh wait, we haven't come out of that one, have we?

The problem with that story—perfectly accurate as it is—is that it suggests that the underlying social movement was in some sense inherently doomed and thus inherently flawed. It may or may not have been, but the failure of the Summer of Love (and let's be honest, in terms of the Haight-Ashbury scene, it was an unambiguous failure) shows nothing other than that psychedelic counterculture doesn't work as a mass commodity fetish. The problem is that the underlying and more noble logic has yet to crawl out from under the weight of its branding. And this is true on both sides of the culture wars. Those who still hate the hippies and all they stood for point to the bad aspects of the Summer of Love. Those nostalgic for the hippies mostly point at the superficial. The underlying logic—the parts of it that are a natural outcropping of what was going on in 1966 (covered in a "Pop Between Realities" essay back in the Hartnell volume)—are the parts that are largely removed from the history.

The thing is, anyone who had even thought about psychedelia could have told you that. I mean, just look at something like Timothy Leary's *The Psychedelic Experience*, which I quoted way back in the essay on *The Power of the Daleks*. Leary, like most of psychedelia, is a punch line these days, but there's an uncanny power to his actual work (as opposed to his reputation). *The Psychedelic Experience* is a description of LSD couched in terms of *The Tibetan Book of the Dead* and full of phrases like "ego-death." This is not what would be described as "effective marketing." "Come to San Francisco and experience ego-death" was not going to spark a mass influx of youth. But that's the point. Psychedelia isn't supposed to be "fun." LSD isn't a pleasurable drug. It's a drug about intense spiritual experiences. There's a reason it was the most immediately available metaphor for the trauma of regeneration, and a reason that once drugs like speed and heroin took off—drugs that offered a much more straightforwardly pleasurable high—the usage of LSD fell off a cliff and never recovered.

So why drop acid? What's the point if it's not going to be pleasurable but rather an intense and self-destructive spiritual experience? It's worth referencing back to the essay on 1966 underground culture in London in the previous volume. Specifically, remember how psychedelic culture in London was adjacent to the Situationalist International style of Marxism imported from France. Situationism was, for all its flaws and failures, a movement focused on the material. Its failures amounted to being anarchistic without a clear sense of what to do next. Let's talk about that approach some more, then. Jumping back to San Francisco, one of the most interesting facets of the Summer of Love was what the pre-existing population of San Francisco—the ones whose actions sparked the feeding frenzy—did to try to keep things under control.

Take, for instance, the Diggers. This is the sort of group that was at the heart of the Summer of Love, and they are maddeningly forgotten in favor of the flashier parts of it. Combining SI techniques of guerilla theater with a commitment to building things instead of tearing them down, the Diggers took their name from a seventeenth-century English movement to abolish private property. Opposed to the entire idea of commerce, the Diggers responded to the wave of people by opening a free health clinic to go alongside their free "store" that distributed essential goods in a parody of traditional commerce. Throughout the Summer of Love, the Diggers mixed in-your-face theatrical stunts (it was they who declared the whole scene dead in October with the "Death of a Hippy" performance).

We should pause briefly to highlight the role of the theatrical in this thicket of concepts. Almost no matter where you go in 1967, you'll see counterculture movements with an oddly theatrical flair—a tendency to go out and do bizarre things. Events like the Human Be-Ins that prefigured the Summer of Love are all about this. Organized strangeness was important. There's a whole wealth of theory behind this approach, but the thing I want to underline is this—all of it stems from ideas in avant-garde theater that would have been wholly familiar to anyone working at the BBC. Absurdist and existentialist theater—a bread-and-butter concept—was a direct predecessor to people like the Diggers, which means that something like Doctor Who (which had, admittedly disastrously, already attempted absurdism) was not all that far from this vein of culture.

The Diggers, in other words, were an illustration of the fusion of psychedelia and social action. Their goal was to create functioning social institutions that were unmistakably products of psychedelic counterculture. Hence the entire idea of a free store—an entity that at once provides an essential social service and directly confronts the inadequacies of the larger social order. It's an intensely politically radical idea—let's do away with money—that is not merely proposed but put into action, and put into action in a way that is useful.

With that approach in mind, we can head back home to London and start to see the impact of this when you get far, far away from the mass of smelly hippies and virtually indistinguishable smelly hobos. (The "Hobo or Hipster" game started here.) Psychedelia was in full swing in England as well, but there, separated from the commoditized San Francisco events, it functioned more or less as intended. The psychedelic was there to help you see the world in a way more conducive to changing it.

In the British tradition this is fundamentally connected to a tradition within fantasy, and particularly children's fantasy, of doorways to other realms. This is something that Miles and Wood call particular attention to in their essay. They relate psychedelia in 1967 to an entire British tradition reaching back to the Romantics and Victorian culture. The heart of which, in their argument, is that there is a relationship between exotic external spaces and exotic internal spaces.

What's crucial is that this wasn't just about the occultist tradition we talked about last time we were in this web of concepts. Once you get to 1967 you start to get a different facet of it—the desire to make functional playgrounds and odd spaces in the middle of normalcy. Psychedelia became a tool to bring the unusual and the revelatory in contact with day-to-day life. This—more than any particularly psychedelic feeling to the imagery—is why *Alice in Wonderland* became such a fantastic metaphor for the scene. It's not that there's any inherent connection between talking caterpillars and acid. It's that there is an inherent connection between tumbling down a rabbit hole into a bizarre new world and acid. There's nothing particularly acidy about Alice in Wonderland except for the basic idea of having a strange new world intrude on the normal one and the confusion of internal and external spaces implicit in its heady mixture of childhood logic and magic worlds.

The relevance to Doctor Who here should be obvious. The Doctor provides a psychedelic intrusion into an existing society, and in doing so causes a revolutionary moment that reforms the society. That's the plot of ... well, pretty much half the stories since Troughton showed up. Troughton is a societal drug trip with his own personal portal to another world. The perfect emblem of the real psychedelic culture busily being eaten alive in San Francisco.

Is this at all deliberate? Oh, probably. The artistic community of the BBC was exactly the sort of place psychedelia would have been influential. It's basically inconceivable that no one involved creatively with the show dropped acid in this period, and it's a fun game to guess who it might have been. Yes, there are other competing tendencies— the '60s were every bit as much about the scared reaction of the existing seats of power in society as they were about youthful revolution. For every David Whitaker the series has, there's a Kit Pedler who seems to want to hide under a rock until all this social and technological change goes away. And so Doctor Who is frequently going to be at war with itself. We'll see that really clearly in the next two stories, one of which is a maddeningly reactionary piece of xenophobia and the other one of which is a rather sweet piece about Buddhism (by the authors of a maddeningly reactionary piece of xenophobia in Season Six, but we're getting ahead of ourselves).

But on the other hand, there's a distinct arc that the series has taken. The Doctor's anarchic tendencies—which we've seen in play since at least *The Romans*, are starting to gel into a coherent approach to the series that answers the question "what is this series for" in a much more interesting way than any of the forms of entertainment/education that have preceded it. If nothing else, the link between psychedelia and children's literature helps us here. Psychedelia, at least by one reasonably fair definition, is about using childish ways of looking at the world for practical purposes. Children's literature is about couching adult concepts in ways that work for children. Doctor Who, with a foot in each camp, manages something truly extraordinary. It's a show that teaches children that the world is a scary place without teaching them to grow up. Contrary to its earliest conceptions, it's very pointedly not about teaching the facts of other worlds, it's about teaching the logic of them—about grappling with the basic question of what it's like to fall out of the world. In hindsight this was always there—it's certainly been what *TARDIS Eruditorum* has been tracking since day one. But here there's a sense that the show is starting to figure out what it does best.

What's With All the Mute Black Strongmen?

One of the first things my blog found itself known for was its commentaries on race and Doctor Who. This is a crown I'd love to pass on to someone who isn't white, or even just to Lindy Orthia, whose edited the fantastic *Doctor Who and Race* anthology. But since I do have the reputation, I suppose I should own that for a page or two and make some sort of general statement on the subject.

It is true that throughout these essays I tend to come down pretty hard on racism and sexism in Doctor Who, including in spots where other people would defer. In particular, my bits on both Kemel and Toberman have come under repeated criticism. So I'll make a couple of quick comments. First of all, I don't think that there's any "tropes of the genre" defense that justifies having a mute black strongman. Yes, mute black strongmen are tropes of a lot of genres. That's why they're offensive stereotypes. You don't get to "offensive stereotype" without going through "common element of a lot of stories" first. We'd be in far better shape, frankly, if there were more mute Jewish strongmen and more scheming and selfish black men in television. That's what racism is most of the time. It's not all white-hooded KKK members and Enoch Powell shouting about rivers of blood. It's people getting so inured to things that they stop being capable of noticing on their own that the only times they put a black man on the show are when they need a mute strongman. I don't think Davis and Pedler wrote Toberman in while cackling about how this will put black people in their place. I think they wrote him in, along with the rest of the residents of Shiftystan, without even managing to string the thought "Gee, what are we saying about other ethnicities here" together. Racism, like most forms of discrimination, isn't about conscious malice, but about unconscious failures to even notice that there's a problem. More often than not, discrimination is just a particular flavor of stupidity.

Second, it has to be admitted that the period in Doctor Who in which racist stereotypes are at their worst coincides uncomfortably with the tenure of Gerry Davis as script editor. He entered midway through *The Massacre* and served on both *The Ark* and *The Celestial Toymaker*, with the latter being largely his rewrite in the final version. He also wrote the novelization of that story that uncomfortably overemphasizes the Toymaker's ethnicity, mentioning it three times in one sentence. He continued to preside over *Evil of the Daleks* and Kemel, and then wrote *Tomb of the Cybermen*. And with that story he goes away and Doctor Who stops having nearly so many racist stereotypes (though it manages a corker in *The Web of Fear*). On the other hand, a usual defense that comes up here is that at least there were racial minorities on Doctor Who in these years—something that often isn't true elsewhere in the classic series. This is true, and the accounts of people who were comforted even by poorly done racial minorities on television are real and need to be taken seriously. But even given that, surely one can appreciate that black kids got to see a heroic character in Toberman while still wishing he hadn't been portrayed as an imbecile.

Third, yes, sometimes I give a pass on discrimination and sometimes I don't. Usually it comes down to whether there's something else to look at. I can deal with Kemel better than Toberman because with Kemel I can look at the other good, intelligent parts of *The Evil of the Daleks* and because there's reason to think that Kemel wasn't supposed to be a mute black strongman. (What he was apparently meant to be—a mute Turkish strongman—is not necessarily an improvement, but it's at least a stranger image). Kemel is a racist note in an otherwise fantastic story. Toberman is a racist note in a lazily written, poorly plotted story. And if my tone regarding the overt sexism and orientalism of *You Only Live Twice* in a few essays' time sounds like damning with faint praise, it is. When a movie is aspiring to nothing more than some action and thrills, ethical failings are a bigger problem than they are in a movie that's mostly accomplishing something subtle and interesting. I can set aside racism to look at interesting explorations of humanity much more easily than I can to look at a car chase. Or, put in the bluntest terms, racism mixed in with good bits is better than racism mixed in with mediocre or bad bits.

Which is to say that racism [or any other discriminatory - ism] is not some horrific stain that ruins everything it touches forever. It's just a thing humans do that's bad. Treating racism either as something that we should just give otherwise good things a pass on or as something that taints something beyond all redemption is a fundamentally flawed approach. If nothing else, I, along with every reader of this book, at some point, has stupidly blundered into a racist or discriminatory act. And unless we die very soon, we will do so again. When we do, we should accept the criticism and work to do better in the future. But we should also take care to judge the failures of others by the same standards. Which means neither flinching from the criticism nor rejecting the laudatory parts of something because of a racist bit.

Which is, in the end, my defense against most of the heat I get about criticizing racism in Doctor Who. Because to be honest, most of the heat I get comes in various forms of a desperate desire to "save" a beloved television show from accusations of racism—as if my criticism somehow invalidates other people's pleasure. Which is strange, as it doesn't invalidate my pleasure—as should be obvious, I adore *The Evil of the Daleks*, and while I hate both *Tomb of the Cybermen* and *The Celestial Toymaker* I don't hate them entirely for their racism. Yes, it exacerbates the problems with both, and it gives an uncomfortable pause in *The Evil of the Daleks*. But at the end of the day, the defensive desire to rescue Doctor Who from its own history serves as an unpleasant attempt to ignore the realities of race in Britain in the 1960s, and in doing so exacerbates the problem by allowing the racism to go unchallenged and unremarked upon. Better to like something in spite of its flaws than to delude one's self into pretending they're not there.

My Writing Gets Worse and Worse (*The Tomb of the Cybermen*)

It's September 2, 1967. Scott Mckenzie is at number one with "San Francisco (Be Sure to Wear Some Flowers in Your Hair)," the basic subject of which we discussed last essay. The Beatles' anthem for the same events, "All You Need is Love," is still at number six, having peaked at number one back in July. A week later, Engelbert Humperdinck, who has increasingly become the very image of the establishment for the purposes of these metaphors, takes number one a week later, and holds it for the remainder of this story (and a third of the next). The rest of the charts remain pleasantly psychedelic, however, with Keith West, Flowerpot Men, and The Move keeping the dream alive.

In real news ... basically, hung over from the summer, the world spends September taking a breather. Seriously, it's slim pickings. The Vietnam War drags maddeningly all, The Doors have an iconic performance on *The Ed Sullivan Show* ... and that's about it. Whereas on television ...

Well now, that's actually a good question. What did happen on television that month? I mean, specifically related to Doctor Who. The story of what aired those four weeks has changed over time, and for the first time really since *The Gunfighters*, we have a case study in evolving views of the show.

Let's begin with the objective facts. To kick off Doctor Who's fourth season, the Cybermen were brought back for their first of three actual title appearances in the classic series.

This time, they're in a tomb on the planet Telos, where apparently they shuffled off to have a nice long nap after the whole Moonbase thing went tits up for them. And then, in 1974, seven years after transmission, the BBC junked the tapes to free up space, leaving it as one of the missing stories.

Novelized in 1978, *The Tomb of the Cybermen* got in under the wire to be one of those stories that fandom mythologized, and it pulled off the job with aplomb. To wit, Peter Haining's book *Doctor Who—A Celebration*, a book responsible for setting the initial consensus on much of the classic series, declares the story to be "the peak of its kind." Howe, Stammers, and Walker, in the *Second Doctor Handbook*, give it two nines and an eight, calling it things like "one of the true classics of this era" and "another cracking good story."

The difference between their reviews and the one in Haining's book (by Jeremy Bentham) is that Howe, Stammers, and Walker are writing post-1992 (i.e. after the story was discovered in Hong Kong by a television station that had failed to properly dispose of them back in 1970). Still, they represent an orthodoxy regarding the series and the Troughton era in particular that it is impossible to avoid. See, prior to being found, that viewpoint was that *The Tomb of the Cybermen* was one of the series' best stories, it was missing, and large swaths of fandom would readily bargain with their or their family's vital organs to get it back. So before we look too deeply at what we get when we see the episode, we should ask why this story had such a universally good reputation sight unseen.

It's easy to pick on David J. Howe here, because of the three commenters in the handbooks and the *Doctor Who: The Sixties* coffee table book, he's the one most willing to just lay his prejudices on the table. He unabashedly likes Doctor Who for the monsters, and thinks that when it does things like "historical" stories it's boring. He's the archetype of the account of Doctor Who's history that says that the historical was killed because nobody liked it (demonstrably untrue, looking at the ratings of *The Highlanders*), when as we've already discussed, the truth of it was considerably more complex.

From the viewpoint of a fandom that actually has access to the historicals (of which, remember, only three [plus *100,000 BC*] exist in their entirety, making them something that depended on audio and reconstructions to understand), it's difficult to even figure out how someone would get to that conclusion. But we have to understand, the idea that fans might actually engage in detailed analysis of the whole of Doctor Who is a comparatively new idea. Prior to that, views about the series were heavily controlled by the published literature on the matter, which was itself heavily controlled by a particular school of superfans among whom Howe is distinct only inasmuch as he actually admits to his biases.

We also need to pause and make it clear that whatever flaws Howe, Stammers, and Walker's accounts of Doctor Who may have, the quality of factual research they conduct is impeccable. However odd their critical opinions of the show may be, they've conducted the best scouring of BBC archives to date to get accounts of the production of stories. As first drafts of history go, they're phenomenally good.

All of which said—and let's be fair, this is obviously what we've been building to for five paragraphs now—they're dead wrong. You can start to see the wheels come off in the coffee table book, actually. Just look. When talking about the start of Season Five, they say, "the changes made by producer Innes Lloyd and story editor Gerry Davis had succeeded in revitalising the series, and this was reflected in a ratings increase from an average of around five million viewers per episode at the start of Season Four to an average of around seven million at the end, accompanied by a rise of about ten percentage points in the average appreciation figure, which now hovered around the 55 mark."

This is wrong in almost every regard. Yes, it's technically true that the series gained ratings over Season Four, having started in the toilet for *The Smugglers* at 4.5. But this is a misleading way to measure things. If we take the start of Innes Lloyd's new direction as *The Moonbase*—the beginning of a run of three base under siege stories in a row, then the series shed 2 million over those three stories, managing to come in at 6.4 million for *The Evil of the Daleks*—the lowest rating the Daleks had ever had by a considerable margin. And these are the stories where the supposed new direction is really happening— not the run from *The Power of the Daleks* through *The Moonbase*, which, as we've seen, are generally not base under siege stories.

But more to the point, Innes Lloyd's watch started way back in *The Celestial Toymaker*, which made 8.3 million. That's an aberration—*The Ark* which was before this story had 6.5 million viewers, and *The Gunfighters* after that had 6.3. But remember—those are the sorts of numbers that *Evil of the Daleks* got. *Evil of the Daleks* could barely beat the ratings of *The Gunfighters*, which is ostensibly one of the great failures of Doctor Who. The fact of the matter is that from *The Gunfighters* to *The Smugglers*, Lloyd managed to drive away twenty-five percent of the show's audience. Yes, he won a fair portion of them back over the course of Season Four, but he was the one on whose watch they'd all left. (Mind you, a lot of that was just down to ITV running *Batman* opposite Doctor Who.) And calling the AI figures "around 55" is a bit ambitious, given that their peak was 56 during *Evil of the Daleks*. Mind you, 56 was a number the series hadn't seen since ... *The Ark*. So again, Innes Lloyd has, by the start of Season Five, managed to mostly undo the ratings damage he'd inflicted on the show. It's tough to call this a revitalization. It's more a semi-successful application of defibrillator paddles.

But the real lunatic moment of the *The Sixties* comes when they say "The effectiveness of *The Tomb of the Cybermen* can be attributed in part to the fact that its central plot was a variation on the successful formula established in the previous season." In other words, *Tomb of the Cybermen* is awesome because it's a base under siege, and bases under siege are awesome. This point is so strange that we're just going to have to put it aside for a bit and come back to it.

All of this said, it should surprise nobody that once this story was found in 1992, its reputation suffered a bit. To some extent, this is just because nothing could possibly live up to the reputation the story had accrued. In legend, this was a piece of sublime horror. In practice, it was, as all Doctor Who in the 1960s was, rush-produced television with a few moments where it transcended its limitations. But Doctor Who fans have been forgiving of far worse. Yes, the reputation of this story was overinflated, but not so overinflated as to justify the degree to which a fair segment of fandom has turned on it.

But treating this story's newfound battered reputation as just a matter of the effects doesn't capture what happened here. The first major blow was probably Paul Cornell, Martin Day, and Keith Topping's *The Discontinuity Guide*, which made the quite sensible observation that, shortly after the big "Cybermen break out of their tombs" sequence, the plot stalls out entirely and the last two episodes feature them climbing back into their tombs and going back to bed. This is true, and once you notice it, it's hard to quite enjoy the story the same way again.

Then there's the villains. Not the Cybermen, who do a perfectly competent job of showing up, having the classic bit of stock music "Space Adventures" blare, and then faffing around patiently until the Doctor defeats them. No, I mean the human villains: Klieg, Kaftan, and Toberman. The first thing to notice about the villains is how the show helpfully made them all easy to identify: they're the ones who aren't white.

Not only are Klieg and Kaftan both nonspecifically ethnic (belonging to that classic sci-fi ethnicity "Shifty"), but Toberman ... oh, man—a basically mute, giant black strongman. This from the guy who functionally wrote most of our favorite piece of racial sensitivity to date, *The Celestial Toymaker*. And the one who wrote the novelization of that story, where he manages to get the word "Chinese" three times into one sentence describing the Toymaker. (He is, as it happens, "lounging in a black Chinese chair behind a lacquered Chinese desk inlaid with mother-of-pearl and scenes of Chinese life." Also, the Toymaker is Chinese. If you were wondering.) So yay. Casual racism. Ooh, and the residents of Shiftystan are the ones who are obsessed with logic, just like the Cybermen. So that's funny too.

On top of that ... the plot here is ... well, OK. Klieg's plan is that the Cybermen, because they're totally logical, should be willing to help Klieg and his logic-obsessed lackeys take over the planet. This is perfectly normal by Doctor Who standards. Then we have the Doctor. When he shows up, the entire archeological expedition is about to give up and leave due to the deadly electric doors. Problem solved. Nobody is going to wake the Cybermen. Unless the Doctor were to do something staggeringly stupid like help them open the doors and get to the Cybermen, we should all be fine and we can just go home.

Needless to say, he opens the doors. And continues helping them. His eventual explanation? He wanted to know what Klieg was up to. Yes, the Doctor has helped unleash the Cybermen in order to confirm that the bad guy wanted to unleash the Cybermen. So that's maybe not his best plan ever. Thankfully, he's got plenty of people willing to lend a hand to make sure he doesn't look like the stupidest guy in the story. Victoria spends her debut adventure as a companion as a sniveling peril monkey that occasionally wakes up and tosses off a bon mot at a bad guy or sexist jerk, and who has exactly one good scene with the Doctor—an emotional bit in the third episode in which it is obvious that someone realized that Victoria never had any real characterization and was hastily added to the TARDIS crew.

Thankfully, the Cybermen are happy to be idiots as well. Their plan, and I promise you I am not making this up, is as follows. See, they're running out of power. So they've retreated to their base on Telos and gone into hibernation, setting up a bunch of fiendish and deadly traps so only very smart people can get to them, at which point they can convert the smart people into Cybermen. Accordingly, once the humans make it to them, they crawl back into the tombs to conserve power until they can kill all of the humans. Oh, and they try to convert Toberman.

But the grand prize in "how exactly is it you don't kill yourself getting out of bed in the morning with that level of stupidity" goes to Klieg himself, who, in the climax of the story, decides that if he has a Cyberman gun then he'll be their equal and they'll have to listen to him. It is worth pondering why, exactly, Klieg thinks that the gun—something the Cybermen presumably have rather a lot of—is such a massive threat to them. Of course, everyone acts as though the gun is particularly deadly. Mind you, it leaves the first human it hits alive, so if it is deadly, this means that the Cybermen—a seemingly monolithic race of conquerors—have designed their weapons to be more deadly to themselves than to the people they're conquering. As the Cyberleader said in *The Moonbase*, clever, clever, clever.

So once the story itself came to light, we didn't like it quite as much as we thought we would. But there's one big problem here—all of this should have been visible from the novelization, telesnaps, and other stuff that existed before 1992. The story makes no sense, is flagrantly racist, and has no climax. All of these problems were not surprises at all. When we lionized the story, we did it in spite of all of these obvious shortcomings.

How did we, as a fandom, manage to do this? Much of it comes to one of the fundamental fault lines in Doctor Who fandom—whether or not one prefers Doctor Who made for Doctor Who fans, or Doctor Who made for casual viewers. Monster stories are unabashedly for Doctor Who fans—or at least, they were by the time Howe, Stammers, and Walker were working. For one thing, they provided facts. You could separate a Doctor Who fan from a civilian because Doctor Who fans knew all the Cybermen stories and could describe how the Cybermen were redesigned for each one, whereas normal people just remembered finding it creepy when they burst out of their tombs, but couldn't honestly tell you if that was the time they were on the moon or not.

The danger of this view will begin to become apparent later this season, and will begin becoming something of a massive problem when it means that we are actually expected to take things like *The Invasion of Time* or *Warriors of the Deep* (or, God help us, this story's "sequel," *Attack of the Cybermen*) seriously just because they have returning monsters in them. Which is ultimately where monster fetishism falls flat—the fact that the show conclusively demonstrates in the '80s that returning monsters do not automatically equal compelling drama.

But there's something deeper going on here. Fundamentally, the view espoused by Howe, Stammers, and Walker—that this story is great because it executes the formula well—requires us to view Doctor Who as a show that plays it safe. Doctor Who, in this view, exists to do stories that feel Doctor Who-ish. This is a view that describes most television shows well. Certainly it describes well the *Adam Adamant-Avengers-Batman* style of show that Doctor Who is overtly aspiring to in this period. The thing is, the one show it doesn't describe well—or at least it didn't before Innes Lloyd showed up—is Doctor Who, which previously thrived on the fact that it would put something like *The Crusade* right after *The Web Planet*. Whereas frankly, nothing since *The Moonbase* has felt like a strange or surprising way to follow what came before it. The only things that have been surprising are when stories subvert their own apparent internal logic, like when *Evil of the Daleks'* logic went down a Victorian rabbithole.

This latter view amounts to a great rethinking of the Troughton era, in which it's criticized for exactly what Howe, Stammers, and Walker praised it for—being an endless succession of identical base under siege stories. I am not the first person to complain about this, and the fact of the matter is, it's a fair critique. Coming at them in sequence, which we can finally do now, there's almost nothing new to say about *TheTomb of the Cybermen* that we didn't say in *The Faceless Ones*, *The Macra Terror*, and *The Moonbase*. The show, at this point, is almost beyond criticism, good or bad. Every story simply tries to perform the formula correctly. Generally it succeeds. This time is a little more racist than usual, and with a bit of a stupider plot, but there are some good set pieces. I'll leave it up to you to decide whether "nice sequence of the Cybermen breaking out of their tombs" makes up for "horrifyingly xenophobic and racist" in the grand scheme of things.

Frankly, it's tough to complain that the BBC junked most of these stories. With no interest in repeating black-and-white material in a color market and no home video during this time, why keep nearly a dozen basically interchangeable stories? What does any one have that the other eleven don't? Why would we consider rescuing another one of these to be a greater contribution to culture than, say, rescuing any of the missing *Top of the Pops* performances, or any other BBC show from the era that's got holes in its archives? To be quite honest, unless you're an obsessive Doctor Who fan, why the hell would you care about the show in this era?

And now we're kicking off Season Five, praised as "the monster season" by the establishment of fandom. What this really means that out of seven stories, six of them are bases under siege and five of them feature monsters that make a repeat appearance (although two of those are the Yeti, who make their first and last two appearances this season). So we're going to need to either find some answers to the question of why we care or get very depressed and very cynical. Or, you know, both.

But, watching *The Tomb of the Cybermen* in sequence, those answers really don't present themselves. The scenes with the TARDIS crew are fun, which they'd better be given that we now have nothing resembling an audience-identification character. Instead we have our charismatic lead, his comically thick Scottish sidekick, and Victoria the peril monkey. They're all well performed, although if we're being honest Frazer Hines's schtick is starting to get a bit thin. As with Ben, any actual performance notes are buried under his accent.

Deborah Watling is, admittedly, a revelation, adding a level of plucky charm to the companion that we haven't seen in ages. But it comes right at the point where it almost stops mattering who you hire in the role. Polly was a normal person, and when we saw her in terrible danger we were supposed to respond with something resembling empathy. Victoria is a pretty person, and when we see her in terrible danger we may as well just break out Laura Mulvey and start explaining how the male gaze works. Yeah, Watling does well with it and the character is likable and fun, but this is the companion stripped down to its most brutally functional form—the cute thing that gets menaced.

The cast, in other words, is forced to hold the show together on sheer charisma. Thankfully they have it, but it's maddening to see the show just kick up its feet and decide that the cast can carry it. Yes, they can, but that's not the point.

But this does lead us to the one thing that does make this base under siege different from any other base under siege—a second reconsidering of the story that we need to take seriously. See, it's a known fact that when Matt Smith began reviewing performances of past Doctors in preparation for the role, he fell in love with Patrick Troughton. And specifically, he fell in love with this story, supposedly calling Moffat in the middle of the night to rave about it. (He also supposedly wrote a piece of Doctor Who fanfic to prepare for the role. Enjoy imagining that any given piece of ridiculous id-vortex Doctor Who fanfic could have been written by Matt Smith.)

So yes, at this point we're left just ignoring most of the story and watching Troughton to see how he might have influenced Smith. But since Troughton is the only consistently watchable thing in this story anyway, that's hardly a flaw. For all the stick I gave this story above, I have nothing bad to say about Troughton at all. The man was a genius. So let's look at how Troughton plays the Doctor, and how that influenced Smith.

What's key about Troughton's performance in this episode is the way in which Troughton lurks around on the edges of scenes. He spends large amounts of time in scenes positioning himself on the outskirts of the sets. Even in this story—a story in which the Doctor's logic and plans are particularly ill-considered—Troughton manages to continually make it so that his Doctor is always taking concrete action, maneuvering characters into doing what he wants. Even when he's given tedious sequences of technobabble and exposition, he actively engages the Doctor with the other characters in order to get them to react in certain ways. Pointedly, he shapes the scenes from a marginal perspective—not through the domination of the screen space.

The really key scene in illustrating this is the much-praised scene between the Doctor and Victoria in the third episode. It's a scene in which Troughton overtly has a supporting role—he's supposed to be providing a platform for Deborah Watling (by far the best known actress to be cast as a companion to date) to get a star turn. And Troughton dutifully spends the scene finding readings that give Watling a justification to do wide-eyed, sympathetic close-ups. Troughton has one of the handful of really emotional moments his Doctor gets in this scene, and he pointedly lets it be understated in comparison with Watling's performance.

This not being the Matt Smith book, I won't go into the same lengthy reading of a scene from his tenure (such a reading is available in the video version), but this very much describes how Smith works, making the Doctor a character who shifts around rapidly, always taking action that is carefully measured to engage with the other actors. The capacity to do a generous star turn is something very few actors can manage, but Troughton is extraordinary with it in this story, and we have to give it credit for the fact that this story has an outsized influence through him alone, despite its myriad of massive, massive flaws.

My Guru, If You Will (*The Abominable Snowmen*)

It's September 30, 1967. Mr. Humperdinck continues to rule over the charts untroubled by the psychedelic whippersnappers in the rest of the top ten (of which there are at least three). He continues this for two weeks, at which point he is abruptly unseated by the Bee Gees with "Massachusetts," with The Move's "Flowers in the Rain" immediately behind. For the next four weeks, it's just a question of which bits of psychedelia fail to unseat the Bee Gees, who have a trace of psychedelia in the lettering on their single but are otherwise, let's be honest here, about as far from that model as you can get.

"Flowers in the Rain" and "Massachusetts" are also, interestingly, the first two songs played on BBC Radio 1, which debuts during this story. Radio 1 is one of four new radio stations that comprised the BBC's long overdue concession to the existence of rock and pop music as well as the death knell of the pirate radio stations. You also, during this story, have the murder of Jack McVitie by the Kray Twins, a key event in the unraveling of the dominant system of organized crime in London in the 1960s. In other news, it's mostly the Vietnam War, I fear, though you have the memorable instance of Allen Ginsberg and Abbie Hoffman attempting to levitate the Pentagon during this story. Which is actually, probably a decent way into this one.

One of the problems looking back at the 1960s is that for all we romanticize psychedelia and the hippies, for a wide variety of reasons, hardly anyone actually wants a return to the days of psychedelia. The romanticization of the era has as much to do with entombing it safely in the past as it does with actual regard for it. And the March on the Pentagon is kind of a perfect example of this. For large swaths of the world, the attempt to levitate it while Ginsberg performed Tibetan chants is simply incomprehensible, and is evidence that, however nice an album *Sergeant Pepper* was, perhaps the whole acid thing went just a little further than is useful. It's seen as so absurd as to be completely harmless and unworthy of serious thought. I mean, levitating the Pentagon? Really?

In fact what we have here is a case of failing to understand your audience. Anyone who was tuned in to the psychedelic movement at large would have recognized the Pentagon levitation as an act of guerilla theater in the classic psychedelic vein. Did Hoffman and Ginsberg actually expect to levitate the Pentagon? It's tough to imagine that they did, given that it's not like they had a lengthy track record of levitations to go on. I mean, even if you decide to just completely embrace the idea that it is possible to levitate objects via meditation and chanting, nobody starts with the Pentagon. I don't care how many drugs you've done, if you're actually making efforts at psychic levitation, you don't start with a colossally large building while the cameras are watching. You start alone, quietly, in your room, and establish that you can actually do this. The fact that they went right for the Pentagon suggests rather strongly that success was not at the top of their list of concerns.

On top of that, levitating the Pentagon is a terrible idea. I mean, not for the obvious reasons. Well, OK, yes, for the obvious reasons as well. But most people stop thinking about the matter after "but that's impossible" and never really pick it up to consider it more deeply. The plan was to levitate the Pentagon five feet and shake it once to exorcise the demons. Think for a moment about the practical result of elevating a massive building for five feet (what would hold all that stone together?); what would happen to the people inside when the building is shaken, and, for that matter, what about the massive damage done by the broken water and gas manes throughout? To say nothing of what would happen when the building were returned to its now broken foundations. This is a plan, in other words, that clearly nobody ever once considered the practical consequences of. Which makes sense only if one of two things is true. Either Ginsberg and Hoffman are simply idiots, which an even cursory review of their work shows they are not, or they never intended for it to work.

No. The Pentagon levitation makes sense only if you consider it as a bit of theater. An attempt not to levitate the Pentagon but rather to give the bureaucrats inside the Pentagon the bracing experience of having a mob of people angrily trying to levitate you. In other words, it was not so much an attempt to cause massive property damage as it was an attempt to make the lives of people working in the Pentagon wildly stranger than they would otherwise have been.

There are two things to point out here. One is that there's something fundamentally odd about Tibetan Buddhism being one of the major engines of this sort of psychedelic guerilla theater. The other is that under this interpretation, Doctor Who is wildly more in tune with psychedelic culture than anybody gives it credit for being. The base under siege, in which people who are firmly part of the military-industrial complex are suddenly confronted with horrible and inexplicable monsters, is in fact a dramatization of the very idea of psychedelic politics—confronting the entrenched structures of power with the utterly mad.

By staggering coincidence, then, we get *The Abominable Snowmen*, a six-parter in which bizarre monsters lay siege to a group of people and, in the process, their entire worldview. Specifically, in which giant robot Yeti attack a Tibetan monastery.

There are some things that happen to you when you become a dedicated Doctor Who fan, not all of which are good. One of them is that, after a certain point, you stop blinking at sentences like the one at the end of the last paragraph. So I'll invite you to read it again, and then reflect on just how completely insane it is that the plot of this story centers on the idea that the mythical Yeti are actually (or at least largely) robots controlled by a vast extra-terrestrial intelligence. Even if you review the previous four seasons and change you won't see anything that can seriously be considered a straightforward antecedent of this. It is an idea like nothing we've previously seen in Doctor Who.

Plus we have the Tibetan monastery—the first trip to a real non-Western human culture since *The Aztecs*. This, then, is not unprecedented, but it's still visibly and tangibly outside the mould of what we expect from the program. That said, the setting can't really be considered a sudden return of multiculturalism to Doctor Who. As we can already see in this post, Tibetan Buddhism was iconic for psychedelic culture. The link is all but explicit in the story, which, we should note, makes a complete hash of the names to the point where, when Terrance Dicks novelized it a few years later, Barry Letts (an eventual producer of Doctor Who and actual Buddhist) told him to change the names around to actually make sense as a supposed Buddhist parable), since the master of the monastery, Padmasambhava (a name that, as Miles and Wood point out, would only have been kept in the script if there was a reason for it), is named after the author of the supposed *Tibetan Book of the Dead*, the book that was cannibalized into Timothy Leary's psychedelic handbook *The Psychedelic Experience*. Of course, Padmasambhava is possessed by evil, so maybe that's not a glowing recommendation for psychedelia.

Indeed, there's something kind of unsettling about this faux-Buddhism (both here and in the larger psychedelic culture). There is, after all, an actual religion with around a half-billion followers who, understandably, might object to the degree to which their entire spirituality is actively co-opted by a bunch of rich white people to, at best, provide a spiritual component to their socio-political revolution and, at worse, provide a thin justification for being drug addicts. Certainly British and American New-Age Buddhism has at best an awkward relationship with the actual thing, having about as much relationship with it as a stage magician does with actual occultism. If we're being honest, its appeal is probably that Buddhism, being a fairly unstructured religion with a very nebulous concept of spirituality, lends itself better than most major religions to being the glue that holds an otherwise disparate set of beliefs together. But all of this is dreadfully culturally imperialist, and it's tough not to be a little bit uncomfortable about it.

All the same, after the disaster of xenophobia that was *The Tomb of the Cybermen*, it's really difficult to get too bent out of shape over something that's merely misguidedly respectful of another culture. However tacky New Age-flavored Buddhism is, it's hardly a fundamental betrayal of the show's principles or a massive affront to good taste in the same way that a story full of Shiftystanians is. And Troughton has the typically good sense to play the Doctor as someone with a deep and abiding respect for Buddhism, which helps take the edge off of the more troubling aspects.

The result is that the monastery turns out also to make a surprisingly effective base for sieging. The monks appear to have a genuine sense of crisis. Having the Yeti attack a literal icon of psychedelic culture and launch a spiritual attack on the monastery as a whole is a clever idea. The use of a vaguely Lovecraftian "Great Intelligence" (Yog-Sothoth, if the horrible Lovecraft retcon of Andy Lane is taken seriously, which, frankly, is nearly impossible) means that the stakes of this have an odd weight to them—it matters if this base falls or not. If the archeological expedition on Telos fails, at the end of the day, we'd have some dead bodies and some probably-still-trapped Cybermen. If this monastery falls, the sense is that the moral foundation of Buddhism, psychedelia, and possibly the Doctor himself would be gravely wounded.

The problem is that for all the cleverness, we run into the fact that the Yeti are, in this story at least, an appallingly dumb idea. The idea of the Great Intelligence controlling Yeti is neat. And the story ultimately hedges and has real Yeti exist. So what's the point of the robot ones? Why introduce a ludicrous idea like this? Surely the idea that the Great Intelligence, which already demonstrates mind control powers, is simply controlling the local fauna makes more sense than silver control spheres for robot Yeti. But instead, because the show creates monsters according to a very narrow paradigm, we get a bad *Scooby Doo* premise. Because for all the good ideas the show has, it is, at this point, much like the Model T coming in any color you like as long as it's black, Doctor Who is, at this point, a show that can be about anything as long as it's a base under siege. This is a pretty good base under a pretty dumb siege, and the result is at least extremely watchable.

If this sounds like damning with faint praise, it almost, but not quite, is. Yes, it's hard to just praise this issue. It's another base under siege. It's another six-parter that should have been four. (The modern invention of psychic paper would have trimmed the first two episodes out entirely.) It's got all the problems that the show is increasingly having—the plug and play mentality. But following a catastrophically xenophobic exercise that plunged the show from "kind of repeating itself a bit" to actually being something that it's just tough to love, this story is, if not back to lovable, at least enormously likable. It's at least got the Doctor seemingly caring about making the world a better place, and it's got some lovely atmosphere between the lack of music and the setting, and you get the sense that the series is at least trying. Which, let's face it, was starting to come into doubt.

I Never Had a Life like That (*The Ice Warriors*)

It's November 11, 1967. The Foundations, a British Motown group, are at number one, because these things happen in the UK charts. Two weeks later they get unseated by Long John Baldry's "Let the Heartaches Begin." Knowing nothing about this song, I listened to ninety seconds of it and … well, look, we all make mistakes in life. But on week two of this rather unfortunate moment in pop history we can already see relief riding triumphantly up the charts, arriving decisively when The Beatles' "Hello, Goodbye" shows up. What are the UK charts going to do when they don't have The Beatles to save them from their own ill-advised taste?

Whereas in real news, the Vietnam War continues to be a massive problem that is seemingly about to bring down Johnson's Presidency, the value of the UK Pound finds itself a cliff and leaps off of it with impressive zeal, and the Concorde makes its debut. Of these, the devaluation of the Pound is of the most interest to us, as it is a part of a larger economic recession hitting the UK in this period, and setting a fair amount of the national mood firmly on "pessimistic."

Whereas on television we have *The Ice Warriors*. You may have noticed, over the past few essays, a growing frustration with the "base under siege" subgenre. But in all my complaining I haven't entirely dealt with what's wrong with the genre other than that it's repetitive (which, admittedly, it is). So since *The Ice Warriors* is a quite good piece of storytelling with only a few particularly overt flaws (of which the title characters are probably the biggest), it seems like the perfect place to look at the underlying problems here.

The easiest way to see the difference is to fire up *The Rebel Flesh/The Almost People* from what is, at the time of writing, the most recent season of Doctor Who and compare it to this story. (I should note that the original blog post of this entry was written between the two parts of that story, so the comparison is not arbitrary.) Both of them are bases under siege. In fact, as several people have pointed out, the Ganger two-parter feels in many ways like a Troughton story. But if you look at the stories side by side, there's not really any competition to be had between them. Even allowing for advances in editing technology and budget, the fact of the matter is that Matthew Graham's story is miles better than *The Ice Warriors*.

Why? Because *The Rebel Flesh* feels like it has people in it. What's interesting about this is that *The Ice Warriors*, as 1960s bases under siege go, tries hard on this front. It uses the social realist techniques we talked about before to give a sense of its world. The Doctor doesn't show up for six minutes, and instead we get a clear picture of what the base is like. An extended opening-credits sequence with stock footage of icy caverns gives a similar sense of what the world at large was like. On top of that, *The Ice Warriors* has an absolutely first rate cast, which gives everything a serious edge that is lacking in other stories. And yet despite this, *The Ice Warriors* feels miles less human than *The Rebel Flesh*.

The difference can be seen in the nature of the first scenes. *The Ice Warriors* opens with a crisis—people pounding on control panels, flipping switches, and responding to alarms. It's all well acted, but it's important to accurately describe what it is happening here—people who are in charge of something are dealing with a massive external crisis of some sort. Whereas at the start of *The Rebel Flesh*, we have working class people encountering an industrial accident. And that's the heart of the difference. *The Ice Warriors* creates a world full of big, important people. *The Rebel Flesh* creates a world of ordinary people.

In fact, the approaches are almost exactly backwards. By the end of the first episode of *The Ice Warriors*, we've gotten an explanation of its world. It's an insane explanation (excessive harvesting of plants has reduced carbon dioxide levels across the world leading to a second ice age. So yes, this one comes off a bit oddly in 2011), but it's an explanation nevertheless. Whereas *The Rebel Flesh* never comes close to explaining the purpose of the acid the crew is harvesting or giving a particularly detailed picture of anything beyond the day-to-day lives of the workers.

On paper, this sounds like *The Ice Warriors* would be the better story, but surprisingly, it doesn't work out that way. Because in *The Ice Warriors*, the world remains just that: an explanation. When any of the crises in which "the ionizer is failing" or "the glaciers are advancing" flare up, there's still no context for it. We have no sense of where the people in this world are, what they do, or how their lives will be impacted by the glaciers. Sure, we get great poetry like Clent's line about how one winter, spring never arrived, but what we never see is any sense of the human consequences. The glaciers and the ice are just this week's binary computational blocks—the meaningless technobabble people shout about when it's time to be excited. They sound spectacular, but there's no underlying drama to them.

And that's where far too many of these bases under siege fall flat. The appeal of the base under siege story is the same as the appeal of the film *Twelve Angry Men*—the fact that if you want interesting drama to occur, taking a bunch of people and stranding them somewhere with a problem is one of the easiest ways to construct it. *The Ice Warriors* goes further towards that than anyone is going to give it credit for. It creates an effective triangle of loyalties among Clent, Penley, and Garrett. It has the end crisis be about humans solving an internal conflict inside the base, not about shooting aliens. It's trying very, very hard to make this a serious drama about characters, and the people involved deserve real praise for coming out miles ahead of every previous iteration of the base under siege. In particular we should mention: Peter Bryant, the script editor soon to be promoted to producer; Brian Hayles, who, on his second outing, reveals himself to be actually a quite solid writer who makes one wonder what *The Celestial Toymaker* was like before it lost two of its three supporting characters and got rewritten by Gerry Davis; and Derek Martinus, by this point an old pro at the series (he directed *Mission to the Unknown*, *The Tenth Planet*, and *Evil of the Daleks*).

But in coming out ahead, oddly, the story ends up exposing its faults even more clearly. Once we see all the parts of this story working as well as they possibly can, we can finally see what doesn't work in sharper relief. Yes, this is an interesting drama about three people, but there's no stakes and no sense of a larger world beyond a vague texture to it. The same three people could be having the same argument in any setting without needing to change the story significantly. The base under siege is suddenly revealed as an arbitrary container into which a drama gets slotted, as opposed to a story. There is literally nothing that constitutes a reason why this plot has to be the one that happens at Britannica Base while the last one had to happen in a monastery. Which is a problem given that the appeal of the base under siege story is that it gives you high concept settings and memorable monsters to market. When it turns out both of those are completely irrelevant to what makes the story work then it becomes difficult to really justify the genre.

Though perhaps we should thank God this story doesn't depend on the Ice Warriors, given that they're the sorriest excuses for recurring monsters the show has come up with yet. They're Cybermen with more annoying voices. If we're being honest, the fact that they are literally green reptile monsters from Mars has to mark the point where the show has simply given up on monsters and concluded that the audience will accept anything. Unlike last time, when this sort of complete ambivalence to all notions of quality in monsters at least left us with a crowning monument to insanity, here it leads to what are easily the most obvious and uninteresting monsters Doctor Who ever thought worth recycling.

While on one level this is a good thing—the story is forced to work on other grounds, and so you get things like actual tension among the crew, or, in my favorite scene in the story (and one of my favorites in Doctor Who thus far), Clent praising a subordinate for his dedication in volunteering for this mission, only to embarrassingly find out the guy was drafted. It allows for things that give us at least the feel that there is some outside world, or the most interesting idea the story has, Storr the scavenger.

But Storr ends up being yet another exhibit of how this story almost, but not quite, figures out how to tell itself. The idea here is perhaps the most magnificent in the story—the idea that, in this ice age, there are people scrambling about trying to survive who don't give a toss about these expensive efforts to "ionize" the glaciers, they just want to figure out what they're doing right now. In other words, Storr is a character that does exactly what this story needs—he gives us a human way in.

Except they don't follow this idea to its full potential. Instead, Storr is portrayed as an ultra-luddite who exists to shore up the moral credibility of the story. Because the story ends up hinging on the base crew rejecting the computer and thinking for themselves, it needs a character like Storr who is obviously wrong in completely rejecting technology so that it can end up holding a suitably milquetoast middle ground. And so the most interesting idea it has—actually asking what a new ice age would be like for people—gets killed off in the fourth episode because we need to establish that the Ice Warriors are dangerous. Again.

Part of the problem here is also, if we're being honest, the TARDIS crew. I've noted before that the TARDIS crew has no audience identification characters anymore. The three companion roles originally set out—ordinary man, ordinary woman, and starchild—have been reduced to their crassest plot functions: action man and peril girl. Neither of them bring any sense of the ordinary, and in fact the major source of alienation they should be having—the fact that both of them are from Britain's past—is usually ignored save for a token scene for each of them, usually Jamie calling something a metal beastie and Victoria being prim about something. So where before when we introduced a major monster like the Daleks, we could focus on Barbara's terror at them, now when we have Victoria in her major peril scene we just revert to classic Laura Mulvey male-gaze territory.

This is the second time I've mentioned Mulvey, so let's stop and explain. Laura Mulvey is a 1970s film theorist who came up with an idea called scopophilia. Mulvey's claim is that the editing and camera angles of cinema reflect a male pleasure of looking at women based on fragmenting their body and objectifying them. And it's worth comparing the lengthy sequence in which Victoria runs around in caverns away from the Ice Warriors to the first iconic monster-menacing scene, Barbara being menaced by the Daleks in *The Daleks*. In *The Daleks* the camera focuses primarily on Barbara's face and on her terror at the unseen Daleks. Here Victoria is portrayed less as a character for us to empathize with and more as a character for us to watch being imperiled—she's kept either in long shots where we can't read her face or in tight close-ups that focus on her eyes instead of being kept in medium shots that really communicate her terror. And it marks a really unfortunate abandonment of a model of characterization in favor of treating the characters as mere plot functions.

I know it sounds like I'm very down on this story, but I'm not. It's just that this story requires one of those strange things you have to do with Doctor Who every once in a while—praising with faint damnation. I'm always wary, lest I turn into late career Lawrence Miles, of criticizing a story for not being something other than what it sets out to be. But here that's necessary. The problem with *The Ice Warriors* has nothing to do with anybody working on it, and everything to do with the fact that it's an episode of a show that has, by this point, given up on trying to surprise the audience. It has collapsed entirely into the standard action-serial mode and made its home there. Its primary virtue is that despite this, it has enough people trying to make it good that it reliably ends up being far, far better than a standard weekly action serial needs to be. The show has essentially given up on producing A-quality storylines in exchange for avoiding ever producing complete duds, reasoning that it's better to be a show that gets a B consistently than one that gets an A occasionally and a C or lower a lot too. More than anything, at this point in the show, one finds one's self wishing for something like *The Gunfighters*—a glorious, misguided mess. One finds one's self desperately wanting to admire the ambition of a story instead of the execution. Especially here, because the execution is so solid that it is at times actively painful to see everyone wasting it on this.

Still, we can start to find a silver lining here. We're seeing the opening seeds of what's going to eventually elevate the series out of this. Writers like Brian Hayles are, even if only out of the need to pad their stories two episodes each, learning to give us fleeting glimpses of ordinary people. Writers like Haisman and Lincoln are beginning to key onto the idea that if we're going to make it so the TARDIS crew has no identification figures we need to make them larger-than-life mythical heroes. Both of these are major steps towards a mode that works.

But hey. The next story is by David Whitaker, who has by now established himself as the best writer the series sees in its first five seasons. So we probably have something good happening there. And after that, we get a change in producer, which is probably needed around now. (Not that I think Innes Lloyd has been bad for the show—I honestly think his reign is, on balance, pretty much all good things. But I do think that we're rapidly reaching the end of new ideas he can bring to the table.) If the show were always this good when it was going through a bad patch, it wouldn't have been cancelled. The show is frustrating because it's not living up to its vast potential and the talent of its cast—not because it's bad. There are worse problems to have.

Pop Between Realities, Home in Time for Tea: *The Prisoner, You Only Live Twice*

Despite the superficial similarities here—two iconic British espionage stories from the same year—this is an entry of staggering contrasts. They may both feature secret agents, be British, and be from 1967, but that's about where the similarities between James Bond's *You Only Live Twice* and *The Prisoner* end. Past that we find ourselves staring the culture wars in the face.

Let's start with Bond, since that's the one that's kind of long overdue in this project. The thing to note regarding *You Only Live Twice* is that it is a movie that expects nothing out of its audience. It would be easy to describe it as a movie which has a sort of cynical contempt for its audience, but that's overly simplistic; it is not as though it thinks little of its audience and thus concludes that it can be lazy. No, the movie thinks little of its audience and then works overtime in order to please them. It's a triumph of a fundamental aspect of popular culture: the extremely well-made piece of trash.

There's something almost giddily entertaining about the movie's complete lack of irony. Later the James Bond movies begin to poke fun at the series' tropes by using things such as Bond's refined tastes as the material for comedic scenes. And over time this becomes necessary—as Bond became an artifact of the past and the tropes became reflexively known to the audience this sort of subversion became the natural response. But this movie is caught in a bizarre midpoint in the franchise between establishing the tropes and subverting them. It's well established enough that everybody knows that Bond likes vodka martinis (though here he seems quite pleased to get one stirred) and is a rakish womanizer. But it's not well enough established to play Bond complimenting his host on the choice of vodka or describing at some length the proper temperature for sake to be served at for laughs. Instead these scenes are presented with a sort of earnest conviction that the audience really just wants to see Sean Connery explaining the proper presentation of sake. And apparently, given how the movie did, they were right.

But perhaps the most astonishing thing about *You Only Live Twice* is its structure. When some of the production documents for the first Indiana Jones movie leaked onto the Internet a few years back, one of the things people excitedly pointed at was the fact that Spielberg and Lucas talked explicitly about using the structure of a serial and putting a cliffhanger in at regular intervals. This is indeed a clever trick, but for some reason people seemed to think that Lucas and Spielberg were the first people to think of doing it in a movie, as opposed to the first people to have their discussion about it leaked onto the Internet. Because once you're past the opening credits sequence of *You Only Live Twice*, with very few exceptions, the movie is structured as a serial comprised of five-minute episodes.

Almost like clockwork, every five minutes, Bond is plunged into terrible danger. (And on the first five-minute mark where he isn't, he's plunged into bed with an attractive Asian woman instead.) The movie is basically just a string of plot exposition and motivation that links together the action sequences. A given five-minute stretch of the movie will almost always consist of Bond getting out of trouble, discussing the trouble he just got out of with someone, discussing what they should do next, going to do it, and then getting into trouble to set up the next cycle.

This is not actually a bad thing. I mean, yes, two hours of it can be a little draining, and you start to wonder about anyone who just marathons these films or sees any significant depth to them, but for what they are—chains of set pieces—they're staggeringly well done. Admittedly, watching it in 2011 involves identifying whichever portion of your brain engages in any feminist or racial/cultural criticism of media and clubbing it until it falls silent forevermore, but if you judiciously apply some *Tomb of the Cybermen* topically before watching, you can fall into a sort of pleasant ethical numbness in which it's possible to actually enjoy yourself.

In the end, though, *You Only Live Twice* is an extremely well-produced chain of action sequences full of crass racism and cultural imperialism. Two things about this are important for our purposes. First, for everything I've complained about in Doctor Who recently, it could be a lot worse. The show may be in a rut, but it's still miles more ambitious than just phoning in action sequences for their own sake, and it's still got a moral center that makes the moments of casual racism jarring, unlike the Bond film where they seem all too natural. Second, and this may sound obvious, but there's a difference between the stylistic bits of the 1960s and the moral/philosophical bits. *You Only Live Twice* is unmistakably made in the 1960s—you can tell just by looking at it. But its debt to the 1960s is only in its sense of what's cool.

It is instructive to compare the film to *The Abominable Snowmen*. Both stories pick East Asian settings because they're cool and trendy at the time. In *You Only Live Twice*, this is used as an excuse to see James Bond enjoy the luxurious decadences of Japan, in particular the women. In *The Abominable Snowmen*, on the other hand, the Doctor is used to give a real moral force to the viewpoints of the Asian culture in question, albeit to an overly simplistic and superficial version of those viewpoints. This isn't just an artifact of late 1960s culture either. In a fundamental sense Doctor Who and James Bond have a very different philosophy that will always set them apart. There's necessarily something a little more in tune with '60s youth culture about a mischievous vagabond than there is about a government employee who's frequently referred to by his ID number.

Speaking of people who are numbers, he said, in a

desperate attempt at a transition, let's talk about *The Prisoner*. On the surface, *The Prisoner* is just another ITC serial, ITC being a production company that turned out legions of TV shows, both good and bad, over the '60s and '70s, often with an eye on the export market, in sufficient volume and with sufficient fidelity to a formula to constitute a genre unto itself. But amongst their massive output were several shows of legendary quality—including, oddly enough, *The Muppet Show*. One of the shows that was not quite legendary but was still quite good was called *Secret Agent* or *Danger Man*, depending on where you lived. When that series ended, its star, Patrick McGoohan, moved on to another series partially of his own devising called *The Prisoner*, in which a nameless secret agent (assumed by many to be his previous character) quits, is kidnapped, and is sent to a strange and mysterious island where he is referred to only as "Number Six." There they try to break him and get him to explain why he quit, and he, for seventeen episodes, refuses. The result is seventeen episodes of surreal psychedelia that are widely and rightly regarded as one of the best television series ever.

Far too much of the praise for *The Prisoner* is reserved for its final episode, "Fall Out." It's not that the final episode is bad by any stretch of the imagination. It's just that the final episode is, bewilderingly for anyone who's watched the thing, treated as though its focus is the scene in which Number Six pulls off the mask of Number One and discovers his own face behind it. While this scene does happen, it's worth considering how it actually plays out. First of all, his own face is the third face (and I would argue, mask) of Number One he sees—Number One is first seen wearing a black-and-white mask of the sort that all the people running the Village are wearing in this episode. Then, when Six pulls off that mask, One is wearing a gorilla mask. It's only after both of these masks are ripped off that we see the third mask: Six's face. But the total number of seconds we see it on screen is negligible—it's barely possible to see that it's Number Six. At that point, the two fight briefly and Number One runs off.

The point, in other words, is not that Number Six was Number One all along. It's certainly not, as some people oddly insist, that the famous opening credits of *The Prisoner* have been giving the ending away all along. (Although read as a script, the exchange "Who is Number One?" "You are Number Six" could be interpreted as providing an answer to the question— "You are [Number One], Number Six." However, as delivered, the line is unambiguous in identifying Number Six by his number. It's never read in such a way as to covertly give the game away.) In fact, the point of the final episode is precisely to avoid any sort of sensible explanation of what is going on. The episode makes no sense, weaving its way through a sort of trial sequence straight out of Eastern European absurdism, plenty of psychedelia, and a basically meaningless and borderline impossible resolution. Those who view the entire final episode as a delusional dream in the style of *Brazil* (the closest thing to a film adaptation of *The Prisoner* we are ever likely to see) are on far more plausible footing than most, but the fact of the matter is that it's tough to assume anyone involved in making that episode was making it with the intention that there was some sort of clear or definite answer as to what was going on. It wasn't supposed to make sense, and if you think it did, you definitely did it wrong.

No, as good as the finale is, the show is far more interesting when it's not cranking the weirdness all the way to eleven. This is the thing anyone coming to the show for the first time will notice. Sit down with "The Arrival" on the basis of its reputation alone and you'll get about twenty minutes of Patrick McGoohan wandering around a holiday camp. In fact, it seems largely like a remake of *The Macra Terror*. Then the booming voice organizing things orders everyone to stop. Patrick McGoohan looks intently and panickedly at a fountain, in which a small white orb is floating.

Even if you know that *The Prisoner* features a big white balloon that is the Village's security system, there is absolutely nothing that prepares you for actually seeing Rover. The camera cuts back to McGoohan doing a double take, and suddenly there it is—a giant white balloon that chases a man down, asphyxiates him, then bounds cheerily away. And all that can really be said is that there has never, before or possibly since, been anything quite like this on television. And when we finally get the bewildering spectacle of Patrick McGoohan trying to fight with Rover … look, let's just come out and say it. *The Prisoner* manages to make a weather balloon look scarier in 1967 than Doctor Who had ever managed to make anything at all. This is the moment where *The Prisoner* definitively beats out *The Macra Terror*. *The Macra Terror* had to spend a ton of money on not-entirely-well-made giant crabs in order to evoke the same terror that *The Prisoner* accomplishes via the most laughably silly-looking prop ever.

This is where *The Prisoner* is most effective—when it's closest to standard espionage territory. The show's excursions into full-out psychedelia are lovely, but nothing compared to what was already increasingly passing for mainstream entertainment. The Beatles' TV movie for *Magical Mystery Tour* aired almost smack in the middle of *The Prisoner*, and was miles further down the rabbit hole. *Yellow Submarine*, essentially the same film only done well, is only a few months out from here. Plenty of things had the psychedelia base covered better than *The Prisoner*. What's interesting about *The Prisoner* is that it often presents itself as a fairly normal spy show and then allows its strange psychedelic elements to encroach on the business as usual of espionage.

Once this is understood, the show becomes far easier to grasp. Even its ostensibly flashy and weird episodes—things like "Living in Harmony," in which the show abruptly and with no explanation reboots itself as a Western (complete with a new credit sequence) only to have *The Prisoner* intrude on the Western about five minutes from the end. The biggest problem came when people misunderstood this structure and expected that, eventually, all the spy stuff would have a James Bondy explanation. "Fall Out," far from being the peak of the series, was just the series telling those people off.

Still, we should note, perhaps with some pride, that the idea of bizarre genre juxtapositions in a vaguely psychedelic sci-fi show has some antecedents in British television, namely Doctor Who. Yes, the most obviously similar story, *The Macra Terror*, was made too late to have an influence on *The Prisoner*. (Indeed, if anything it's more likely that Ian Stuart Black had heard a bit about *The Prisoner* while it was in production.) But on the other hand, does "Living in Harmony," in which the awkward juxtaposition of a classic British genre (the James Bond genre that *The Prisoner* is still living within) and the American Western is used, not owe at least some debt to *The Gunfighters*, which did the exact same joke in April of 1966, right around when *The Prisoner* was being conceived?

Once we look at it that way, other similarities show up. *The Rescue*, for instance, is far closer to the plot of an episode of *The Prisoner* than anybody bothers to give it credit for. The absurd presentationalist techniques of *The Web Planet* are absolutely crucial to how *The Prisoner* works (build up an utterly insane world and then spend time in it without anyone acting like this is at all strange). And one can vaguely imagine that if *The Celestial Toymaker* had been made with its original having-a-point script that it would have been firmly in *Prisoner* territory. Even *The Chase*, in inadvertently inventing postmodernist narrative techniques through sheer incompetence (as I argue back in the Hartnell volume), seems to be paving the way for *The Prisoner* to come along.

But all of this points to a somewhat disturbing possibility. All of the examples we've used of the ways in which Doctor Who seems to lead towards *The Prisoner*, with the exception of *The Macra Terror*, are from William Hartnell stories. *The Prisoner*, when it started airing, was a far more intelligent and mature successor to William Hartnell's Doctor Who than Doctor Who was, even with its enormously talented lead actor. And this is a bit of a tough thing to celebrate. On the one hand, we Doctor Who fans can, in seeing *The Prisoner*, know how cutting edge our show was in the years leading up to it. On the other hand, we're forced to admit here that our show has been left in the dust, and has a lot of catching up to do.

Look How Cool This Stuff Is (*The Enemy of the World*)

It's December 23, 1967. The Beatles are at number one with "Hello Goodbye," and also at number three with the *Magical Mystery Tour* EP, which, being an EP, is charted as a single instead of an album. They'll hold number one for five weeks, reiterating the vague tendency for creativity in Doctor Who and The Beatles to coincide. At week six, as the season's one experiment with something other than bases under siege concludes, the bottom falls out and Georgie Fame takes over with "The Ballad of Bonnie and Clyde." In the meantime The Monkees chart with "Daydream Believer," as do Cliff Richard, Tom Jones, The Four Tops, and Engelbert Humperdinck.

In terms of news, we have the first use of the term "black hole," one of the pieces of science most friendly to science fiction. Prime Minister Wilson endorses the "I'm Backing Britain" campaign asking people to work an extra half hour without pay, which ends up being a complete turkey. The Prague Spring gets underway, which is a bit unusual given that it's January. And the Vietnam War keeps it up.

While on television we have *The Enemy of the World*. For a long time, this was the big overlooked story of Season Five, which was long beloved as "the one with the monsters" such that the one without any and with a goofy sounding "identical dupicates" premise looked, in the words of the Peter Haining book, "odd." It had a few proponents in reconstructions—Lawrence Miles marks it as his favorite Troughton in *About Time*, and I praised the hell out of it as well. But with its slow middle episode as the only surviving part for a long time and a general failure to be what a lot of people wanted from the Troughton era it labored in a measure of obscurity—*Doctor Who Magazine* had it at 139th between *The Idiot's Lantern* and *The Doctor's Daughter*. Then, four years later, it jumped to 56th.

There's no mystery to how this happened. In October, 2013 it was announced that *The Enemy of the World* and most of *The Web of Fear* had been recovered in Nigeria and would be out shortly on iTunes. And suddenly, in a mad 50th anniversary rush, a pair of 1968 Doctor Who stories shot to the top of the iTunes charts. And while *The Web of Fear* remains the more popular story, once everyone got an actual whiff of this they realized that yes, it was absolutely brilliant. Even 56th is harsh, frankly—this belongs in the company of *City of Death, Caves of Androzani*, and *Kill the Moon*. It's that good.

The basic conceit of this story is simple: it's the inevitable "Doctor Who Does James Bond" piece. Whitaker holds to the James Bond paradigm we have already discussed, dropping an action-based cliffhanger every five minutes for the first fifteen minutes of the story as the Doctor, Jamie, and Victoria are chased by hovercraft and helicopter, and then, for good measure, attacked by gunmen. This is clever—far cleverer than just using some generic James Bond trappings. Whitaker begins by mimicking the structure of a James Bond movie, then dropping the Doctor into it. But then he pulls his first grand trick by having Troughton also play the Bond villain.

This certainly could be silly, and it's true that the "identical double" setup has diminishing returns over the course of the series. But Whitaker takes good advantage of it, making Salamander into a well-constructed double of the Doctor. Whitaker's Doctor, as we've discussed, is a mercurial figure, not just in the banal sense of being eccentric and clownish. Salamander, on the other hand, is far from mercurial—indeed, he seems positively saturnine—an angry, sullen, and malevolent figure.

But Whitaker's real genius with the story comes in its pacing. The obvious promise of the story is clear from the moment the premise is revealed—the audience wants to see the Doctor and Salamander meet. But Whitaker takes until the closing seconds of the story to actually do this, instead reveling in the anticipation of it in the way that so much of 1960s Doctor Who does. More broadly, the pleasure implied by the Doctor being put through a James Bond-style plot isn't just seeing the James Bond material but seeing how the Doctor is going to subvert it. And so Whitaker largely keeps the Doctor away from the narrative, allowing the tension to build up as he explores ways of colliding Doctor Who and James Bond other than giddy pastiche.

The most striking aspect of this approach is, in many ways, the cliffhangers. Virtually all of them consist of characters learning pieces of information, generally ones the audience already knows, but being in no immediate danger. The first and weirdest of these is the one at the end of the first episode—a strong contender for the strangest cliffhanger of the classic series. In it, shortly after the Doctor has found out about Salamander, Salamander's security forces show up, forcing the Doctor to duck into a bathroom and then to hastily attempt an impersonation of Salamander. The thing is, Salamander is Mexican. (Indeed, in one of the few somewhat tacky bits of the story, Troughton plays him slightly blacked up, although it's important to realize that in black-and-white television is that this is possible without tipping into the sort of racial parody of, say, *The Talons of Weng*-Chiang.) And so part of impersonating Salamander means doing his accent.

I've talked before about Troughton's counterintuitive but brilliant line readings. Here he outdoes himself. It is important to remember, first and foremost, that Salamander is also played by Troughton. Troughton, in other words, can do the voice perfectly—it's his voice, after all. (The voice is not so much a Mexican accent as a generic "foreign" accent that softens the racial elements of the character.) But Troughton opts to ply the Doctor's imitation as a botched imitation, striding out and confidently greeting Bruce the security guard in the worst Mexican accent imaginable. This is, on its own merits, already a strange and sublimely weird moment. But then to have that be the cliffhanger—on an episode that has featured fifteen minutes of tense vehicle chases—is simply mind-wrenching. It's a classic case of using cliffhangers to signal changes in direction of the story, instead of just to put the characters in danger (which gets farcical rapidly—the preceding story has an absolutely ludicrous cliffhanger in which the Doctor is given the choice of answering the question "Who are you" or being exploded. In a move that I am sure shocked every single viewer, he answered the question next episode), and Whitaker does it for the whole story. But these cliffhangers get at what Whitaker's story is actually about. It's not a story about the chases and thrills as such, but a story about what kind of story it is. And so these cliffhangers, as characters get information that changes their understanding of their world, are effective precisely because they suggest that the basic shape of the story could change at any moment.

Here we also get at another aspect of Whitaker's cleverness. He is, after all, the writer of the pseudo-Shakespearean *The Crusade* and the shockingly literate *Power of the Daleks*. He's also well aware that he's writing for the BBC, and so while he gets a lot of action into the first fifteen minutes, there's only so much James Bond movie he can actually put into the story. He needs to find something else, and he fills it with the sort of methodical intrigue of his best work. The trappings may be James Bond, but the substance, as Miles and Wood point out, is akin to Roman court intrigue, with complex double and triple crosses going on all over the place. And there's a weight to things. The third episode—for a long time the only one we had—is almost purely an exercise in worldbuilding that turns the focus to the characters on the margins of the world.

Its premise has Jamie and Victoria working Salamander's kitchen for an episode where and trying to pry information about Salamander from his food taster, Fariah. Fariah is notable as the show's first black female character, and, more to the point, she's an amazing in her own right—it will be a long time before Doctor Who does a black character of any gender this well again. The second episode manages a clever bit where it initially looks like she'll be a miserable serving girl, then slowly reveals that she's actually quite an important character and a strong woman until, when she dies in the fourth episode, it's genuinely upsetting because of how good a character she was. But the point of the third episode is not primarily Fariah, but a character who makes his only appearance in it—Griffin the Chef.

It's tough to quite explain Griffin the Chef. Basically, he's a character who has absolutely no stake in any of this "save the world from the evil dictator" business, dislikes everybody, and just wants to be left alone to cook, which he does very well in spite of the fact that virtually every other sentence out of his mouth is an observation about how bad his food is and how he's going to get fired or executed for it. Basically, he's a comic relief character. But he benefits tremendously from actually being genuinely funny. More to the point, however, he's exactly what so many of the past few stories have been lacking—a regular person. Griffin is in the story so that we have the perspective of an ordinary guy who just wants to manage to survive this insane world where people routinely poison and shoot each other. And it's absolutely wonderful. Griffin steals every scene he's in, and the inclusion of the third episode is a huge part of what elevates *The Enemy of the World* from "quite good adventure" to "sublimely good story." Because it goes miles towards making us actually see the whole world that Salamander is the enemy of. It's not, in this case, an expected pleasure. But it's crucial to what Whitaker does because it bothers to firmly establish the milieu in its own right and makes the nature of the inevitable subversion of the world isn't straightforwardly obvious—this is far more complex than its source material. As characters' places in the world shift around due to the cliffhanger revelations the nature of the eventual explosion when it all comes together shifts too.

Structurally, the build of the story is focused on running through a series of lesser elements people would want out of the concept as it builds to the Doctor and Salamander. So for instance, first the Doctor opts send Jamie and Victoria halfway across the planet to do an espionage plot in order to prove that Salamander is a bad guy. This makes perfect sense. Yes, we want to see the Doctor in the James Bond plot, but Jamie McCrimmon, 007 is a solid idea too.

But these tricks cannot get Whitaker to six episodes on their own, and so he holds back his most majestically odd decision. After three episodes in which the Doctor sits on the sidelines of the story demanding evidence of Salamander's evil before he'll act, it is finally Salamander who gets to push the story in a completely unexpected direction. It is worth noting how strange the fourth episode is in general. Hines and Watling get the week off, leaving Troughton as the only regular in this episode. On top of that, Troughton spends the lion's share of the episode as Salamander, so the Doctor is hardly in it. This is practically *Mission to the Unknown* in terms of how absent the regulars are. So instead of bringing the Doctor to the action, the show frustrates that desire as much as possible. This is obviously a gambit, and one only worth making if you have a strong payoff in mind.

Whitaker does. Salamander is at this point in an interesting position: he doesn't seem like the sort of character who can break the rules of the narrative. But he's still a mirror of the Doctor played by Troughton, and so that card can still be played straightforwardly and without rancor. Whitaker slams it on the table in triumph, unraveling the story in a single stroke. Salamander literally slips out the back door of the James Bond plot, entering his mysterious "records room" that nobody else is allowed into and suddenly ducking out into another story entirely. See, it turns out that Salamander has had a bunch of technicians stored away in an underground bunker, and has convinced them all that there was a terrible nuclear war up on the surface and that they have to hide down there and orchestrate natural disasters for him so he can defeat the last armies and render the planet habitable again.

This may sound stupid, but there's one other detail—the bunker full of people is basically a bunch of grumpy British people. After a story full of exotic names and foreign locales, the bunker consists of people with common British names playing their parts in their native accents. In other words, as Rob Shearman (who I'm surprised ends up kind of neutral on this story, as it seems so very much up his alley) points out in *Running Through Corridors*, "Having shown us a world stage which is so relentlessly cold, he now wrongfoots us by presenting the people who've so passively allowed that world to come into being—and they're not Eastern Europeans hiding behind exotic names. They're us."

What Shearman doesn't give Whitaker nearly enough credit for is this—months before the end of *The Prisoner* has actually been seen, he's managed to stick a gigantic pin in the entire premise of that show. *The Prisoner* is, after all, about an insane world with an illusion of normalcy hidden within the real world. And in its final episode, part of the point is the inescapability of the Village and the idea that there isn't actually an "outside" to it. Whitaker is offering a very droll undercutting of this premise by having us suddenly stumble upon a Village-like structure inside a James Bond story. By doing this, he points out one of the tricks that allows *The Prisoner* to work, namely that the Village can only function because of the series' implied connection to McGoohan's previous series. The Village only makes sense because it's not hidden in the real world, it's hidden inside what we assume to be the crazy James Bond world of *Danger Man*. It's far easier to have a blurry boundary on the Village when the world outside it is as fundamentally insane and fictional as the world inside it. But on top of this, Whitaker has just spent the previous episode making his world less insane and fictional. It may be full of James Bond stock characters, but there's a real texture to the world that cuts against the idea that there might be something like the Village in it. Salamander, it turns out, has been hiding a whole other story inside the James Bond plot.

But what's really brilliant about what Whitaker does here is that it completely changes how the end of the story goes. By the time in the fifth episode that the Doctor finally gets around to intervening in the James Bond plot it's already been subverted by Salamander. Whitaker has made us wait for four episodes to see the Doctor get to play in a James Bond story, and by the time the Doctor finally gets there, the main villain of that story has already shown himself to be far more than just another Bond villain, and in fact has shown himself to be a mercurial character who subverts narratives as well.

This means that Whitaker can get away with a resolution that is different and more interesting than he's been setting us up for. Because the Bond villain has already breached the narrative, Whitaker is much freer to do as he pleases in letting the Doctor into it. And so when Salamander's security forces swarm Kent's compound, setting off a Bond-like showdown, Whitaker can have the Doctor completely defuse it and point out that everybody is insane—a far more drastic action than he could have pulled off previously.

But Whitaker resists the temptation to simply turn this story into an out-and-out parody of James Bond stories— although that is one of the things the story does. Instead, he lets one of the Bond characters—an intermediate henchman named Benik—become a truly terrifying figure, menacing Jamie and Victoria in an overtly creepy and sexualized way, and chillingly admitting to being a simple sadist who just likes to hurt people. Yes, eventually the Doctor barges in and defuses the situation with a Salamander impersonation, but Whitaker lets the scene run long enough to be deeply unsettling, and even when the Doctor arrives, he continues his Salamander impersonation with Jamie and Victoria in order to demonstrate how genuinely afraid of Salamander they are and thus how evil he must be, pulling the task off so well that subsequently he has trouble convincing Jamie and Victoria that it's him via a cute variation on one of Troughton's trademarks, with the Doctor searching for his recorder to prove that he's himself and finally just miming a recorder performance as proof. This is quintessentially Whitaker, with his far more ambiguous and inhuman characterization of the Doctor as someone willing to push and manipulate his friends if he needs to.

So by the time we get to the sixth episode, all Whitaker really has to do is run down the checklist of big confrontations and get us to the end. Or at least, that's what we would think if it weren't for the fact that Whitaker uses his last cliffhanger to throw yet another curveball, with Astrid stumbling upon Salamander's underground bunker, thus connecting two parts of the narrative—the James Bond setup that got the Doctor into it and the late game subversion of the James Bond narrative—that the audience surely did not expect to see connected. Once Salamander has torn down the James Bond plot the last thing the audience would be expecting is for the Bond girl to get pulled into Salamander's subverted plot.

So when the big face-offs that the story has been promising the audience get going in the sixth episode all bets are off. Whitaker has spent five whole episodes making it so that we truly don't know what kind of story this is or who has power within it. And so every confrontation bristles with potential and tension. The Doctor faces down Benik again. Astrid the Bond girl faces down Salamander's secret Britain. The companions face down the dumb Bond henchmen. (OK, that last one is a bit of a snide comment on Whitaker's part, perhaps.) We know how all of these should go in a story that follows the expected set of rules, yes. But we don't know whether that's the type of story we're watching.

Which means that Whitaker can pull another big twist and reveal that Kent has secretly been a Bond villain the entire time, and that he was originally in league with Salamander on this whole "secret bunker causing natural disasters" thing. And the Doctor has known this all along, and that's why he's been so reluctant to help Kent. Aside from being a beautiful lampshading of this story's biggest flaw—the degree to which the Doctor delays getting to the action—this sequence and the resultant confrontation between Kent and Salamander reiterates a key point—Salamander is smarter than this narrative too. He is every bit the evil Doctor and a proto-Master, and he even gets a nice Mastery laugh in after killing Kent. Kent tries subverting the James Bond narrative by being a secret double agent, and he gets cut down by Salamander largely because Salamander has already become so much bigger than the mere James Bond antics Kent is playing at.

What this means is that there are huge expectations for the big one. It means that when Salamander and the Doctor finally do face off, it's going to have to be epic. And for a lot of people, the story fails at this. Those people are wrong. Generally, their objection is that this final confrontation scene is too abrupt and too tacked on. I will grant that it is surprisingly short, apparently because the effect needed to get Troughton on the screen twice proved much more difficult than expected. But what these commentators miss—and it's an easy thing to miss when you're as used to later Doctor Who as anyone who goes and watches reconstructions of Troughton episodes is—is that Salamander has done something we've never seen done before: he's breached the TARDIS.

Other than a brief incursion from a Zarbi way back in *The Web Planet*, the TARDIS has been sacrosanct. Sure, it might get stolen, batted around, or, in *The Tenth Planet*, mildly possessed. But no villain has ever just strode into the TARDIS and tried to steal it. The TARDIS has always been completely safe. And Salamander gets within a few inches of stealing it. Never mind how brief the scene is, or the strange question of how Salamander found the TARDIS. (It's a David Whitaker script. As always, we deal with symbols, not reality.) The jaw-dropping thing is that he's there, and he attacks the Doctor inside his own ship.

Again, this follows perfectly from the setup. Salamander is capable of transgressing against the narrative just as the Doctor is, and steadily breaks the story from its James Bond narrative. The obvious follow-up is that he should finish by turning around and trying to break the Doctor's story as well. That's the appeal of a villain who can transgress against narratives— the villain is able to threaten the Doctor with narrative collapse. Once you set up the idea of an exact counterpart of the Doctor, you have to let him face the Doctor on the Doctor's home turf. If the counterpart isn't a strong enough character to threaten the Doctor in the TARDIS itself, he's not a strong enough character period.

Yes, venting Salamander out into the Void is a bit abrupt. (Although if you look at the start of *The Web of Fear*, it spends a few minutes wrapping this up and then moves on to an unrelated plot. One gets the sense that Whitaker's episode overran and that they tacked the last few minutes of his onto the start of *The Web of Fear*.) But on the other hand, this is, again, David Whitaker. He created the TARDIS as we know her way back in *The Edge of Destruction*. He established her as the fundamental reason why the Doctor's alchemy is superior to the Daleks'. So having the TARDIS herself destroy Salamander is wholly appropriate. He may be able to nearly trump and beat out the Doctor in his own story, but the one thing he cannot hope to compete with is the magical box itself. Just as the TARDIS justifies the Doctor's triumph over the Daleks, so too is it able to redress the narrative imbalance threatened by a second Doctor in the story. The TARDIS becomes Doctor Who's trump card—the thing that protects the narrative from all danger.

The result is sublime. A story that starts seeming like a James Bond pastiche and ends up delivering a commentary on James Bond, *The Prisoner*, and Doctor Who, has some sublimely weird and mind-blowing double crosses in the final act, and gives us more of a sense of a world than we've gotten out of Doctor Who in months. It also lets Patrick Troughton really stretch his acting chops. It's proof that Doctor Who still can do anything, assuming it's allowed to try. *The Enemy of the World* is a story that starts looking positively mundane, ends up with its villain nearly threatening the entire narrative structure of Doctor Who, and stops off at Griffin the Chef on the way. It was always a classic. Now everyone gets to know it.

Help, Brigadier, Help! (*The Web of Fear*)

It's February 3, 1968. The Love Affair is at number one with "Everlasting Love," a piece of production-line pop given a reasonably psychedelic spin in album art. It's unseated by Manfred Mann covering Dylan, who are in turn unseated by Esther and Abi Ofarim's "Cinderella Rockafella," a novelty blues song by an Israeli double act. (Look, you have to get used to these things. Eventually I'm going to have to talk about how "Do the Bartman" hits number one in between KLF and The Clash, and I'm going to have to do it with a straight face, so if you can't deal with Israeli novelty blues, we're in trouble.) Engelbert Humperdinck lurks around lower in the charts, as do The Move, the Bee Gees, and Donovan.

As 1968 progresses, it becomes increasingly hard to read events outside of a larger narrative. When we see three college students killed when police break up a civil rights rally at an all-white bowling alley in South Carolina, or when the Tet Offensive ends, it's very hard not to read these as part of the ongoing progression towards the collapse of the idealism of the 1960s. The charts, indeed the whole of the culture seem to reflect this—these songs are not quite the unambitious conservative pop of Engelbert Humperdinck, but are also not exactly The Beatles, The Who, or Jimi Hendrix.

While on television, we get *The Web of Fear*. Once again, we're stuck with a story where the history of it is frustratingly and maddeningly layered. But in this case, unlike something like *The Gunfighters* or *The Tomb of the Cybermen*, the layers are alarmingly stable. For a long time, based on its reputation, *The Web of Fear* was one of the holy grails of missing stories. Then the bulk of it was found and everybody still loved it. Indeed, this is one of those essays where I have to revise it around a completely different claim than the one I initially made. The first draft of this essay suggested that "the people who want this story back don't actually want the five missing episodes that aired in early 1968, so much as they want something that never actually existed in the first place." Except, well, they got four out of the five and seem perfectly happy with it, so evidently not.

On the one hand, this is unsurprising, as that was a provocative take that was unlikely to hold up to reality. After all, loads of people still insist in the face of four episodes of hard evidence that *Tomb of the Cybermen* is brilliant. But there was something to the case. *The Web of Fear*'s reputation was clearly based on a host of things that not only weren't the actual episodes, they were unrelated to the actual episodes. Most obviously, *The Web of Fear* features the debut of what will eventually become a major element of Doctor Who, which means that an extensive future that simply didn't exist in 1968 is routinely projected onto this story. Really, this is true of both this and *The Abominable Snowmen*. Even though the Yeti never appear again except in cameo, these two stories remain important because they introduce someone who goes on to have a large role in the series. I am talking, of course, about John Levene, who is inside one of the Yeti costumes in each story and goes on to play Sergeant Benton through Jon Pertwee's tenure as the Doctor.

Sorry, that probably whizzed over some people's heads. Let's back up. Starting in Season Seven, about two years after this story aired, Doctor Who gets a complete revamp in which it is set entirely on Earth with the Doctor teaming up with UNIT, an international military force, to fight aliens in modern-day Britain. That's mostly a matter for Volume 3, but as it turns out, one of the major characters in UNIT is Brigadier Alistair Gordon Lethbridge-Stewart, better known as The Brigadier.

The Brigadier appears in the Season Six story *The Invasion*, which was in part an effort to test out the UNIT concept before they committed to it for the whole series. But he wasn't actually supposed to be in that story. In that story the recurring character was supposed to be Anne Travers, daughter of Jack Travers from *The Abominable Snowmen*, who also appears in this story in which the Doctor teams up with an unnamed group of soldiers to fight aliens in modern-day Britain. But that didn't work out and so the director of *The Invasion* (and *The Web of Fear*), Douglas Camfield, picked a different character from *The Web of Fear* to bring back.

Or, more accurately, he picked an actor—Nicholas Courtney—he knew he worked well with (Courtney had also previously played Bret Vyon in the Camfield-directed *The Daleks' Master Plan*), and instead of making him a brand-new military character (which probably would have resulted in a kerfuffle about whether Hainsman and Lincoln, the writers of *The Web of Fear*, were due a royalty payment on what was obviously a knock-off of their character) just decided to give his character from *The Web of Fear* a promotion. Then when *The Invasion* worked pretty and became the standard concept of the series, Courtney's character became a regular who appeared in the next seven seasons, made three reappearances in the '80s, then continued to appear, played by Courtney, in numerous audios and spin-off materials through the '90s before making a final comeback in *The Sarah Jane Adventures* in the '00s and, rather ghoulishly, becoming a Cyberman in the Peter Capaldi era.

The short version of this is "*The Web of Fear* is the debut of the Brigadier, but he's only a colonel in this story." Indeed, this dimension of the story helps explain why Episode Three, featuring Courtney's debut, was, in Philip Morris's account, nicked from the Nigerian television station where he had found them before he could get them back to the UK—it's demonstrably the most valuable episode of the lot, and by all appearances someone stole it and it's in the hands of a private collector. But all of this obsession over Nicholas Courtney's appearance obscures one really important aspect that the long version of the history does not: nobody involved in the making of *The Web of Fear* knew they were introducing the longest-running supporting character in the show's history. And watching it with one eye on the Colonel as a fundamental part of the series mythology means that we miss the character that's actually introduced in this story. (All of which said, John Levene really is inside one of the Yeti, though, and really does have a long run on the series.)

And this isn't even the only way in which this story became a weird metonym for the Pertwee era. One of the major descriptors of the Pertwee era, repeated ad nauseam by Pertwee for years after he'd left the role, was that there wasn't anything scary about an alien on an alien planet, but that there was something scary about "A Yeti on your loo in Tooting Bec." (Tooting Bec being a more or less random part of South London.) Ignoring, as every fan has learned to do, the implications of this image and what the scariest part about a Yeti using your toilet would actually be, and further ignoring the entire question of whether Pertwee's basic point is sound, there is something very strange about this description that nobody really points out when they recite it: Jon Pertwee never fought the Yeti.

That's how effective and memorable this story was. It is so effective that for the rest of his life after he left the role, Jon Pertwee pointed to a story he didn't even appear in as the ideal image for his era of Doctor Who. Add a particularly good early novelization and you have a story that was primed to be loved because of its larger role in the series, with no real concern for what went on in the episodes needed.

As we've seen, there are plenty of stories like this that, when exposed to scrutiny, faltered, whether it be everyone seeing *Tomb of the Cybermen* or just *The Celestial Toymaker* running aground when people saw the reconstructions. This, on the other hand, lived up to the hype. Why?

The answer is not hard: Douglas Camfield. We've encountered his work before and will again—he did *The Crusade*, *The Time Meddler*, and *The Daleks' Master Plan*—and he's been consistently good, a track record that will continue through remaining four stories. Indeed, Stanley Kubrick was sufficiently impressed by how he shot Katarina's death in *The*

Daleks Master Plan to call him up for advice on how to recreate the effect in *2001: A Space Odyssey*. He's both technically adept and capable of thinking filmically in a way the bulk of other Doctor Who directors simply aren't.

And so *The Web of Fear* turns out to be the rare Doctor Who story on which the memory does not cheat and it actually was as good as a nation of spooked ten-year-olds remember. The corridors of the Underground are dark, moody terrors, the Yeti are shot well and in ways that actually make them scary, and the action sequences, particularly the big Covent Garden sequence, are as well-shot as anything else in the entire classic series.

Camfield is surely what puts this story in a different class than the ones around it, but Haisman and Lincoln do some things that are sharp as well. First, it turns out that an out-and-out military setting is more effective than other settings for bases under siege. Much of the frustration of a lot of these stories is the fact that they require crewmembers on the base to be stupid over and over again in order to drag out the plot. In *The Ice Warriors*, for instance, the core conflict is the fact that Leader Clent is an ineffectual idiot who insists on listening to his computer over common sense. The plot is driven forward in a large part because Clent can be relied upon to screw everything up when necessary. This is what I mean when I refer to an idiot plot—the fact that the plot advances because of characters who consistently behave like idiots.

But here we're free of that. We instead get a bunch of soldiers who actually do sensible things to try to stop the Yeti. Yeah, we have Evans, who is pretty reliably moronic, and Chorley, who is also not the brightest crayon in the box, but mostly we have people behaving in a manner that is not entirely inappropriate to the task of being attacked by monsters, which is depressingly refreshing. Instead of having an idiot plot, most of this story is wrapped up in paranoia as everyone tries to second guess who the Great Intelligence's plant in the camp is, with the leading suspects being, at various times, the Colonel, Evans, and Chorley. (And, interestingly, for one brief scene,

Jamie.)

The other thing that's very clever here is that the Doctor doesn't actually get to the situation until the third episode. He spends the first episode interacting with no supporting characters other than Jamie and Victoria, and Troughton takes the second episode off while Jamie and Victoria get acquainted with the situation. So by the time the Doctor actually gets to the action (in the third episode) everybody knows who he is, has been expecting him, and things can get up and running. The degree to which this works highlights the degree to which the stultifying tedium of the Doctor trying to get people to listen to him for half the story is a bad idea. (These days we use psychic paper for this.)

The only downside is that there's something ever so slightly awkward about the Doctor working alongside the military; it's just not quite the right set of allies for him. That's overcome here by the fact that the Doctor has been shoved into this trap and so has little choice in who else is there.

Notably, these two upsides and one downside form some basic aspects of the UNIT era. The downside needs to be dealt with through other means, but the combination of the exile and the clever idea on the part of Malcolm Hulke and Barry Letts in *The Silurians* to have the Doctor be at odds with UNIT makes inroads on that, problematic as the ending of that story is. (But that's another volume.) As for the upsides, UNIT means that there are, in theory, lots of capable people who do things and that the Doctor can come into the situation at full speed.

(In practice, of course, the Doctor spends the early '70s getting sandbagged by stupid bureaucrats and watching in astonishment as his crack military sidekicks act like the keystone cops. And he was frequently irritatingly OK with military tactics. But that doesn't mean it's a bad idea, it just means that some writers can't follow a bloody recipe.)

In other words, this story was effective in its own right and solved several of the problems of the Troughton era. It's not surprising, then, that future writers looked to it for solutions. Even aside from AI figures and ratings, writers are not stupid people and can see if a story works. Any writer—and especially Terrance Dicks, who comes onto the show as assistant script editor with this story—could see that this one works, and learn from it.

That's not to say, however, that there aren't some obvious problems here, which helps explain why I was wrongly skeptical about how much people would like the actual episodes. First of all, it's kind of staggering that the premise of this story works. The idea that an extraterrestrial intelligence created robot copies of the Yeti for its own use was already a bit of a stretch in *The Abominable Snowmen*. Now we've transplanted the Yeti to a place where Yeti don't belong, and given them, for no obvious reason, new powers. This isn't just weird. It's something that to really care about you have to be invested in Doctor Who. Pitching this one to someone unaware of the historical importance of it elicits raised eyebrows at best, even if they're a fan of the contemporary series. Even if we ignore the reason everyone is so obsessed with this story— Nicholas Courtney—we have to admit that this is the most sequel-like story Doctor Who has served up yet. The story flat out assumes you've seen *The Abominable Snowmen* and are already comfortable with the idea of Yeti, and even given that it's a bit of a stretch.

But the bigger problem is the ending. Not just the obviously frustrating bit where the Doctor's plan is foiled by the fact that every single supporting character downs Leader Clent's stupid pills early in the sixth episode and becomes oblivious to the Doctor's repeated assurances that he's got this under control. No. The fact that the reveal of the traitor is— and this is a reveal that is stressed as a major point for nearly five episodes—turns out to make no sense; it turns out to be a soldier whose dead body is animated by the Great Intelligence. The problem is that we know there's a traitor in the camp long before he dies. So it makes no sense whatsoever why he dies. Either the Great Intelligence is killing its own servant for no obvious reason or the reveal fails to explain the actual mystery. Either way, it doesn't work.

For the most part, these facts were obscured for a very long time. With the story missing, we mostly had Terrance Dicks's novelization to go on. Dicks is a damn entertaining writer, and offers the novel a classic Terrance Dicks first line: "The huge, furry monster reared up, as if to strike." (As I've said elsewhere, whatever can be said of Terrance Dicks's writing, he is a wizard of first lines.) Plus he clears up several of the issues the script has. Knowing full well what Lethbridge-Stewart would become in the series, he dispenses with all pretense that the Colonel is a viable suspect for the Intelligence's plant (whereas in the actual episodes he's the prime suspect for much of the story), thus making the story much more satisfying to those who like it because of him. He also fixes the Arnold plot, making it clear that Arnold was under the Intelligence's control all along, thus making the ending sensible. The fact that this was for a long time the most readily available version of the story means that all of this helped a lot. And combined with the mythologizing of fans who thought Season Five's endless parade of bases under siege marked an all-time high for the series and who thus prone to worshipping at the feet of its best-made one even before all the proleptic continuity and you had a story that was always going to be a classic.

And ultimately, the sorts of plot holes that are there just aren't that damaging. Certainly the new series has set up plenty of howlers just as big if not bigger—*Curse of the Black* Spot anybody? And it's worth remembering that many of these problems would vanish under the cloud of forgetting that weekly serialization brought, so that Arnold's early improbability as a suspect in the early episodes is forgotten by the time the sixth episode rolls around.

But while there's a lot to love here, there's also serios problems. Most obviously, Silverstein, the collector who appears in the first episode, is easily the single most racist caricature of a character to date, rivaling anything else in the series outside *The Talons of Weng-Chiang*. More broadly, whatever this story's virtues, its rapturous reception remains fundamentally rooted in the assumptions that bases under siege are a series highlight and that the most important thing the Troughton era does is set up the early 1970s. Sure, this is the high point of a particular way of doing Doctor Who, but that particular way was never the whole of the 1960s, and positioning it as though it were the telos of the era says more about everything that focus erases and pushes to the margins. *The Web of Fear* is fine, and now those who want to obsess over it can. For the rest of us, let's move on to something more fun. Like ridiculous continuity wankery.

All Right, Fine, UNIT Dating

I suppose I can't just ignore one of the biggest continuity controversies in Doctor Who. The heart of it is simple—over the course of the decades in which UNIT, first established in *The Invasion*, is mentioned, there are at least two completely contradictory timelines for when the main UNIT era (which runs from this story through to *The Seeds of Doom* in the Baker era) takes place. Entire forests have been slaughtered in the attempts to adjudicate this debate and try to come up with a coherent explanation. Even the series routinely lampshades it, with anyone mentioning a UNIT event expressing a degree of uncertainty as to whether it took place in the 1970s or the 1980s. Unfortunately, they're all essentially doomed simply because the statements made are so basely incompatible. In *The Web of Fear*, it's said that 1935 was "more than forty years ago," setting the Brigadier's first encounter with the Doctor no earlier than 1975. In *Pyramids of Mars*, meanwhile, Sarah Jane Smith identifies herself as being from 1980, which is broadly compatible with that date. But in *Mawdryn Undead*, the Brigadier is shown to have retired from UNIT prior to 1977.

The impossibility of reconciling these has not stopped people, of course. Tat Wood, usually saner than this, suggests in *About Time* that Sarah might have been estimating when saying "I'm from 1980," which is hilariously thin. Equally entertaining is David McIntee's suggestion that *Mawdryn Undead* should be taken as having happened in a parallel universe. Lance Parkin throws up his hands in *A History* and just uses "UNIT Year 1" as shorthand for whichever of 1979, 1974, or 1969 you want to pick.

From a philosophical standpoint, I laid out many of my views in the previous essay. Given that the events shown in the

UNIT stories clearly never happened and the future they represent is an impossible one, the very act of "dating" them seems strange. More broadly, Tat Wood, when not attempting to suggest that Sarah Jane Smith didn't know what year she was from, makes excellent points in *About Time* that the small cultural details such as clothing styles and the transition to decimal currency give the UNIT stories a grounding in the present of their transmission that ought be taken seriously. Show the UNIT stories to anyone in hindsight and they'll identify immediately that they're from the 1970s. That feel permeates them far more thoroughly than the hazy evidence that the writers intended a near future setting.

And even if they did intend a near future setting, science fiction has long had versions of the "five minutes in the future" setting. More to the point, portraying a fanciful version of available technology can hardly be taken as a sign of futuristic settings, unless someone seriously intends to suggest that the audience defaults to reading *The Avengers* and James Bond as set in the future (and, in many cases, still set in the future relative to today). Clearly one of the basic codes of reading for action-adventure serials is a certain allowance for fantastic technology.

This gets at what, to me, is much closer to the core of the UNIT dating issue, which is whether you want to treat the milieu of the UNIT stories as being "our world" or as being a spy-fi type world that the Doctor sets up a semi-permanent residence in. And the problem is that the stories go back and forth. Even the two Troughton stories featuring UNIT characters don't agree on this. *The Web of Fear* draws its power from the fact that it's the familiar London Underground that's being attacked—a component of our world. And quirk of its dialogue aside, everything about *The Web of Fear* says late '60s. Simply put, *The Web of Fear* is much more compellingly read by a contemporary audience as a five-minutes-in-the-future story than it is as a seven-years-in-the-future story.

In contrast, *The Invasion* is blatantly near future and the phobias engendered by International Electromatics only work if they're fears about the next newfangled piece of technology.

But even there we run into the problem of discarded futures. If we limit our date-reading to the evidence of the Troughton era, *The Invasion* is set in 1980. As a story about computers and electronics set in 1980 goes, it's ludicrous. It does far better as being a late 1960s piece of spy-fi, which is a genre that assumes exactly the sort of incrementally advanced technology that *The Invasion* needs to play off of. The point of *The Invasion* isn't to imagine futuristic technological developments but the sorts of things that are thought to be inches from market. We're talking about the difference between "five minutes into the future" and "the next Apple product launch into the future" here.

But that's still, at least, a difference. Even if we reject the twelve-year gap implied by *The Invasion*, we can at least allow that the "several years in the future" crowd is opting for a version of the same spy-fi argument that prefers to treat the world of Doctor Who as a coherent place with an imaginary history instead of as a set of fictional conventions. Even if I differ with them sharply on that—and obviously I do—there's still the core question of whether or not the UNIT stories are taking place in "our world" or a deformation of our world.

But by and large the answer seems to be "our world." Yes, there are exceptions, but as Tat Wood points out, there's only about four UNIT stories, one of which is *The Invasion*, that really require offsetting into a world that is defined by the ways in which it differs from ours instead of the ways in which it's the same. And perhaps more importantly, three of those four are at the extremes of the UNIT era—*The Invasion, The Android Invasion*, and *Battlefield*. Within the core of the UNIT era—i.e. the Pertwee era—only one story, *The Ambassadors of Death*, is at all wonky, and that one wasn't originally planned as a UNIT story. (And, on top of that, is one of the ones that gives the most fits to any attempt to treat the UNIT era as having a relationship with real world dating, depending as it does on a British space program that never happened.)

The remainder of the UNIT era, including *The Web of Fear*, is manifestly our world with some convenient spy-fi touches to spruce up the action a bit. In other words, as close to our world as Doctor Who can reasonably be expected to be assuming that it's dealing with big military and political scale events. Separating it from that context to move it to the future does nothing but sever Doctor Who from social commentary in a period where it actually and seriously was attempting to comment on the real world. Simply put, situating the UNIT era in close relation to when it was broadcast causes the stories to make more sense. Given that any attempt to pin down a firm UNIT date causes contradictions, the interpretation that benefits the stories the most seems straightforwardly to be the best one.

Time Can Be Rewritten: *Twilight of the Gods* (Christopher Bulis, Virgin Books, 1996)

Let's start by admitting that *Twilight of the Gods* is not a very good book. Bulis is in many ways the Terrence Dicks of the Virgin and BBC Books lines, a comparison I mean as a jibe instead of a compliment for once. Bulis reliably penned a book a year, and has written for all of the first eight Doctors at one time or another. All his books are reasonably competent adventures, but in lines that frequently distinguish themselves with creative and unusual takes on Doctor Who the writer most associated with fast output and straightforward adventures was never going to look very good.

All of which said, this isn't much of a reason to criticize Bulis. "He writes Doctor Who novels that are straightforward and fun adventures" isn't so much damning with faint praise as just regular old praising. And for most novels so it would be—possibly not enough to be something I feel like covering in the book, but worth praising. Unfortunately, this is a book where what Bulis is good at and what the material requires are at cross-purposes. *Twilight of the Gods*, you see, is a sequel to *The Web Planet*.

Those of you who have read the first volume of this series are presumably aware that I am among the minority that absolutely adores *The Web Planet*. I think it's an absolutely fantastic piece of experimental television—one of the most radical things the classic series ever attempted, and absolutely amazing for what it is, which, as I argued, is in no way "a piece of quasi-realist drama." Instead it's a story about finding strange things to put on television and about pushing the limits of the medium.

In that regard, then, it's a very strange choice for a book—which is, I suppose, ironic given that *Doctor Who and the Zarbi* was one of the three original novelizations. So much of what makes *The Web Planet* interesting is its use of unusual visuals. There's not really a prose equivalent to this. Even if Bulis had written a highly experimental novel with unusual and idiosyncratic stylistic techniques—and he really didn't—it wouldn't be a match for *The Web Planet*. There might be some virtue to that approach anyway, but it's tough to see in many ways. An experimental novel might be the only worthy sequel to *The Web Planet*, but the truth is that anyone wanting to be as experimental as the book would require would probably prefer not to be shackled to a bunch of concepts that have little to do with narrative experimentation.

The root problem, and it's one that at least partially affects all spin-off Doctor Who material, is that some of the things that are fundamental to Doctor Who are factors of its medium. Doctor Who, in all of its eras, is in part about visual eccentricity. And the logic of images isn't something that translates to audio or to books. This is on the one hand a very obvious statement, but it's easy to overlook the specifics. *The Web Planet* worked because it harkened to a long visual tradition including of things like Méliès's *A Trip to the Moon*. Its special effects were based in part on Victorian stagecraft. The tradition it belongs to, in other words, is not a literary tradition in the first place. And *The Web Planet*, for all its alleged faults, is an iconic piece of Doctor Who, if for no other reason than that it was one of the most-watched Doctor Who stories ever. So the intensely visual experience it represents isn't something that can be ignored lightly.

So *Twilight of the Gods* is, in that regard, fundamentally misconceived. But even on top of that Bulis's book and what he's good at fall badly short of what a sequel to *The Web Planet* needs. Again, part of this is simply the inherent silliness of the idea. *Twilight of the Gods* is attempting the impossible task of being a sequel to a story defined by its weirdness. It's the sort of story that the nostalgia-drenched approach of novelized sequels is almost exactly wrong for. But the real problem is that Bulis is very good at exciting potboilers and *The Web Planet* isn't one of them.

So Bulis writes a book with one of the most clichéd and standard-issue plot concepts in Doctor Who: two warring factions of aliens. Let's, once again, contrast this with how *The Web Planet* worked. There the focus was on the strange perspectives of various creatures—the Menoptra, the Optera, and, to a lesser extent, the Animus. But the warring Rhumons have no such compelling perspectives. The two factions divide straightforwardly along human political grounds—one group is made of religious fundamentalists, the other group of communists. There are no strange philosophical bits about existing only in light or silent walls to be had. The Optera and the Zarbi are almost completely excluded, while the Animus adheres to the ludicrously dull theory of the Virgin era whereby various vast cosmic intelligences of the classic series were secretly minor characters from H.P. Lovecraft's Cthulhu mythos. (Canonically the Animus, apparently, is Lloigar—which isn't even one of the good ones, having been created by August Derleth.)

In other words, where *The Web Planet* was about making things strange, *Twilight of the Gods* is almost entirely dependent on the intensely familiar. In one sense, despite this not being a base under siege like virtually the whole of the season it's set in, it's a more perfect fit for the Troughton era than Bulis realizes. Over little more than a year the series has gone from a show that attempts the strange and the alien on a regular basis to one that is based on the repetition of a formula. Yes, it's a very good formula, but it's still, as we've been noticing, an increasingly depressing one. Bulis is using a different one, but for the most part this book fits perfectly into the Troughton approach, only with the added garishness of making fetishistic sequels to previous stories. Which, actually, coming after *The*

Web of Fear, isn't that inappropriate either.

But the result falls badly short in another regard as well. Troughton's Doctor is a literally mercurial character defined by a charming anarchism. Bulis's book, on the other hand, has the Doctor going on a lengthy monologue about how communism is doomed to fail except in small doses. Aside from the fact that this is part and parcel of the book taking on the most clichéd set of ethics for a science fiction book imaginable—generic suspicion of extremism coupled with overt atheistic tendencies—there's something crushingly generic about this.

Admittedly Bill Strutton apparently intended *The Web Planet* to be a parable about the evils of communism, but he at least had the decency to do a really rubbish job of it. The idea that the Doctor would be prima facie opposed to the idea that systems of government other than modern liberalism could possibly work anywhere in the universe jars depressingly with *The Web Planet*'s joyful exploration of the idea of the alien. *The Web Planet* was interesting because it was willing to go so much further than other stories in asking what alien cultures might think. *Twilight of the Gods*, on the other hand, goes to great lengths to deconstruct the Menoptra's religion and show that their gods were just aliens. It's one thing when Doctor Who pulls that trick with human mythology. That creates a juxtaposition between the science fiction world of Doctor Who and existing mythology that's interesting. But pulling the "their gods are just aliens" trick on a bunch of aliens is just dull anti-religious sentiment. It wants to take the alien and make it more human.

The crowning misery of this is the final scene, in which the Doctor, after admitting that he doesn't usually stick around, proceeds to make an over two-page speech about how they should structure their society and live their lives. On the one hand, this is something I'll complain about increasingly over the remainder of this book that Troughton's Doctor doesn't do enough of. On the other, as Bulis admits, Troughton's Doctor doesn't do these sorts of things, and nothing in the monologue sounds even remotely like his Doctor. For instance:

It is time to leave the ways of cosmic childhood behind you, and with it all those beliefs and superstitions that have proven wanting. When you do set out on that long voyage, you must do so in unity and harmony; either for mutual protection, or in preparation for judgement by races more powerful than you can yet imagine. Go forward bravely with open hearts and minds, but also humbly. Do not try to force your preconceptions onto others, for you still have much to learn.

The fact of the matter is, this is Troughton sounding like badly written *Star Trek*. This would be bad enough on its own merits, but to have a sequel to *The Web Planet*—a story that *Star Trek* would never dream of attempting the weirdness of—falling into this genericness is hard to take.

But in some ways, as I noted, what else would be possible? We may only be about three seasons from when *The Web Planet* aired, but even where we are in the book we're miles from when a story like *The Web Planet* could possibly happen. By 1996 it's almost completely unfathomable that anyone would try for that kind of utter weirdness. For all of its faults, *Twilight of the Gods* is interesting in its failure simply because it reveals just how quickly some of the original, bewildering spark of Doctor Who faded. It will, of course, find other sparks—indeed, the mercurial glee of Troughton's Doctor (this book sadly excepted) is its own kind of spark, as will be the glam aesthetic of the Pertwee era, the gothic postmodernism of the early Tom Baker era, and many more things to come.

But the sort of thing that led to the glorious weirdness of *The Web Planet* is long gone from Doctor Who. This book, if nothing else, serves as something of a tombstone.

Time Can Be Rewritten: *The Dark Path* (David McIntee, Virgin Books, 1997)

It's March of 1997. Depending on the week, either No Doubt is at number one with "Don't Speak," or the Spice Girls are with "Mama." Other options in the top ten include the Backstreet Boys, Boyzone, R. Kelly, Ant and Dec, Bush, and the Bee Gees. If you think one of those things is not like the others, I certainly don't disagree.

If you are the sort of person who is aware of the general shape of the 1989–2005 period of Doctor Who then the phrase "March of 1997" already gives you some clues as to what's going on here. If not, what we've got here is the second to last month of Virgin Books before they lost their license to BBC Books. In this period, Virgin, facing their own end with little to gain or lose save reputation and a sense of artistic integrity, basically proceeded to cut loose with some of the best and most challenging books of their line. All of this, however, was frankly dampened by the kind of funereal atmosphere that hung over everything. Not everyone had loved the Virgin line, but it had some strong admirers who were crushed to see it go. The prospect of the BBC starting up an in-house line of Doctor Who books based on the TV Movie was hardly inspiring, especially given the murmurs that the line was to be the anti-Virgin—an explicit reaction against the Virgin era's excesses and a return to simpler, less challenging prose. In practice the BBC Books line would be weirder and more interesting than that, but it looked bad from the outset.

Meanwhile, Virgin was releasing its last books in a sort of maudlin celebration of the line's potential. In the second to last month, they released two books. One, Marc Platt's *Lungbarrow*, was an ambitious retconning of the history of Gallifrey and the apparent culmination of the last plot strands left lingering from when the series was on television. The other, *The Dark Path*, was a long awaited attempt to tackle a massive continuity point and deliver what is one of the most wanted, untold tales in Doctor Who, or at least, one of the most speculated about.

As a result, there's something almost actively insane about reviewing it within the Troughton era. The supposed conceit of the Missing and Past Doctor Adventures is that the stories they tell could be inserted into their assumed eras. As we've seen that's always been a bit of a myth—even the most faithful recreation we've looked at, Gareth Roberts's *The Plotters* (covered back in Volume One), takes liberties that could not have been taken in the Hartnell era. Other times it's nearly shattered—*The Man in the Velvet Mask* is flagrantly and deliberately a vision of the Hartnell era distinct from what we see on the screen. But both of those were still fundamentally comments on the Hartnell era. One attempts to work within the format of the Hartnell era to tell a story that wouldn't have made it to screen with the actors in question or in the year it would have aired. The other attempts to show a counter-narrative to the Hartnell era.

But this is nearly impossible to even couch in terms of the Troughton era. Not just in terms of being impossible to air in 1968, but in the sense of fundamentally not being about concerns that make any sense in the context of Doctor Who in that era. It's worth attempting to parse it as a Second Doctor story just to see how it fails. The Doctor, Jamie, and Victoria land on a remote human colony. There they meet a man named Koschei, who is an old friend of the Doctor's and a member of his species. The Doctor and Koschei work separately on the problem that this colony has—something they call the Darkheart, which is apparently an ancient tool of a species called the Chronivores that, among other things, can destroy planets and rewrite species DNA so that they are and always were human. Ultimately Koschei, tempted by the prospect of bringing his dead lover back, goes mad and abuses the power of the Darkheart, and the Doctor ends up trapping his old friend in a black hole as his friend taunts him, saying, "in time you too will call me Master." Oh, and Koschei hypnotizes Victoria, but the novel cleverly keeps from revealing exactly where Victoria's natural sympathies for Koschei leave off and the hypnosis picks up.

And apparently, if the cover of the book is any indication, Koschei looks like the actor Roger Delgado, a character actor from the 1950s–1970s who worked extensively in live television with roles in things like *Quatermass II*. So apparently McIntee had in mind who should play him.

Is this out of line with the Troughton era? Not entirely, certainly. True, we haven't seen any members of the Doctor's own species at this point in the show for about two years—the last one we saw was the Monk in *The Daleks' Master Plan*. But so what? We have seen them before. The plot has an obvious hard SF edge from the 1990s, but that's no more of a reach than we're used to in the Missing Adventures. Putting Troughton in an adventure based on a 1990s conception of science fiction is firmly within the point of what the Missing Adventures line should be for.

Perhaps most interestingly, the book walks a very meticulous line. The back of the book may talk about Time Lords and temptation, but within the text of the book the words "Time Lord" never appear. This is a subtle thing, but oddly remarkable because seemingly every author of spin-off fiction adheres to this rule. I've not done an exhaustive search, and there probably is an exception or two scattered across the history of Doctor Who, but for the most part there are virtually no novels from the Hartnell or Troughton eras that actually call the Time Lords by name, despite the fact that there are several in which they appear. And there's no inherent reason for this. Yes, in *The War Games* both Zoe and Jamie don't know what a Time Lord is, but there's no reason why Koschei can't identify himself as one to Victoria in this book. Nor is there a reason why (to use a book from the Hartnell era) Irving Braxatiel can't mention the word to Vicki in *The Empire of Glass*. Especially given how freely the term is thrown around after *The War Games*.

And yet every author seems to demure here. And they do it for what is, from the perspective of anyone approaching the show through any means other than the one I am—that is, anyone who read *The Dark Path* in 1997 instead of pretending to read it in 1968—a completely bizarre reason. Namely, they do it because everybody knows that *The War Games* is the story that introduces the Time Lords. And even if they impose Time Lords at an earlier point in the narrative (and it's also interesting that there are, to my knowledge, no stories with Time Lords prior to *The Time Meddler*, again despite the fact that a story in which Ian, Barbara, and Susan meet one is completely plausible and would not wreck any continuity as such), they don't do so in a way that "spoils" the reveal of *The War Games*, even though their entire audience knows the reveal by heart and it's been essentially decades since anyone was surprised by it while watching *The War Games*.

It is important to stress how utterly weird this is. Seemingly by popular convention among writers, and with no editorial edict (since the back of the book blabs freely about Time Lords), the writers of Doctor Who books have universally and without any explicit comment opted not to spoil a plot point in a classic Doctor Who story in any material set prior to that story, even though the entire readership of that material knows full well what that plot point is. There is no more reason not to mention Time Lords in *The Dark Path* than there is in the book starring the Fourth Doctor that follows it, *The Well-Mannered War*. Both are, in reality, released into a world that knows that the Doctor is a Time Lord and has known it for nearly thirty years. And yet one, because it is ostensibly set prior to where that reveal happened in the series, dances around the term.

What's really strange, though, is that the exclusion of the words "Time Lord" is just about the only concession to the continuity of the series in 1968 that the book makes. It is, on the whole, exceedingly proleptic. See, the thing I've avoided quite coming out and saying is that Koschei isn't just some member of the Doctor's species that shows up. He's very clearly the Master—a character who doesn't make his television debut until about three years after where this story is set. In that regard, it's one of the only Doctor Who stories I am aware of in which the plot revolves around the Doctor encountering something belonging to a future era of the show.

There are a few exceptions. Obviously every multi-Doctor story is in some sense forward-looking. Cameos are also not uncommon in books—for instance, *The Dark Path* also features some remnants of Pertwee-era future history (it appears to exist during the transition from the Earth Empire seen in *The Mutants* to the Galactic Federation seen in *The Curse of Peladon*). And there are a number of instances like *The Empire of Glass* and *Interference* in which a past Doctor encounters a plot point from the concurrently running current-Doctor novel series. And occasionally a two-part story will move backwards along Doctors so that, for instance, the Fifth Doctor novel, *Goth Opera*, is written as a sequel to the Seventh Doctor novel *Blood Harvest*. But the number of instances is strangely small given how many past-set books and audios exist. And the number of these that do it in such a way as to have the intrusion of the future be the major point of the story is vanishingly small. I can, off hand, think of one book in which the Fourth Doctor encounters Nyssa achronologically, Simon Guerrier's astonishingly good *The Time Travelers*, in which the Doctor encounters a future London ruined because he hasn't fought WOTAN yet (and stumbles upon a consequence of *Remembrance of the Daleks*), and arguably, the appearance of River Song in the Russell T Davies era.

There are no doubt a few others, but the point remains— despite the fact that the Doctor travels in time and routinely knows a lot about situations he seems to encounter for the first time, people break this rule almost as rarely as they break the "no mentioning the Time Lords" rule. Yes, some of this is rights issues—you can't have the Fourth Doctor facing down the Weeping Angels, even though they'd fit smoothly into the Hinchcliffe era, just because Tom Baker records few audios and the Big Finish audios don't get to use new series concepts. But on the other hand, the number of seemingly obvious combinations that have never gotten employed is bizarre. Nobody has thought to give Troughton a base under siege by the Wirrin? No encounters between the First Doctor and the Cybermen prior to *The Tenth Planet*, despite the fact that he knows who they are in that story? Pertwee never gets to face off with the Rani? I mean, come on, you know you want to see Pertwee, the Delgado Master, and the Rani in a three-way showdown. It's about the only good idea for the Rani there is, and mysteriously, it's the one that's never actually been tried.

The common idea underlying these seemingly pointless conventions is that, strangely, the developmental history of the show cannot be fully decoupled from its continuity; there is something about the idea of Time Lords or the Master that cannot be separated, even for the purposes of continuity games, from their history. There is, in other words, something about Doctor Who that requires an approach like this one, in which continuity and real world history are accepted to be fundamentally intertwined.

The most obvious glue to hold these things together is the audience. Which for a majority of the history of the show has meant, at least in part, fandom, and for a significant portion of time basically means nothing but fandom. Doctor Who fandom is staggeringly well developed, as discussions of things like *The Web of Fear* have hopefully indicated. To the point where there are a large number of fairly well-trod fan debates that various novels have, essentially, attempted to stake territory out for. And more to the point, where various eras of the show and elements of those eras are signifiers of whole aspects of fan debates. One of the biggest of these is the entirety of the Pertwee era, which forms the earliest chronological major fault line. (A small number of fans like to create a Hartnell/Troughton fault line, but they're just being difficult.)

You can hopefully see where this is all going. What this means is that it is next to impossible to read *The Dark Path* as anything other than an overt and explicit effort to throw Troughton up against aspects of the Pertwee era in a more deliberate manner than *The Web of Fear* and *The Invasion* possibly could—to compare them, in other words, with the advantage of history.

The heart of this confrontation occurs with the confrontation between Koschei and the Doctor at the end, in which Koschei attempts to argue that he is morally superior to the Doctor, asking him "Don't you ever get tired of always reacting to what has happened? Only picking up the pieces, but never being able to prevent the breakage in the first place," and insisting that, unlike the Doctor, he offers "order" to the universe. Unsurprisingly, the Doctor responds to this with absolute horror.

But notably, the Master is calling the Doctor out on the grounds that the Doctor is inefficient in fighting the anarchy of the universe. This is certainly true, especially in the Troughton era, but it's true in no small part because Troughton's Doctor seems very much like an anarchist. And so phrasing it as a criticism makes no sense. The Doctor is, if anything, an agent of chaos and breakage, not one of fixing things. Unless, of course, we remember that Koschei is a Pertwee villain, who is using Chronovore technology—another Pertwee-era concept. In this case what Koschei is declaring makes more sense— Pertwee's Doctor is, after all, much more closely allied with establishment authority than Troughton's ever was.

Of course, the most overt commentary on another Doctor Who story comes in the form of the Master tempting Victoria to his side by offering to destroy Skaro and save her father. This confronts Victoria with a decision we will see the Doctor face twice in the future of the series—in both *Genesis of the Daleks* and *Remembrance of the Daleks*. And, notably, Victoria succumbing to this temptation (and taking the decision the Doctor took in the latter of those stories) is presented as the wrong decision, since it's later revealed that this was part of the Master's hypnosis of her.

But a subtler issue surrounds this hypnosis. At one point, the Doctor is warned both of the potency of Koschei's hypnosis and that Victoria might not still be trustworthy, to which the Doctor grumbles: "He used to do that at school, and anyone he can hypnotize, I can de-hypnotize." This is interesting on several levels. First of all, it's one of only a few insights into the Doctor and Koschei's interactions at school. Second, it's utterly bizarre. The Doctor grumbles irritatedly as if he's used to Koschei hypnotizing his friends. This is a standard part of their friendship? Koschei hypnotizing the Doctor's female friends? I mean, not to belabor the point here, but as sentences designed to launch an unceasing torrent of slash fiction go, that one is a doozy. (As is the Master's droll observation as to how he managed to entrance Victoria so utterly—her classical education. As if Victoria is a fundamentally flawed companion and human being because of her upbringing. Not that I'm praising Victorian morality here, but that seems a bit harsh.)

All of which points at the larger problem with *The Dark Path*. It's a book about the conflict between a Pertwee villain and Pertwee's Doctor, with themes that apply up to the McCoy era, only it's set in the Troughton era and its only seeming insight on that era is that Victoria is a bit rubbish (which in the end isn't even true). On top of that, its big secret revelation about the Master is ... that he went mad when his human companion turned out to be a Time Lord and then became cranky at him for committing genocide in a mad attempt to save her? That's why he's a villain? Because his girlfriend turned out to be a Time Lord?

I mean, can anyone seriously argue that this book improves anything about Doctor Who's history? That we're better for knowing that the Master and the Doctor had a weirdly kinky friendship based on hypnotizing ladies in college and that the Master went mad because his girlfriend kind of mildly betrayed him? Does this actually in any way deepen anyone's enjoyment of any Doctor Who episodes?

To some extent this is the problem with the concept. The history of the Doctor and the Master is one of the most speculated-upon points in Doctor Who. It's so utterly overdetermined that no account of it can possibly actually be satisfying. No account for why the Master turned evil can quite work, whether it be the sound of drums or his Time Lord girlfriend. No explanation of what the Master and the Doctor were to each other prior to his fall can truly satisfy. Fundamentally, this story attempts to answer a question that cannot actually be satisfied by a single answer.

I am frequently suspicious of Missing and Past Doctor Adventures, I will admit, for exactly this reason—that too often they seem to solve problems they themselves invent. On the other hand, I've been more or less fond of most of the books this project has covered so far. That said, the books I've enjoyed were all ones that offered commentaries on the eras they were set in and on the show itself. Not only does *The Dark Path* not offer any real commentary on the Troughton era, it doesn't really try to. It's just some continuity points and snide commentary on companions strung together without a clear sense of what it's actually trying to do.

Perhaps that's why the "future villain appears in the past" story is done so rarely—because it's hard to do it in a way that's actually a working commentary on the past as opposed to a celebration of arcane trivia. But even still, for all this book's flaws, we should look at it, perhaps, in comparison with something like, well *Fury from the Deep*. To wit, the next essay.

When You're Living Your Life One Day After Another
(*Fury from the Deep*)

It's March 16, 1968, and Israeli novelty blues are still at the top of the charts. It is replaced by Dave Dee, Dozy, Beaky, Mick, and Tich with "The Legend of Xanadu," which sits oddly on the line between novelty and love song. In week three The Beatles ride in to save us with "Lady Madonna," and in week five it's Cliff Richard. Honestly, I'm at a loss—this is not music I'm terribly familiar with. Cliff Richard appears to veer in his career from young rock guy to evangelical Christian. I see things like 1910 Fruitgum Company lower in the charts, which I have never heard of. As I look at the cover I think "Ooh, that looks like a nice bit of psychedelia." And it turns out to be bubblegum pop. Let's call that the defining image of these weeks. Psychedelia that turns out to be bubblegum pop.

In real news, the British Foreign Secretary resigns, seemingly over a drunken row with the Prime Minister, and the Mai Lai massacre takes place. Ninety-one people are injured in a London protest against the Vietnam War, and 200 more are arrested. Aer Lingus Flight 172 crashes, killing sixty-one people. Lyndon Johnson declares he will not seek re-election, which was probably a good idea on paper, though as it turns out, this upcoming US Presidential Election is going to go somewhat badly for the planet. (I am rather more of a hippie than an archeologist.) Martin Luther King is murdered. Political assassinations take place in Germany. And, just to wrap off these uneventful six weeks, on the day the final episode of *Fury from the Deep* is transmitted, Enoch Powell makes the famous Rivers of Blood speech in which he rails against excessive immigration into Great Britain, complains that the British way of life is being destroyed, and warns:

> As I look ahead, I am filled with foreboding. Like the Roman, I seem to see "the River Tiber foaming with much blood." That tragic and intractable phenomenon which we watch with horror on the other side of the Atlantic but which there is interwoven with the history and existence of the States itself, is coming upon us here by our own volition and our own neglect. Indeed, it has all but come. In numerical terms, it will be of American proportions long before the end of the century. Only resolute and urgent action will avert it even now. Whether there will be the public will to demand and obtain that action, I do not know. All I know is that to see, and not to speak, would be the great betrayal.

In other words, this is the bit of history that we're talking about when we talk about the turbulence of the 1960s. Except none of this is turbulence. Turbulence suggests the rapid switching back and forth between Summer of Love-esque bits of youth culture and stuff like Enoch Powell. This is, frankly, just a six-week stretch of sheer and unadulterated horror and unpleasantness.

While on television, we have, to use that increasingly bone-chilling phrase, a classic Patrick Troughton story. No. That's unfair of me. It's really not that there's anything awful about the stories in this era. It's just that there's rarely anything especially good about them either. *Fury from the Deep*, I fear, is no exception. I'd summarize the plot, but you know it. The Doctor arrives at LOCATION_OF_BASE, where it turns out that the base is being threatened by a terrifying DESCRIPTION_OF_MONSTER. Although the base takes a while to trust the Doctor, eventually he is able to save the day. This time, LOCATION_OF_BASE is an offshore natural gas platform, and DESCRIPTION_OF_MONSTER is sentient, mind-controlling seaweed.

As with any base under siege, there are plusses and minuses. We get some sense of ordinary people here, including a civilian wife who is unfortunately menaced. There's a strong female character, although she's the stock-idiot plot role of the new person in charge who shows up when all the old people in charge have either been possessed by monsters or won over to the Doctor's side in order to make sure nobody does anything untoward like actually resolve the plot. Which gets at the larger problem—a base under siege lives or dies on its supporting characters, and these ones are, on the whole, pretty flat.

On the plus side, though, the threat has some scariness this time, with the clearest example yet of the show taking an everyday object and making it dangerous. (This time it's seaweed and stove repairmen that are revealed to be deadly.) The lack of any overt monster is a pleasant change—instead it's bits of foam and rushing water that are scary, which is a nice touch.

In more childish fun, we also have here a Doctor Who story that is oddly suited towards being a stoner party game, since everyone keeps talking about "the Weed" and delivering lines like "someone among us here must be under the control of the Weed!" The last episode even aired on April 20. Better party games in Doctor Who do not exist. (This paragraph of inappropriateness should perhaps be capped off by observing a recurring theme in the Troughton era that appears again here. Just as the Third Doctor is a gadget freak and focuses most of his sciencey bits on gadgetry, Troughton's Doctor usually solves problems via chemistry. In the psychedelic era, when the major drug is the result of chemistry as opposed to horticulture, this is a small but significant clue in where this Doctor's social allegiances lie.)

Staying on the positive side of the ledger, this story is also intriguingly more modern in its storytelling than the rest of Season Five. This story, you see, marks Victoria's departure from the TARDIS. And for the first time since at least Steven, and arguably since Susan, or even, if you really want to, for the first time ever, this fact is actually seeded and dealt with through the entire story. Victoria, as this story goes on, gets more and more frustrated and upset about life with the Doctor and the continual mortal peril she's thrust into. Until, in a deliciously clever end twist, it turns out to be Victoria's screaming that is capable of vanquishing the seaweed, which ends up being the final straw for Victoria, who longs for a life in which she is not continually threatened by homicidal plant life, Martians, Cybermen, Daleks, or Yeti, and so decides to leave the Doctor. The entire story is thus about Victoria's misery and the suffering she goes through—a clever and cutting move given how much the use of Victoria up to this point has been about taking pleasure in watching a reasonably well-known child actress have horrible things happen to her.

But the structural maturity here only serves to make clear the degree to which we do these things better in 2011. Yes, this episode deserves credit for seeding Victoria's departure through the whole story. And also for giving hints that Victoria's screams are effective against the Weed throughout the story. And for the fact that the Doctor's bit of gadgetry in the start— unscrewing a hatch with some new toy he has called a sonic screwdriver—echoes the solution he'll eventually use to defeat the monster—a sonic attack. All of this is very good and intelligent and shows a level of thinking about the work as a whole that Doctor Who has, for all its moments of greatness, mostly lacked in anything not written by David Whitaker.

But it's not enough. *Fury from the Deep* may show us Victoria's misery a lot, and even have her misery play into the climax, but it's not *about* her misery as such. Compare it to the nearest equivalent in the new series—*Last of the Time Lords. Last of the Time Lords* may be by far the weakest of Davies's season finales, but it goes out of its way to earn Martha's departure at the end. Martha goes through absolute hell, and the whole story revolves around the fact that she has to do this because the Doctor, Jack, and her family are all captured. Every plot development extends from Martha going through awful things, so that when she finally says this is too much and she has to go, we believe it and know why. And yes, it's clumsy and has an awful moment where Dobby-the-House Doctor metamorphoses into a magical love Jesus through the healing power of Doctor Who fandom, but it's still a better handling of an emotional journey than *Fury from the Deep*.

But here we get to the bizarre thing. For all of its flaws, *The Dark Path* is a better story than this too. Which is odd, because this is probably the third best story of its season and one of the better Troughton stories overall. But this story, which is ostensibly about putting Victoria through the emotional wringer, still doesn't deal with her nearly as interestingly as *The Dark Path*, even though that novel ends up being a kind of ridiculous snub of Victoria. Why? Because that novel took the time to make sure multiple plot developments hinged on Victoria's actions. Because there are specific character traits of Victoria's—her upbringing, her father's death—that cause her to make the decisions she makes. Her fate at the end of that book is meaningfully a consequence of her own actions, and had it been the story of her departure, it would have made far more sense than this one did with no changes other than her leaving at the end.

Here, on the other hand, ultimately Victoria is a passive object to whom bad things happen until she gets fed up and leaves. Even the ultimate defeat of the Weed does not extend from her actions. She screams into a microphone, and the Doctor solves the problem. This is admittedly part of the point—she's been a passive object throughout her tenure—but the story ultimately just reiterates it instead of providing any commentary on it. Compare this to how this would surely be done now, with her getting captured and dragged to the nerve center and about to have something truly awful happen to her when she lets out a piercing scream and saves the day. Note how in that version of the story, it's Victoria's actions that resolve the story. This shouldn't be a story that also happens to be a bad day for Victoria. It should be a story about Victoria's bad day.

For another comparison, think about the supporting characters of *Fury from the Deep* and the ones in *The Rebel Flesh/The Almost People*, which aired around the time I was writing the original version of this essay. In *Fury from the Deep*, every character is defined almost entirely in terms of how they'll respond to a terrible seaweed crisis. The closest thing to another motivation anyone has is Frank worrying about his wife, and even that mostly only affects how he does or doesn't want to evacuate the base or stop drilling. Whereas in *The Rebel Flesh/The Almost People*, characters have significant traits that don't in any direct way relate to crisis management. Jimmy has a kid whose birthday it was. Jennifer imagined a stronger, better version of herself growing up. These are traits that define the characters as people instead of crisis-management plot devices. They're traits that are not, on the surface, at all relevant to the Ganger crisis that takes place. But *The Rebel Flesh/The Almost People* also uses these facets of the characters in order to reach its plot resolution. The fact that Jimmy is a father and that Jennifer has always imagined a better version of herself both end up shaping how they respond to the crisis in ways that go beyond mere competence. Whereas competence is all *Fury from the Deep* ever thinks of its characters in terms of—how good at crisis management are they, and are they going to make the situation worse or better when they act?

And this gets to something I want to point out, both because I've been fairly critical of aspects of the Troughton era here and because I kind of took McIntee's book to task last essay. Generally speaking, Doctor Who has consistently improved over time. Yes, there are stories in the 1980s I'm going to be as savage towards as anything we've already talked about. Yes, the TV Movie is one of my least favorite things ever. Yes, there are truly staggeringly bad bits throughout the run, and there are stunning classics throughout it as well.

But by and large, over time, we've gotten better as a culture at making television. We've learned and mainstreamed more and more interesting techniques in writing novels. Techniques that were high literary techniques in the 1960s are business as usual in the 1990s, and unsurprisingly, that helps the novels a lot. Similarly, the improvements in filming and editing technology that have taken place over the last fifty years have helped Doctor Who. But so have better understandings of how to tell television stories. Mass entertainment is much better, in 2011, about grabbing emotional throughlines and making sure they impact the rest of the story than it was in 1997. And 1997 was better than 1968. And so *The Dark Path* has more mature and interesting storytelling techniques than *Fury from the Deep* even though it's a deeply, deeply flawed story.

And this applies in general. Most of Doctor Who in the 1980s is, from a technical and aesthetic standpoint, superior to Doctor Who in the 1970s or the 1960s. Virtually all of the new series is miles better than any of the classic series. Obviously there are high levels of variation in the short term—a given story may well be worse than one a year or two before. But in the long term, an average piece of Doctor Who in a given year is likely to be better than an average piece from, oh, let's say five years earlier, and likely to be inferior to one from five years later. That doesn't mean that the Hartnell and Troughton eras aren't amazing, but let's be honest—they need to be watched as historical phenomena. Even the best episodes of 1960s Doctor Who—an era where it was one of the best things on television—don't pack the same emotional punch as many mediocre dramas made in 2011. None of this is a criticism of the classic series—I think learning to appreciate and enjoy historical modes of storytelling on their own is a tremendously important skill. I think there's a ton to be learned by seeing how 1960s Doctor Who is good. Because even if later Doctor Who is better, there are still things that are good in 1960s Doctor Who that aren't done again, and there's a lot to be accomplished in looking to old ideas and figuring out how to make them work in new contexts. This is part and parcel of the mission of the new series—reinventing the ideas of the past for the present. And it's a thing of real beauty.

I say all of this because, well, there are stories I don't like and eras I don't like. The Pertwee era, which is increasingly looming over this volume, is one I'm openly not that fond of. And I've been harsh on the Troughton era, aside from my continual point that Troughton is a jaw-droppingly good actor who can make anything compelling. But despite that, it's better than the Hartnell era was even at its best. Have a look at the lengthy clip of Mr. Oak and Mr. Quill menacing Maggie Harris that survived for this episode. Look at the use of close-ups and cutting to tell the story, and how they create and sustain tension. There's very, very little in the Hartnell era that works that effectively. The Hartnell era needed to kill Sara Kingdom and have a Dalek ultimate weapon to get the kind of menacing atmosphere that *Fury from the Deep* manages with evil stove repairmen. That speaks to a show that's gotten better, just as a mediocre and flawed emotional throughline in a 1997 novel works better than one that was miles ahead of everything around it in 1968.

Fury from the Deep may not be a very ambitious story, but in terms of how it's put together, it grabs the audience and engages them in a way Hartnell-era stories didn't and couldn't. And Pertwee stories will improve on this, and so on and so forth. Whatever wrong turns the show takes, and I'll point out lots of them, this is something we don't reflect upon often enough—by and large, the show really does improve. Some years go downhill from the ones before them, and some are shockingly bad compared to what else was on at the time. But in terms of how it tells its stories, the picture is almost uninterrupted improvement.

But enough of that. Let's go to a more unambiguously positive note. This story is our farewell to Victoria, as I said. No, wait. That came out terribly wrong. Because there's nothing nice about Victoria leaving. She's the most successful female companion the show has had in ages. And we ought to take a moment, as she goes, to praise her.

The thing that is so effective about Victoria compared to the two preceding female companions is, ironically, the thing that makes her least palatable in 2011. No effort is made to have her be an ordinary, viewer-identification figure. We talked about some of this when talking about *The Ice Warriors* and the male gaze. Instead of being the eyes through which we see fantastic things, Victoria is instead usually a bit objectified and used as what I have derisively referred to as a peril monkey.

The thing is, and this ties in with my point about *Fury from the Deep* as compared to *The Dark Path*, it works terribly well. In part because we have such a magnetic lead and in part because we are nearly five years into this Doctor Who thing and thus pretty comfortable with the basic premise, we don't need audience identification figures in quite the same way anymore. And so the female companion has been reverting, over the last few years, into a plot role as opposed to a character role. The female companion is simply there to get captured and menaced. This is itself a problem and something the show will have an almost continual love-hate relationship with. Starting with the next story, it tries to solve it a bit, with mixed results. Just under three years from now, it's going to succumb to it in a major way, only to have it suddenly turn around and end up better than the mixed results of Zoe and Liz Shaw. From there on out, it swings back and forth, and it still swings to this very day.

But what's crucial about Victoria is that she's actually a companion designed to do what companions do on the show, as opposed to what people wish they did. The decision to cast a well-known, former child star as the companion pays dividends, because the show is unrepentant about using close-ups of Watling's face and using her charisma to let her get in nice plucky moments between her imperilments.

Yes, it's frustrating that the female companion is such a peril monkey. And if all of the outrage weren't so painfully obvious, I'd stamp my feet and point out that it sure would be nice if she got as many save-the-day moments as Jamie. Or, you know, any. But here's the thing. Since Barbara left, female companions have tended to be good ideas that get shoehorned into peril monkeying. It's very much been a matter of "take a solid actress and a neat concept for a part, and then have them stand there and get menaced by monsters constantly." And it's been a frustrating waste of talent and an insult to the characters. However much of a male-gaze-focused damsel in distress Victoria might be, the fact of the matter is that seeing a character who was actually supposed to be a strong and independent woman like Polly reduced to hot beverage service is considerably more irritating than seeing the damsel in distress done flawlessly from day one. By starting the companion off as a fairy-tale damsel in distress—which is what Whitaker did with her way back in *Evil of the Daleks*—the show made it so that when she dishes out sassy put-downs to sexist men in *Tomb of the Cybermen*, it counted for something. It was not just, as those rare moments of spunk in Polly were, brief moments where the character worked as intended. They were moments when the character worked surprisingly well.

But for all that she's an appallingly sexist peril monkey, it's difficult to get around the fact that Victoria is the best-done companion in some time. It's telling that, ever since the series unceremoniously dumped Vicki in 1965, its track record with female characters and particularly their departures has been dismal. Katarina and Sarah Kingdom were both unceremoniously killed, while Polly and Dodo were functionally dropped in mid-story. Whatever else might be said of Victoria, she at least was a companion that required more than that. The departures of Polly and Dodo were jarring, but to attempt that with Victoria would have just felt wrong— much as it felt wrong when Vicki, the last solid female companion, was dropped so suddenly and degradingly. Victoria, at least, was a companion who went beyond her plot function. And while it's infuriating to see such a token female character during a period of such active feminism in the larger culture (although to be fair, the heyday of feminism is actually the mid-'70s, and the companions in that era reflect that), for better or for worse, there is some small measure of progress here.

With Victoria, in short, the show stopped trying to have the female companion be the audience's eyes, and instead had the female companion be likable. And that means that future companions can push up against the limits of the role in ways that past ones couldn't. And it is one of the best decisions the show made in its first five years. It's every bit as much of a watershed moment for the series as Patrick Troughton's revamp of the role of the Doctor. So farewell to Deborah Watling. Basically, you rule.

That's Just Wizard (*The Wheel in Space*)

It's April 27, 1968. Louis Armstrong is declaring how wonderful the world is, and is at number one doing it. He continues proclaiming this for four weeks, before being unseated by one of the great anthems of pedophilia, Union Gap's "Young Girl." What a wonderful world indeed. So wonderful that nothing too terrible happens during these six weeks—just your usual nuclear tests, Vietnam war protests, deadly tornadoes, nuclear submarine sinkings, and Manchester United winning the European Cup. This last one I actually quite like, as a Manchester United fan, but I'd be lying if I said it was a hugely relevant point. Oh, and the May 1968 events in Paris. Those are kind of important. They're also, however, the subject of the next essay.

While on television … Hooboy. This may be the most misunderstood story by Doctor Who fandom I've yet covered, which is impressive given all that I've said about *The Web of Fear*, *The Tenth Planet*, and, really, several other stories. But this one is wholly misunderstood. For one thing, *The Wheel in Space* has what are possibly the two least likely cowriters in Doctor Who: Kit Pedler and David Whitaker. Attentive readers probably have some sense of how weird this is, but if you don't, imagine Alan Moore rewriting Arthur C. Clarke and you're at least in the general ballpark.

See, Kit Pedler is … OK, let's be honest. He's not much of a writer. I mean, this surely isn't a huge revelation. Every writing credit he has on Doctor Who (and, so far as I can tell, every fiction writing credit he has period) is co-authored, which, while not an immediate sign of anything, is suggestive (He does have solo credit on the first two episodes of *The Tenth Planet*, but from there on out it's co-authoring flat out, so I'm willing to bet that the script editor, Gerry Davis, who gets co-creator credit on the Cybermen despite not having a writing credit on their two debut episodes proper, did a fair amount of work on those two as well.) One imagines that Pedler's involvement in his scripts amounts, in most cases, to declaring a location where the Cybermen will show up (The moon! A tomb! Panama!) and ... possibly nothing else, actually. I mean, we should give the man credit—the Cybermen were a brilliant idea, and apparently *The War Machines* was his as well, which ... OK, well, the Cybermen were a brilliant idea.

But at the end of the day, Pedler is an optometrist with a flair for creating "hard SF" premises, with an emphasis on the scare quotes. By all appearances he was brought into the program mostly because Gerry Davis liked working with him. Since Gerry Davis walked away from the series for seven years after leaving as script editor, this left Pedler without a co-author for Cybermen stories. So clearly they had to find someone else to do it. Thankfully, the show has a lot of candidates—one can readily imagine Ian Stuart Black, Victor Pemberton, or Brian Hayles getting tapped for this role, for instance, or current story editor Derek Sherwin. All would make sense. Heck, just about any past writer on Doctor Who would make sense to hire for the job of turning Pedler's plot ideas into stories. I mean, the only one it's tough to imagine pairing with Pedler is ... David Whitaker.

I mean, it's tough to stress how utterly weird this pairing is. On the one hand, we have the archetypal base under siege crafter—the one, actually, who invented the genre—with a hard SF bent. On the other hand, we have someone who is apparently an alchemist who likes penning lengthy deconstructions of the show's entire premise. I mean, Whitaker apparently believes that you can eat metal by draining its life energy and corroding it. He is the last person who should be writing hard SF. He's the writer who has most methodically resisted the base under siege structure to date, whereas Pedler hasn't written anything but. The two of them together is a juxtaposition worthy of … well, Doctor Who, actually.

For my part, I have to admit that I have fallen completely in love with David Whitaker's work. I think he is an absolute genius. And so yes, I may have gone out of my way to love this bizarre bastard child of a story. But my God, I love it. I'm in no way convinced my love of it translates to it being good television, but I'm pretty confident that it's a great watch in 2011 and a delightful treat to anyone who is the sort of person to whom "traditional base under siege story" is a meaningful phrase. The thing is, I'm pretty convinced that Whitaker is offering a deliberate parody of, or at the very least a withering comment on, the standard base under siege story that has shown up in every story of Season Five he didn't write.

The first question, I suppose, is whether this is plausible. Certainly *The Enemy of the World* suggests that Whitaker is a writer with enough of a grasp of narrative structure to subvert it like this. And certainly the collapse of the series into an endless chain of cookie-cutter stories is almost diametrically opposed to everything he ever tried to do with the series and exactly the sort of thing that seems like he'd react against. It is, quite simply, difficult to believe that Whitaker was terribly happy with the brief of expanding out Pedler's script.

The problem, at least in 1968 terms, is that Whitaker deals with his problems with the base under siege format by systematically and meticulously demonstrating every single one of its flaws, often in ways that feel more like the grueling slogs of absurdist theater than like mainstream sci-fi drama. For instance, the first episode consists mostly of Jamie and the Doctor wandering around the TARDIS and a rocket. Nearly a full twenty minutes pass in which they're the lone characters, in fact. If you compare this to other stories around it—things like *The Ice Warriors* or, as we'll see on Monday, *The Dominators*—the most obvious thing is that this is a total reversal of the direction the series has been trending. Of late the series has decided to introduce its situation, establish a level of crisis, then drop the Doctor into it once the crisis is already cooking.

Instead we get twenty minutes of *The Web Planet*-style exploration. Except instead of exploring a vast and strange alien landscape we just explore a cramped rocket. We're faced here with two possibilities. Either David Whitaker has turned into a complete hack overnight or he's just decided to embrace completely messing with the audience. The former frankly seems improbable, while latter shouldn't be discounted. After all, both possibilities involve the assumption that Whitaker does not actually like the story he's being paid to write. (He has said in interviews that he tried to restructure the story so it had characters, which is fairly scathing as such comments go.) So why wouldn't we assume that the writer of *The Edge of Destruction*—a story that was, in point of fact, blatantly influenced by absurdist and existential theater—would bash out a Brechtian assault on audience sensibilities in which he stubbornly refuses to give the audience what they want at any turn while repeatedly yelling at them for wanting it in the first place?

Which just about sums up what the lengthy exploration of the cramped rocket does. Whitaker, maddeningly, approaches this story like he's writing a Season Two story, even though all the plot elements are Season Five elements. So he insists on doing an episode of wandering around exploring, even though the show has long since given up on creating interesting worlds to explore and now just goes with cramped metal corridors full of monsters. The result is to highlight just how boring the metal corridors are. And indeed, they're very, very boring. Mission accomplished, so to speak.

Likewise, the basic structure of the base under siege these days is that the first episode ends with a big monster reveal. Thus far every story this season except for *The Web of Fear* (which reveals its monsters early) and Whitaker's own (monsterless) *The Enemy of the World* has used the monster reveal as its first cliffhanger. This is a trick that originated way back in *The Dalek Invasion of Earth*. (No, not *The Daleks*—there

the point is that the monster isn't revealed until the second
episode.) The whole point of the cliffhanger of the first episode
of *The Daleks* is that we don't know what's menacing Barbara,
we only know her terror), but there it worked because the
Daleks had a special status as the first monsters to return—
because their appearance was a genuine moment of thrill and of
pleasure. It works precisely because things like the Daleks rarely
come back. When every single story has a giant monster in it
the revelation of it is not a surprising thrill. So Whitaker flatly
refuses to give us our big Cyberman cliffhanger in the first
episode, instead waiting until the third episode to reveal them
in full. Even when he does reveal them, he refuses to do a
straight monster reveal, instead reverting to the original *The
Daleks*-style cliffhanger of showing only a part of the monster.
Once again this amounts to using the structure that defined the
show back in its second season on its new and "improved"
formulaic take. *The Web Planet*, after all, does not make its initial
cliffhanger about the Zarbi.

This structure of refusing to use the normal set pieces of
the base under siege recurs throughout. Whitaker declines to
give the Doctor and the Cybermen a major confrontation,
declines to give us a major "Cybermen burst out of the tombs"
set piece, and even declines to have the Cybermen in most of
the story. There are plusses and minuses to this. It means that
the expected thrills aren't there, which renders the story
frustrating in spots. On the other hand, the Cybermen are
scarier here than they've ever been save for perhaps *The Tenth
Planet*. The slow and creepy revelation of the Cybermen was, by
most contemporary accounts, scary and effective. On the other
hand, the fact that the Cybermen are so routinely defeated by
the Doctor and have steadily become dull and generic monsters
means that their revelation drips with anticlimax. The more
obvious it becomes that it's just Cybermen the less interesting
the story becomes, and Whitaker, by drawing out the revelation
in a masterfully suspenseful fashion, ends up demonstrating
just how vapid the content of the revelation is and how

unworthy of an attempt to generate serious tension or suspense the idea of "Cybermen are attacking yet another base" is.

Similarly, the focus on building the world of the Wheel is a mixed bag. It makes the story move at a glacial pace in spots. But on the other hand, instead of just callously running up the death toll of supporting characters, Whitaker spends episodes building the culture of the Wheel so that when the deaths start we actually feel their impact. This is exceedingly welcome. Even the standard, overly skeptical base commander is given an overhaul, with his excessive dependence on traditional scientific evidence being presented explicitly as a mental illness, whereas in previous stories the idea that the commander of the base would be an idiot would just be taken for granted.

This last point gets at one of the most interesting things about this story. It is much, much more human than any previous Cybermen story. The most interesting dimension is probably Zoe, the incoming companion. Miles and Wood make an interesting argument about how Zoe represents 1968's view of how information processing would work in the future, even though 1968 didn't really know that information processing was going to be such a major part of the future. Zoe is the arch-technocrat, filled with an encyclopedic level of knowledge so that she can be an effective administrator of society. From a 1968 perspective, this is unsurprising—absent any sense of the digital revolution, a future of technocratic humans seemed the only alternative.

What Whitaker does with this that is so interesting, however, is that he overtly parallels Zoe's situation to the Cybermen's. Zoe frets that the fact that she was only prepared for expected crises renders her effectively useless and like an inhuman calculator. This is, of course, very much like what the Cybermen are. On the other hand, Zoe is likable. Indeed, as Toby Hadoke points out in *Running Through Corridors*, Zoe is very much the image of an obsessive Doctor Who fan (firmly rooted, I would argue, in the trainspotting tradition that developed into the "anorak" stereotype), contrasting her with the Cybermen becomes an oddly brilliant move. So even as

Whitaker is angrily skewering the conventions of the base under siege he's also trying to show a more interesting approach.

This, of course, gets at the other thing the story could be—which, to be fair, is still something considerably more sympathetic than it usually gets credit for being. It could also be that Whitaker is sincerely trying to expand the base under siege, seeing its deficiencies and trying to fix it with the storytelling techniques he knows best only to find that they are dated and inappropriate to the task. There's a nobility to this idea—a sense of Whitaker finding things to do with an idea that enrich it but don't quite work. But it suggests also a narrative in which Whitaker's writing is in decline, or at least becoming old-fashioned. Admittedly, this is his second to last story for the program, and his last one was massively rewritten, so that critique may have merit, but I, at least, find it difficult to believe that a writer who was so astonishingly cutting-edge in his last three stories has suddenly landed over the hill.

No, I think it far more likely that Whitaker is conscious of the fact that he is critiquing the show and demonstrating how far it has drifted from its origins. Yes, his insistence on writing a Hartnell-style base under siege often runs into problems. But I'd argue those problems are the point. Whitaker knows full well that two very different visions of what Doctor Who is are on display here, and the whole point of the story is to show the ways in which they conflict. As a result it's not always fun, but it is fascinating. If nothing else, if you haven't seen the story in a while, fire it up again and pretend it's a Hartnell story. It's still in many ways difficult to enjoy, but in that context, at least, I find it very, very easy to love.

Pop Between Realities, Home in Time for Tea: '68

And that, I think, was the handle—that sense of inevitable victory over the forces of Old and Evil. Not in any mean or military sense; we didn't need that. Our energy would simply PREVAIL. There was no point in fighting—on our side or theirs. We had all the momentum; we were riding the crest of a high and beautiful wave ... So now, less than five years later, you can go up on a steep hill in Las Vegas and look West, and with the right kind of eyes you can almost see the high-water mark—that place where the wave finally broke and rolled back. —Hunter S. Thompson, *Fear and Loathing in Las Vegas.*

The '60s ended.

This may seem like a very obvious thing to point out to anybody with a remote skill in calendar-reading. But when you're immersing yourself in the raging heat of psychedelia and social justice, it's easy to forget that its sense of inevitability was a fragile illusion. Certainly people forgot it in 1968. As ever, reality stands ready to intrude.

However badly the Summer of Love ended, it was still a utopian moment, beautiful in its naiveté. Even in its most crassly commercial version, its iconography holds a strange power. I mentioned a few entries ago the cover of the 1910 Fruitgum Company's single "Simon Says." What is most interesting about this cover is that despite the fact that it is the cover of an appallingly banal piece of bubblegum pop, the cover is still arrestingly psychedelic. Its B-side—"Reflections From the Looking Glass"—is unapologetically and unambiguously a piece of psychedelic utopianism. Even corporate commercialism proved unable to completely repress psychedelia. For one brief and shining moment it really did look inevitable.

Stunning, then, that less than a year later, on the other side of California, youth culture's best hope for the future, Robert Francis Kennedy, was gunned down following his victory in the California Democratic Primary. Two months later the Democratic National Convention in Chicago turned into a festival of ugly riots as various left-wing groups such as the Yippies prepared to make a bold stand and deliver the psychedelic street theater of the Diggers (as discussed in the Summer of Love essay) to the masses, albeit without the utopian community building of the Diggers (which turns out, perhaps, to have been the more important part). From the perspective of anyone with an aesthetic appreciation of guerilla theater politics, this should have been a high-water mark, with the threatened plan to dump LSD in the city's water supply being a particular highlight.

Meanwhile, the increasingly fierce Vietnam protests, spurred on by moral obscenities like the Mai Lai massacre, descended on the convention as well in an effort to derail the candidacy of Hubert Humphrey, seen as too close to Lyndon Johnson's war position. (Johnson, despite being one of the most effective anti-poverty and civil rights Presidents of the twentieth century, was at this point a pariah to the American left over the war, hence his withdrawing from the Presidential race.)

Both forces ran smack into Chicago Mayor Richard Daley, who had previously issued a "shoot to kill" order to quell the race riots following Martin Luther King's assassination. Daley, vowing to maintain law and order, essentially commanded his police force to shut down the demonstrations. The result was catastrophic. Despite later investigations concluding that the resulting violence was wholly down to the overreaction of the police, the end result was essentially right-wing street theater—the successful presentation of revolutionary youth culture as a bunch of violent thugs. From there it was all over save the corruption—a sham trial of the Chicago Seven in which Black Panther activist Bobby Seale was literally bound and gagged in the courtroom following an enraged outburst over his being denied permission to represent himself. The show trials lasted two years, with Abbie Hoffman performing career highlights of street theater in the courtroom. Ultimately, save for contempt of court charges, all of the protesters were acquitted.

The real cost, however, came elsewhere. Humphrey easily won the Democratic nomination and was duly slaughtered in the general election by Richard Nixon. It is impossible to overstate how brutal a slap in the face this was to any revolutionary culture. It would be one thing for a law and order candidate to defeat the more liberal candidate in 1968. But to see the left suffer a crushing defeat even with what was, by their standards, an extremely moderate candidate, and to see them suffer that defeat to Richard Nixon of all people—the very man Kennedy had defeated in 1960, the living, breathing, seething embodiment of the old establishment, must go down as one of the cruelest shutting downs of a political movement ever.

The revolutionary currents of the 1960s have never fully died in America, but this was, in effect, a mortal wound to any hopes of mainstream acceptance. In 1968, seemingly at the cusp of success, the revolution in America died at the hands of Richard Daley's police thugs in Lincoln Park. Psychedelia evaporated in a puff of smoke—the popularity of LSD went off a cliff in the face of the rise of cocaine and never recovered.

The United States is hardly alone in its 1968 flameout. Across continental Europe you got almost the exact same scene. The most prominent example is France in May of 1968, although lesser forms of them broke out across the European continent. But for our purposes, let's just focus on France.

First, we're going to have to understand something of the political situation in France. The first thing one has to realize about France in 1968 was that it was, in one sense, only a decade old as a country. Yes, France, like any stodgy European country, has centuries of history involving a lot of people with numbers at the ends of their names. But following its somewhat stunning decision to slaughter its entire aristocracy in a massive bloodbath, France went on to enjoy several centuries of political instability. This was not helped in any way, shape, or form when they were taken over by Nazis during World War II. The reformed post-War government was rife with problems, and when French colonialism curled up and died in the Algerian War of Independence, the entire government followed suit. Enraged at the idea that the democratically elected government would form negotiations with Algerian nationalists, the French military staged a coup d'état and threatened to invade Paris unless Charles DeGaulle was made President. DeGaulle, rather astonishingly recognizing the fact that being forcibly installed as President gave him rather a lot of bargaining power, refused to take the job unless there was a new constitution that would make him a stronger executive and give him a guaranteed seven-year term.

Fast forward ten years, and the standard revolutionary tendencies of the 1960s are on display. As in any country, many of the flashpoints of this conflict came in universities—unsurprising given that the 1960s were largely a youth movement and universities by definition have high concentrations of youth. A particularly big flashpoint opened surrounding police occupation of the Sorbonne University in Paris, leading to massive demonstrations and massive police retaliation à la Chicago three months later. Allegations flew that the police were infiltrating the protests and committing acts of terrorism by throwing Molotov cocktails in order to give themselves an excuse to brutally crack down on the protests.

Unlike in Chicago, sympathies lay firmly with the demonstrators, at least to begin with. Many of the labor unions in France sided with them and held general strikes in sympathy. From here, the situation went out of control. Instead of subsiding when the ostensible main issue—the occupation of the Sorbonne and the release of prisoners from past protesters—was resolved, the strikes suddenly exploded outward. Despite efforts by labor leaders to bring them to an end, rank and file union members rebelled against their own unions, breaking out into a nationwide wildcat general strike. What started as student protests turned into a widespread attempt to bring down the government.

At the head of this was the Situationist International. Despite at the time being an exceedingly small group, in no small part because of their love of kicking people out for theoretical deviations from Situationist orthodoxy, their work, particularly Guy Debord's *The Society of the Spectacle*, provided the theoretical and aesthetic underpinnings of the protests. Situationist slogans were scrawled as graffiti throughout France: "Under the paving stones, the beach,"; "I'm a Groucho Marxist,"; and "The most beautiful sculpture is a paving stone thrown at a cop's head."

Again, this is not as radical as it might sound to a US or UK reader. Remember, a military coup had brought down the government only a decade earlier, and France was on its fifth governmental structure of the twentieth century and sixth in the last hundred years. Apparently, de Gaulle himself thought his government was toast and began working on a flight to Germany, including disappearing for a time to confer with French generals there. Instead of stepping down, however, de Gaulle called for new elections in June.

Unfortunately, by then popular opinion had turned on the strikers, who were viewed as naive and stupid utopianists. The popular slogans of the uprisings proved popular only among the group of revolutionaries themselves. The revolution turned out to be an echo chamber. Charles de Gaulle's government won in a landslide, and in Europe too, the revolution died. By 1972 the Situationist International consisted of only two members. It dissolved thereafter.

Picking over its corpse, there is much to love. A perusal of the slogans grafittied throughout France feels like a memorial wall to a revolutionary ideology, the POWs and MIAs of a disastrous culture war. But all of it, all of the theories of the inevitability of revolution, came to nothing. The leftists were driven out, their gains reversed, their ideology and members left begging for scraps at the edges of the political discourse. There has not been a moment in the four decades since where global change has ever felt so close.

Through and through, Doctor Who has been allied with the revolution that runs aground here. Admittedly, the show's commitment to social justice has been sporadic, turning at times into simple lack of interest or overt and catastrophic failures of social justice. But on the other hand, it is very difficult to read Troughton's Doctor, who proclaims that bad laws are made to be broken, who is a chemist in the age of LSD, and who is an overt and chaotic anarchist whose basic approach to life appears to be a Situationist form of guerilla theater splayed out over space and time, as anything but a revolutionary liberal. He is a man who is far, far more inclined to bring down a government than build one. In a conflict between youthful protesters and violent cops who are beating them he will and has chosen the youthful protesters every time.

For Doctor Who, then, the summer of 1968 is a vicious blow, even as it tracks the general cultural narrative of 1967–1968 well. A rush of promise in the summer of 1967 followed by a long year of disappointment and generic bases under siege. For all its "classic monster era" status, the fact of the matter is that the seven stories of Season Five feature six that are basically identical and feature no substantive engagement with the real world. This is not merely a complaint that they are not political enough—although I see nothing wrong with demanding that our mass entertainment be political, in no small part because, as the old adage goes, all art is political. Supposedly apolitical mass entertainment is, in reality, reactionary mass entertainment that espouses the default consensus while ignoring all alternatives. No, my complaint is that the bases under siege of the fifth season are not human enough. They are utterly divorced from the idea of material reality and the world they were transmitted into. Yes, we can maybe come up with some excuse for *The Wheel in Space* as David Whitaker launching a much-needed critique of the base under siege, but what do we do from that? Do we try to come up with a redemptive reading of Hainsman and Lincoln's neutered and mildly offensive Buddhism? We'll see in the very next story how poorly that's going to go.

On the other hand, you may have noticed something interesting about the overview of 1968 provided above. The US had its cruel shutting down of revolutions. So did continental Europe. And of course there were things like the Prague Spring to crush the revolutions in communist Europe. But we've yet to discuss anything that happened in the UK.

There's a reason for this; 1968 largely left the UK untouched. The UK peaked in the early days of the revolutionary '60s with mod culture and The Beatles. It is not that it was any less psychedelic or extreme than the US or France, but somehow, these strains of culture interacted differently in the UK than they had elsewhere. There were still major problems and setbacks for the left, but there was nothing like the era-ending crashes of the US and France. Largely, this came down to the fact that none of the revolutionary movements we've talked about were particularly British. British iconoclasm tended to view the aesthetics of street theater less as means to an end than as ends in themselves. You dress in funny clothes and do weird things because that in and of itself is threatening. This survival in 1968 has its own consequences—a decade later, in the next major victory of conservatism, Britain has a wildly worse time of it than anyone else. But for now, at least, Britain survives the purging of the left relatively unscathed.

Or, to relate it back to Doctor Who, for all his anarchism and disregard for authorities, the Doctor is not a revolutionary in the American or French sense of things. Left to his own devices, he seems to want nothing more than to bop about the universe doing cool stuff. Any revolutionary drive he has seems to extend from the degree to which he is a socially unacceptable figure just for wanting to wander time and space. Secondarily, it comes from his traumatic regeneration and subsequent realization that there are genuine monsters who want to endanger the very possibility of "being" someone. But at the end of the day, all the Doctor seems to want is the ability to be the Doctor. Psychedelia and street theater aesthetics are simply who he is. Political revolution is important only inasmuch as it is sometimes necessary to ensure his continued existence.

This is very much in tune with British psychedelia. The British model of psychedelic culture has always valued the individual rabbit hole. Not in the sense of frontier American cowboy individualism, but in a far quieter sense. In some ways, this is even more revolutionary. It is one thing to tear down society and replace it with its opposite. British psychedelia and British revolutionary politics—the last ones standing after '68—offered a stranger and perhaps stronger prospect—the possibility of making psychedelia part and parcel of the larger world. And even if it is not, in 1968, the best show on British television (let's face it, that's probably *The Prisoner*), Doctor Who is the show that best captures and embodies that spirit. As the mercurial and the revolutionary comes crashing down across the world, for this moment, at least, Doctor Who finds itself in the odd position of being one of the last and brightest lights.

I do not take this as a good thing or as a triumph for the show. BBC tea-time science fiction is not the ideal location for the hopes and dreams of the revolution. This is not a criticism of Doctor Who or its potential, but the fact of the matter is that something like Doctor Who ought to be on the mainstream edge of the counterculture, not on the revolutionary edge. When the wheels fall off the revolutionary edge and Doctor Who becomes the last best hope for productive expression of a leftist worldview something has gone wrong. It's a burden Doctor Who is not wholly equipped to bear. But on the other hand, it is the situation we find ourselves in, for better or for worse.

Why Are Earth People So Parochial? (*The Dominators*)

It's August 10, 1968. Tommy James and the Shondells are at number one with "Mony Mony." But if we really want to capture the spirit of this one we need to look at number two, or just jump a week ahead to where it hits number one and look at Crazy World of Arthur Brown's "Fire," which dethrones Mr. James for a single week before he takes it back for one more. From there on out, it's just the Beach Boys and the Bee Gees. So let's go back to Arthur Brown. Personally, I advocate taking three minutes out of your day and looking up Mr. Brown's *Top of the Pops* performance of this song on YouTube. If you cannot spare the time to watch a man with a hat whose most visible feature is the fact that it is a pair of horns which are constantly on fire scream, "I AM THE GOD OF HELLFIRE" on BBC One, well, I pity you. It's basically the greatest thing ever, and should really be recognized as the anthem of a uniquely British psychedelic culture. In any case, Simon and Garfunkel, Sly and the Family Stone, Aretha Franklin, Tom Jones, Herman's Hermits, and Richard Harris also chart, the latter, inevitably, with "MacArthur Park."

As for the news, the last post covers most of it, with the Chicago Democratic National Convention and the Prague Spring both unfolding over the course of this story. While on television we get our second entry into the ignoble rankings of the ten worst ever Doctor Who stories according to the most recent *Doctor Who Magazine* poll of such things. *The Dominators* is, apparently, the ninth worst story ever. But the thing about the bottom ten in a poll like this is that they're not the ten worst stories. They're the ten most hated stories. To come at the bottom of a list like this, you can't just be lousy. You have to be so lousy that there are people who hate you and will make that special effort to give you a zero out of ten.

For most of the ten, there are clear reasons why they're hated. Of the three 1960s stories in the bottom ten, two are ones that have single surviving episodes. Those episodes are watched only by particularly dedicated fans, and if they're dodgy, they are remembered for the constant mocking they elicited. So, for instance, *The Underwater Menace* is basically down there entirely on the basis of Joseph Furst shouting "Nothing in ze world can stop me now," and indeed when the second episode was found, even before anyone saw it, there was a sudden rush of reappraisal of it. Further, there are five stories from John Nathan-Turner's tenure that are slammed as part of a well-rehearsed (and largely, though not entirely, correct) critique of his tenure. Similarly, there's one Graham Williams episode that is slammed because it's the worst story of another era with a ton of detractors. But then you have two episodes that are down there despite having no obvious reason for the hatred—a lone turkey from the new series, and *The Dominators*. *The Dominators*, in other words, is one of two entries in the all-time bottom ten of Doctor Who that has no credible explanation for the hatred other than its actual quality.

That should give you some sense of how bad this is. Clear a space on your shelf next to *The Celestial Toymaker*, because we are about to dive into a story about which the sole good thing that can be said is "they had the good sense to end it an episode early so we got an extra episode of *The Mind Robber*."

As with *The Celestial Toymaker*, the first and most visible problem is that *The Dominators* is a misbegotten wreck at every level of its production. The monsters are rubbish. The writing is rubbish. The acting is rubbish. The costumes are rubbish. Let's start with the costumes. While it is possible that the horrific midpoints between togas and cocktail dresses which the vast majority of characters wear in this story are simply a wardrobe decision that has aged poorly, I have to confess that I am skeptical that the Dulcians ever looked like anything but men in dresses.

For one thing, to believe that the Dulcians were well designed I would have to believe that the Dominators themselves ... actually, we should pause here to note that "The Dominators" is easily the stupidest name for an alien race ever. What on Earth is the etymology of this? Did their planet just happen to be called Dominat? If not, this would be like dogs naming themselves The Furry Barkers, or humans naming themselves The Hairless Pink Things. If so, it seems to open an even stranger can of worms, or as I prefer to call them, Wiggles. (Wait, that one's taken.)

One can only assume, frankly, that they were renamed as part of a corporate rebranding—an interstellar version of the Swiss design craze that brought us Helvetica. It's worth imagining the meeting, if only because it's more fun than the episodes themselves. "So I think you need to refocus on what you do best. Let's brainstorm. What are you guys good at?" "Crushing opposition?" "No, no, Crusher has bad associations in space. Try again." "Ummm ... Exterminating lesser races?" "Sorry, that's trademarked." "Oof. Um. Dominating?" "Yes! Perfect! THE DOMINATORS! I love it!" If that meeting then ended up designing the preposterous shoulder pads that the Dominators walk around with, it is officially the worst corporate meeting since *Microsoft Bob* was greenlit.

Somehow, though, none of this—not the men in dresses that look to be sewn out of excess adult diapers, not the Dominators, not their shoulder pads, none of it—quite prepares the mind for the experience of seeing a Quark for the first time. The Quarks are the first effort to consciously design the next Daleks (in terms of merchandising potential) since the Chumblies. (The Cybermen, although pushed as merchandise, were not actually invented for that.) But where the Chumblies were a bewildering design that at least made interesting noises, the Quarks ... look like children in bad robot costumes. Which they are. Fine. The Cybermen look like grown men in bad robot costumes. But the Quarks take the baffling decision to flaunt this fact with numerous sparkly bits, purposeless spikey bits, and the world's least practical arms. (They fold out of the chest, and seem good for nothing but shooting things.) The Cybermen, whatever flaws their design may have (and there aren't actually that many), at least were designed with some eye towards function. The Quarks look like they were slapped together in a Blue Peter competition. Not that there is anything wrong with Blue Peter competitions, but note that I just said they looked like they were in one. Not like they won it.

(Ah, yes, a note for ignorant Americans. Blue Peter is a weekly children's show that's basically a kids' general interest magazine morphed into television. It has been on the air for a terrifyingly long time, and is completely iconic. The show is such that the Blue Peter badge—given to children for appearing on the show or for sending interesting material to the show—can still, in 2011, be used to gain free admission to numerous British attractions. Also, they frequently run competitions of the "design a Doctor Who monster" variety. Both the Abzobaloff from *Love and Monsters* and the TARDIS console the Doctor builds in *The Doctor's Wife* were based on Blue Peter designs.)

And then, on top of that, after the first episode cynically holds back the Quark reveal as if the appearances of these things are something to look forward to, we hear them talk. And they sound like homicidal chipmunks on helium. Perhaps the idea here was the frisson of childlike objects being dangerous. And in a story like, oh, the one we're talking about in a few essays' time, there's something to be said for this. The thing is, to successfully generate a genuine sense of fear and apprehension via the juxtaposition of the absurd and childish with the serious and dangerous you have to project some sense that you know what you're doing and thus that it might be deliberate. When every other piece of design in the entire episode is a complete trainwreck, the chilling juxtaposition of the childlike and the dangerous just looks like you have no idea that chipmunks sucking down helium are not what people immediately associate with "terrifying robotic killers."

Still, this is Doctor Who. Where we love nothing more than to ignore a ridiculous pile of camp insanity and enjoy the underlying story. So we should be fine, right? Well, perhaps. Certainly it's possible to love the Quarks for all of their flaws. But past that, loving the camp would mostly require anyone involved in this trainwreck to have bothered including an underlying story. Instead they included five episodes in which virtually nothing happens. At one point a rock is rolled down a hill to crush a Quark. It is the most boring piece of styrofoam rolling down a hill ever filmed. It looks nothing like a real rock, and bounces preposterously on the way down before landing off-camera and crushing the Quark. Apparently Morris Barry thought that a bouncing piece of styrofoam would be seen by viewers as an adequate replacement for seeing one of the evil robots blow up.

It's not. But it is par for the course for the plotting of this story. But if you want another example, we can look at the intelligence tests given to the Doctor and Jamie in the second episode which amount to putting blocks in the appropriately shaped holes—while being electrocuted. Aside from the question of what the electrocution was supposed to add to the experience other than establishing that the Dominators are evil—something that was probably decently well communicated by the fact that they are called the Dominators as opposed to the Nice Consensus Builders—we run into the fact that this is an intelligence test that most three year olds pass with remarkable ease. No species that has evolved the ability to talk is going to screw that one up. And yet the Dominators have no trouble believing that the Doctor and Jamie really are that stupid. Perhaps they can't pass the test either?

Of course, there is something of a reason for the crap plotting, much as with, once again, *The Celestial Toymaker*. See, apparently Haisman and Lincoln—the writers of this story— wanted to fill the script with biting social satire, but script editor Derrick Sherwin and producer Peter Bryant felt this was a poor decision. Unfortunately, given that the script was supposed to be about the social satire, what remained after it was taken out wasn't about anything at all. Lest you think the fault here lies with Bryant and Sherwin, however, we should quickly clear up what the satire was supposed to be. See, the Dulcians are all pacifists. Get it?

No, really. That's it. The entire point of the satire was that the Dulcians were pacifists, isn't that stupid. Haisman and Lincoln's entire idea in *The Dominators* is to ruthlessly mock the anti-war movement. And this aired during the Chicago protests in August, remember. This is Doctor Who overtly siding with the people committing police brutality over the people who are being beaten, whose major point is that the things like the Mai Lai massacre were bad.

Admittedly this gets at least somewhat cut in the final version, most obviously by the decision to have the pacifists be old men opposed by the younger generation so that it at least vaguely looks like it might just be a decades overdue critique of Neville Chamberlain. But this is a slender reed to grasp at even before you know that the writers fully intended the story to be an attack on the youth movement. Once you know that it's a desperate patch-up job it just becomes impossible to forgive.

Yes, Doctor Who has critiqued pacifism before—most obviously in *The Daleks*, where much effort is spent getting the Thals to fight. But look at how differently the two stories handle that. In *The Daleks*, the Thals are led to fight against the Daleks when Ian and the Doctor demonstrate to them that there are things they care about enough to fight for. In other words, as noble as pacifism may be, the Thals are led to see that there are things worth fighting for, and furthermore are shown that they clearly already believe this and that their pacifism is based out of the trauma of the last war, but isn't really who they are.

Whereas in *The Dominators*, the Dulcians are an entire culture defined by a genuine and considered ideal of pacifism. And so instead of being shown that, no, there are things they'll fight for, we get a scene in which a Dominator walks into the Dulcian high council. They all try to reason with him and indicate that they are happy to help him extract any minerals he needs and that there's really no reason to be violent, and he murders their leader and tells them that the Dominators do nothing but take and are basically just moustache-twirling villains who will be enslaving them all.

In other words, instead of pacifists being good people who can be made better, pacifists are deluded fools and it's funny to watch them die. It is easily the most cynical and mean-spirited scene I have seen yet in Doctor Who. It is a scene that exists only to take people who are acting out of a genuine moral conviction and mock them for their own morality. It doesn't even pretend to have an interesting story to tell. It's just pantomime villains murdering men in dresses (and in light of all of this it is hard to read the Dulcian wardrobe as anything other than a horrifyingly sexist claim about the hippie movement being a bunch of sissies) because watching hippies get killed is apparently funny.

It's bad. It's mean. It's a story that should never have happened. A story so bad that both Rob Shearman and Tat Wood separately tell stories of being at the 1983 Longleat convention and standing in line for hours to get into the screening room for Doctor Who stories only to be given *The Dominators* as the Troughton story and ultimately giving up on the idea that watching this could ever be fun. Even Troughton seems to be fed up with the story. At one point he's forced to argue that the problem the Dulcians are having with the Dominators is that they're not realizing that the Dominators are completely alien. It's an appallingly xenophobic line. In response to it, the Dulcian points out that the Doctor is an alien too. Now, in the episode Troughton responds laughing and saying "you got me there." But it's worth paying attention to the particulars of his delivery. It's an incredibly fast response—the only moment I've ever seen Troughton flagrantly step on someone's dialogue. Indeed, the line sounds like an improvised drop-in. One strongly suspects that

Troughton snuck it in because he was horrified at his own dialogue and desperate to undercut the idea that the Doctor could be such a xenophobic prick.

Two episodes later you can, quite frankly, see the moment where Troughton quits the series. Forced to do a scene in which the central joke is the use of the "number nine pill" to create a bomb, he gives up all pretense of playing the Doctor and simply begins trying to clown the script into submission in a desperate attempt to make it even remotely watchable. You can frankly see the will to live just drain out of his eyes as he just decides that his playing of the part is going to consist of shouting "oh my" a lot and running around. The "number nine pill," it should be noted, is a reference to a military prescription laxative. In other words, the plot of this story resolves with a diarrhea joke. Actually, it resolves with the Doctor running around with a different explosive trying to dispose of it. You may recognize this as the climax of the Adam West *Batman* movie, which gave us the classic line "Sometimes you just can't dispose of a bomb." While I recognize that the Troughton era is in part an attempt to compete with the charismatic double acts of series like *Batman*, ripping off Adam West for your plot developments has to be seen as the absolute nadir of Doctor Who plotting up to this point.

Here, in other words, Doctor Who has its own private '68. The complete and abysmal abdication of any claim to a moral worldview in favor of a mean-spirited mockery of the youth culture that had previously been the heart and soul of the show. And the blame here falls squarely on Haisman and Lincoln, the mean-spirited thugs who wanted to write a Doctor Who story about how they hate pacifists. This story is so breathtakingly cruel and so shockingly out of step with everything that Doctor Who has been up to this point that, frankly, it calls into question everything Hasiman and Lincoln ever did. Really. Let's re-evaluate their contribution to Doctor Who briefly in light of this, shall we?

First off, we have the Yeti—their big monster. The idea of robotic Yeti was always a bit odd. On the one hand, they've always been in a position of being the best monster that hasn't made a return. But if they were to return, frankly, they'd switch to being the worst monsters that have. There is nothing about the idea of the Yeti that looks on paper like a winner. When you stop to consider that they were created by the same people who made the Quarks—and indeed by the same people who went to war with the production office and threatened to engage in a lawsuit that would have had the probable effect of canceling Doctor Who over the rights to the Quarks—it becomes very difficult to see what about evil, robotic teddy bears is a better idea than the evil, robotic whatever-the-hell the Quarks are. It's just that the Yeti managed to show up in two stories that otherwise had good production values so that the frisson of an inappropriate monster functioned. But in hindsight, we have to take this as inadvertent postmodern genius—one of those moments where idiocy inadvertently works.

We also praised them for the Buddhist setting of *The Abominable Snowmen*. Except one of the things that's striking about that story is that the Buddhist monastery has an oddly militant group of warriors who constantly beg for permission to oppose the Yeti and are shut down by their pacifist brethren. On top of that, there's the fact that Lincoln is apparently fond of broad ancient conspiracy theories about how the French monarchy were secret descendants of Jesus. Taken together, this all gives the sense that we are dealing with people with somewhat less of a grasp on culture and human behavior than one might hope. In fact, I'd argue that in the massive overlap among ancient European conspiracy theories, which tend to all have at least some elements in common with others in the set, it is impossible to distance any of them entirely from the anti-Semitism of conspiracies like the Gnomes of Zurich or the Elders of Zion. Oh, hey, I guess the whole stereotypical Jew aspect of *The Web of Fear* paid off after all.

Indeed, the thing we liked about *The Abominable Snowmen* was mostly how respectful the Doctor seemed of Buddhism. But then, we've already seen Troughton using line readings to undercut the intent of an offensive and xenophobic script once this episode. It is Troughton's line readings more than the script itself that makes the Doctor appear respectful of Buddhism. Looking at the script you have … a bunch of pacifist monks who wrongly ignore the guy who says they have to fight. And the author of the so-called *Tibetan Book of the Dead* possessed for centuries by a malevolent alien. The same *Book of the Dead* that, as I've pointed out, got adapted into one of the major texts of psychedelia. When paired with the unambiguously reactionary nature of this story, it becomes much harder to give that story any benefit of the doubt, firmly establishing it as the thinly veiled swipe at the evils of psychedelic culture, redeemed by quality production and some Troughton line readings, which we feared.

As for their other story, *The Web of Fear*, stereotypical Jew aside, you may remember that I noted that the Doctor and the military make for strange bedfellows—a problem we'll see more and more this season and in the five following. Except that Haisman and Lincoln, in their non-existent understanding of the series they're writing for, seem to think that, no the Doctor loves the military and just isn't very fond of those dirty hippies. And indeed, no effort is made in *The Web of Fear* to ask any sorts of questions about why the mercurial and anarchic Doctor is palling about with soldiers and about the tensions that might engender.

Frankly, once you watch *The Dominators*, it becomes impossible to assume any good will at all on the part of its authors. The sheer mean-spiritedness of this story forces us to reexamine what we liked in their two previous efforts, and once you do that it becomes possible to undo almost every virtue any of them had and read them instead as expressions of the same ugly cruelty of this story. They lucked out and got good production twice and managed to cover up most of their flaws, but with this one, they are, quite frankly, found out as the cynical and nasty hacks that they are. This is their last involvement with the show, and frankly, good riddance.

If I sound pissed off at this story, it's because I am. It is an overt attack on the ethical foundations of Doctor Who. Not only is it an attack on the entire ethos that underlies the Doctor as a character, it's an attempt to twist and pervert the show away from what it is and towards something ugly, cruel, and just plain unpleasant. The sheer sickening stench of this story is enough to turn one off the program entirely. Especially coming off of the long, turgid slog of pointless and cynical bases under siege we've seen over the last year.

Frankly, unless the next story turns out to be a David Whitaker-esque piece of magic and one of the best stories the show has ever produced, it might just be time to pack it in on this program before it goes from worse to completely and utterly unforgivably awful.

We're All Stories in the End (*The Mind Robber*)

It's September 14, 1968. In our traditional sign of some sort of restoration of order, The Beatles are at number one with "Hey Jude." They are unseated two weeks later by a signing to their own record label, Mary Hopkin, a British folk singer, who holds the number one slot with "Those Were the Days" for the remainder of this story. The Bee Gees, The Beach Boys, and Johnny Nash all also chart. As do Amen Corner with "High in the Sky," a song I've not heard of, but that lingers around at number ten for an absolutely terrifyingly long time and so seemed worth commenting on.

In news that doesn't sing, the Apollo missions get closer and closer to the moon with their first manned launch, Apollo 7. The merger between General Electric Company (no relation to the American company General Electric) and English Electric is the biggest merger in UK history. There's a lovely revolution in Panama. And, most significantly, in the one major bit of 1968 catastrophe to hit the UK, rioting breaks out following a civil rights march in Derry, leading to the twenty years of tension and terrorism between the UK and Ireland known as The Troubles.

While on television we have, thankfully, the exact story we needed after the grotesque train wreck that was *The Dominators*. *The Mind Robber* is a thing of absolute beauty. If *The Dominators* was the complete breakdown of all heart, soul, and ethics in the series, *The Mind Robber* is, more even than *The Power of the Daleks*, a story that is about establishing Doctor Who as an unending story. It's a story that is not just delightful to watch, but a story that watching gives one a constant, triumphant sense of right—a sense that this is how and what Doctor Who was always supposed to be.

Even the basic idea has a delightful sense of properness. The basic idea is that, following a TARDIS malfunction, the Doctor, Jamie, and Zoe get caught in the Land of Fiction, a realm in which stories are real. The title, which is admittedly intensely marginal with relation to the rest, refers to the Master of the Land of Fiction, who has apparently lured the Doctor there in order to get him to run things.

Much has been made of many of the obvious aspects of this story. The intertextuality, the degree to which this represents Doctor Who acknowledging a longstanding debt to a tradition of British children's literature, the pleasant and inventive surrealism—all of these are well-worn topics that you can see covered in almost any book on the series. Even if you go for criticism from third generation fandom—things like *Running Through Corridors* or *About Time*—most of what you get are acknowledgments of how brilliant this story is. And it is absolutely brilliant—a story with more creativity, and more of a sense of joy than anything else in the Troughton era.

But that's all been said well enough. So let's, as we try to do here, find some new things to say about *The Mind Robber*. First, I want to talk about a specific approach to Doctor Who that *The Mind Robber* is a particularly key moment in. Because for all the seeming radicalness of this story, it's considerably less of a departure from past stories than one might think. The most obvious place to look towards this is its first episode—a charming piece of surrealism hastily written by script editor Derrick Sherwin to deal with the fact that *The Dominators* packed it in an episode early and thus that *The Mind Robber* needed to expand from its original four-episode conception. This was enormously fortunate for the story. The four episodes of *The Mind Robber* that were originally intended are delightful, but the addition of a real avant-garde piece at the head that serves as a more dramatic break from what had come before.

(The story is one that benefits from a couple moments of odd luck. The sudden illness of Frazer Hines which required his being replaced by his cousin Hamish Wilson for two episodes resulted in a wonderfully disturbing sequence in which the Doctor tries to assemble Jamie's lost face from a set of cut-outs and gets it wrong, temporarily giving Jamie a new face. There is relatively little of the Troughton era that I remember watching as a child, but that scene stuck vividly with me.)

But ironically, the addition of a self-consciously weird episode meant that the story got more grounded in the past of the program as well. Sherwin ended up doing an episode whose sets consisted of the TARDIS and a white void. This meant a lot of TARDIS material, and at this point in the series the TARDIS was largely David Whitaker's baby. Which means that the David Whitaker-style conception of the TARDIS makes an unexpected appearance in a non-Whitaker story. The first episode involves mercury fluid links, sticky switches, bizarre TARDIS control mechanisms, and other classic elements of Whitaker science. We've talked about the nature of Whitaker's alchemical conception of the series before, most notably in *The Evil of the Daleks* entry, but it's worth reiterating the basics. The biggest one is that in alchemy, the symbol and the object are considered to be interchangeable. Furthermore, the Doctor and the TARDIS are clearly associated with mercury, one of the most powerful elemental symbols. (Alchemy as a spiritual practice paid great heed to a syncresis of Hermes and Thoth called Hermes Trismegistus.)

The reappearance of the mercury links, in other words, is not just a callback to *The Wheel in Space*. It's also an invocation of a specific view of the Doctor's identity—one in which one of the most important things to know is that symbols have real power. There's a longstanding debate about Doctor Who as to whether it is really science fiction, or if it's better classified as some form of fantasy. Miles and Wood go to great lengths to arbitrate this, coming up with one of the best distinctions between science fiction and fantasy I've ever seen. Science fiction, they argue, is about man's relationship with his tools, whereas fantasy is about man's relationship with symbols and language.

Whatever its scientific trappings, under this definition it's fairly clear that Doctor Who's sympathies lie more with fantasy, as it's shot through with discussions of symbols. We'll look at the earliest example later, but it extends to the present day. Steven Moffat's first season on the show is a prime example. Look at the depiction of the Weeping Angels in *The Time of Angels*. The idea that "an image of an Angel is itself an Angel" makes no sense as a concept extending from any science. It's purely an alchemical concept—the idea that symbols of the Angels are equivalent to the beings themselves. This is made clearest in one of the most overlooked, creepy lines in the entire series. "What if our thoughts could think for themselves? What if our dreams no longer needed us? When these things occur and are held to be true, the time will be upon us. The time of Angels." In other words, the Angels arose because they were thought of. They stepped out of our dreams and into the world. They are not science, but magic through and through. They are symbols with power. In other words, they are direct evolutions of David Whitaker's Doctor Who. (The resolution of *The Big Bang* takes this even further, in particular the monologue I lifted this entry title from, but that's a topic for another book.)

This is, as is surely clear to anyone who has read this book thus far, the approach to the show that I love most. And *The Mind Robber* is a landmark story in this regard. For one thing, it makes it one hundred percent canonical in the world of Doctor Who that ideas are real. There is a Land of Fiction where things that were created in people's minds have real form. That's a big deal in and of itself. But if we look more closely at *The Mind Robber*, its implications for Doctor Who at large become even bigger.

Let's go back to the Master of the Land of Fiction's plan. He wants the Doctor to take over running the Land of Fiction, and has apparently plucked him from the universe and lured him there for the task. Why? This is actually a very good question. The incumbent Master of the Land of Fiction is a writer of a pulp schoolboy serial (and, Miles and Wood argue, a thinly veiled Charles Hamilton, though the veil here is at least thicker than the last thinly veiled thing related to Hamilton). It's made clear that it's his creativity and ability to write that holds the thing together. So why on Earth would the Land of Fiction want to sack its writer-Master in favor of the Doctor, a character who has never displayed any particular literary ambition, and who has thus far been coded as a scientist, not an artist?

The clue is in the second episode, in which Gulliver makes a comment that the Doctor is a traitor to the Land of Fiction. What on Earth could that possibly mean? On one level, it's transparent. Like all of Gulliver's lines, it's actually from Jonathan Swift himself. But we are, I think, meant to assume that what he says is true, if oddly phrased. The obvious answer is that the Doctor is originally from the Land of Fiction. In fact, if we take Gulliver's line at face value (and there is admittedly some reason not to, though I think the overall tone of the story suggests that Gulliver is essentially honest, even if the constraint on his dialogue makes him hard to follow at times), the Doctor must hail from the Land of Fiction. After all, you cannot be a traitor to a land you are not from.

Virtually everything in the episode seems to confirm this. For instance, Jamie stumbles upon a ticker tape that is actively creating the adventures of the Doctor and Zoe as they happen. (This leads to the one muffed moment of the story, in which the Doctor and Zoe are menaced by Medusa as Jamie reads about it on ticker tape. The cliffhanger shot is the Doctor and Zoe, when, from a modern perspective, it's clear that the far more bizarrely chilling moment would be to cut back to Jamie and have him read out loud about their horrible fate, then cut to credits.) Or, perhaps more significantly, Jamie and Zoe are at one point made fictional, and the Doctor at one point frets that if he writes himself into the story directly he'll become fictional.

Let's say that again to really stress the weirdness of it. The primary threat in this story is that the characters will become fictional. This is, of course, a brilliant use of existential horror and one of the highlights of the story. But thinking about that from a remotely human perspective, it does not actually make any sense. It's impossible to imagine how someone could ever "become fictional." The only way in which a person can meaningfully be threatened by fictionality is if they are already a character in a story. In other words, if they are already in some sense fictional and what is going on is not "becoming fiction" but rather "losing realness." After all, the story does establish that fictional characters cannot be destroyed, and at the end, for no explained reason, the Doctor and company survive when the Land of Fiction is destroyed. Why would this be?

The simplest explanation of all of this is that, on some level, the Doctor has always been a part of the Land of Fiction—intended to be its master and controller. And that he escaped. Thematically, this makes sense. Going back to Whitaker's conception of the TARDIS, if we look at how the ship is explained in *An Unearthly Child*, one of the most unusual things about it is that the Doctor explains the TARDIS via the metaphor of television. This recurs in *The Time Meddler*, where the Doctor describes some controls to Steven, all of which are recognizable as television controls. And in *The Chase*, where what kicks off the destabilization of the narrative is the threat that the Doctor might trade in the TARDIS for watching stuff on television. Indeed, the opening credits of the show are done with a technique called howlaround that is based on exploiting and manipulating the technical limits of television signals. And Miles and Wood write several times about how Troughton's Doctor often peers out of television screens, both in the story (as when he appears on a monitor in *The Wheel in Space*) and outside of it, when he looks at the camera itself. And when he looks out, he appears aware of what he is looking at, a consequence of his tendency to play the character from the marginal spaces at the edges of scenes to begin with so that his power is not diminished by his lack of physical presence. The sense is that the Doctor can cross the thin membrane that separates the world behind the screen from the world in front of it.

In other words, since day one the Doctor has been a character who appears to harness the basic power of television. And he has consistently used this power in order to tell stories. He appears to be someone who can create an infinite number of stories. He has, in other words, always fulfilled the role of the Master of the Land of Fiction, except instead of writing stories by sitting on the sidelines he writes them mercurially— by throwing himself into them and creating them through his own existence in them.

Put simply, months before *The War Games*, *The Mind Robber* has quietly given us an origin story for the Doctor that is almost, but not quite, what we eventually get from the later "official" version. (After all, it is not as though no writer in the first six years had a guess on where the Doctor came from. If I could conjure up David Whitaker and ask him one question, in fact, it would be what he thought the Doctor's origin was.) The Doctor fled from a position of responsibility, stole a spaceship (or, in this case, storytelling medium), and ran off to have adventures. Except that instead of being a Time Lord from Gallifrey, he is the designated Master of the Land of Fiction— the writer and creator of all stories. And he's gone on the run to live the stories instead of simply writing them.

Notably, this never quite gets contradicted, even when this shadow theme of *The Mind Robber* gets revisited as the main plot of the final two episodes of the season. Because the Land of Fiction is outside of the universe, and because the Doctor fled into the universe, he presumably became "real" instead of just fictional. And thus he became something else that served much of the same narrative function; instead of a wanderer in the dimension of narrative, he is a wanderer in the dimension of time. The Time Lords, with their "look but don't touch" ethos and distance from the world, are a fair enough metaphor for the Land of Fiction itself. So the fact that he is something else outside of the Land of Fiction is hardly an issue.

In fact, it's to be expected. After all, we navigate time, internally, through memory and stories, through our minds, which are, of course, far bigger on the inside than the mere lump of grey matter they appear to be externally. What is a Lord of Time if not the master of all things that have happened, and thus of all metaphors and stories? Except, of course, the Doctor storms out, rejecting his people. Why? Because the Time Lords are far too narrow-minded. They are masters only of the stories that have happened. They cannot interfere and create new stories. And the Doctor is a Lord of all stories, whether real or imagined.

But more important than the fact that this theory can survive almost any canon challenge thrown at it is the fact that it makes sense beyond mere continuity. What defines Doctor Who is the fact that its story never has to end. That any story worth telling can be told as a Doctor Who story, and that there is no upper bound to the number of Doctor Who stories that can be told. Of course the Doctor is the destined and designated Master of the Land of Fiction. Who else possibly could be? What other person in the universe, real or imaginary, could possibly have the job of telling every story that ever was?

And that's the genius of *The Mind Robber*. It comes at one of the series' darkest moments—when its formula seems tired, its very ethics seem to be flagging, and when the entire cultural and ideological foundation for it appears to be crumbling the world over. And right in that moment, we get explicit confirmation of something that previously we had only hoped for and suspected. That Doctor Who is an idea that cannot be brought to an end. That there is always another story. Not just because of the flexibility of the premise or because the series has gone on long enough that it's a cultural institution that is always going to be revisited as long as we have well enough recorded history to remember that it ever existed. No. Because the Doctor is every single story there ever was and ever could be, escaped out into the universe, and running loose bringing them into being.

This is, quite frankly, as powerful an idea as has ever been thought of in fiction. An idea that is far larger than fits in any one person's imagination, even if that imagination is bigger on the inside. Something that, quite apart from anyone's efforts to define it and create it, has taken on a life of its own. A symbol that has real power. A thought that has begun thinking for itself. A dream that no longer needs anyone but itself to dream it.

What if, in 1963, these things did occur? What if we held them to be true? There are, after all, truths beyond mere canon.

An Outrageous Amount of Running (*The Invasion*)

It's November 2, 1968. Mary Hopkin is at number one with "Those Were the Days," with Joe Cocker at number two. He overtakes her one week later, and is in turn overtaken by the theme to *The Good, The Bad, and The Ugly*. It lasts until the last two weeks of this story, at which point "Lily the Pink" by The Scaffold, a comedy band featuring Paul McCartney's brother, takes over. Elsewhere in the top ten over these eight weeks one can find Jose Felicano's cover of "Light My Fire" and Hendrix's version of "All Along the Watchtower." Elsewhere in music, Elvis makes his comeback and The Beatles release the *White Album*.

In other news, Richard Nixon is elected President of the United States, bringing, in effect, all hope the left might have ever had over the 1960s to a crashing end, as we have already mentioned. In more subtle news, Douglas Engelbert demos the NLS, or oN-Line System, in an event called the "mother of all demos." Although at the time known only to a small core of technical users, this is one of the most important events in the history of computers, and the technology Engelbert shows off here ends up being the basic underpinning of the modern desktop computer. Among the concepts debuting here are the mouse and the idea of "windows" within a computer system, and the first major debut of word processing on the computer.

While on television we have *The Invasion*. Essentially a backdoor pilot for the Pertwee era of Doctor Who, this story exists primarily to try out a new format whereby the Doctor is the assistant of a military organization called UNIT who battles alien threats on Earth. Here, to kick things off in a big way, the Doctor reteams with Colonel Lethbridge-Stewart from *The Web of Fear*—now given his more famous rank of Brigadier—to fight the Cybermen in London.

This is not, of course, the first time that the series has been set in London. In fact, it's the sixth major instance. First of all, *An Unearthly Child* opens there. From there, contemporary London is avoided until the end of the third season, but futuristic London is attacked by Daleks in *The Dalek Invasion of Earth*. Contemporary London finally gets its day in the sun in *The War Machines*, where it gets attacked by evil computers. From there we nip off to Gatwick Airport for *The Faceless Ones* and the start of *The Evil of the Daleks*, before returning to the Underground (and brief aboveground shots) in the aforementioned *The Web of Fear*.

But something is different this time. For the first time in a story set in a more or less contemporary London (the "more or less" aspect of it will be dealt with later), we have a focus on the idea that London—the very home of the program—is under real attack, with the sixth episode culminating in one of the great money-shot cliffhangers of Doctor Who as the Cybermen burst from the sewers and storm down the steps of St. Paul's Cathedral.

In other words, to understand this story we must first understand London itself. And so it is time here for the book to pay off a debt. On the blog this book is adapted from I've coined the term psychochronography to describe my approach to this project. The term is adapted from the existing concept of psychogeography, in turn yanked from writers such as Alan Moore and Iain Sinclair, both of whom I saw give a talk the week I wrote the first version of this essay, making this a particularly opportune time for some debt repayment. Psychogeography describes a form of writing in which the nature of a place is captured via the experience of moving through it according to logics other than those it was designed for—a concept known in the original Situationist conception as the dérive. Its most common technique under Iain Sinclair is the walking tour, in which the physical experience of walking through an urban space provides the narrative frame for an exploration of its history and future. (Psychochronography, a term of my own invention, attempts to move through stories and histories, providing a "walking" tour of a time period, generally through a specific cultural object.)

To that end, and since I was there anyway on vacation, I decided I'd go full psychogeographic for an entry. A walking tour of the London of 1960s Doctor Who—the major locations of the four of the six London stories to be set in central London, culminating in the steps to St. Paul's Cathedral, in the hopes that through this walk it is possible to understand *The Invasion*. It is an attempt to see what was invaded in 1968, and what remains of it over forty years later. The result, I fear, is an oddity for TARDIS Eruditorum. But Doctor Who, for its first twenty-six years at least, is a story of many things, and one of those things is London. I should, perhaps, allow for some specific explanation. The research for this walk was conducted on June 13, 2011. That said, in revising the piece some nine months later I have not shied from integrating facts and observations based on later events, including subsequent trips to London. Such material is mostly in the St. Paul's section towards the end.

Begin by emerging from Westminster station, a bizarre monument to neo-brutalist architecture renovated around the millennium—the most recent one, to be precise. Exit straight onto the Thames at one end of the Westminster Bridge. Originally slated for a good Dalek menacing in 2150, some four hundred years after its initial construction, plans for this invasion were shelved unexpectedly in 1999 when another one of London's myriad of architectural war crimes to celebrate the new millennium was committed, rendering the original and Ferris-wheel-free footage unexpectedly fictional. London, never a city with an excessive investment in its own skyline, was perhaps uniquely suited for the perversity of slapping up a Ferris wheel for the purposes of a broad city view.

The erection of Merlin Entertainments' London monument rendered this the first of many abandoned futures scattering London. Cross the bridge away from it and towards the Houses of Parliament, mysteriously visible from every window in every American comic book set in London, and you can just about feel it pulsing out the thoughts of the Nestene Consciousness—another future, unimaginable in the 1964 Lime Grove heat to which Jacqueline Hill, Alan Judd, and Ann Davies returned following their run.

Walking on, past the pipers and living statues that make up the mass and fabric of the modern London, past the monument to Boadicea, first-century queen of the Iceni tribe who led a rebellion against the Roman occupation of Britain, torching their settlement at Londinium. Already certain themes present themselves. Boadicea is neither the first nor last person who will be honored for London's destruction, nor is she the first or last woman with which London shall have a strangely ambiguous relationship. These themes, in turn, feed into Doctor Who, the long history of which is perpetually fascinated by massive amounts of devastation and problematic depictions of femininity.

A block past the bridge, turn onto Parliament Street amidst another iteration of that fantasy—the twenty-first century version of trench warfare in which London's streets are vivisected in the name of progress. On one corner, the row of anti-war protesters outside the Houses of Parliament, a mockup of the TARDIS inexplicably sitting next to a sign exhorting Obama to close Guantanamo. Given the distance of Obama from this place, it is difficult to say which is the more inappropriate monument.

Turn away from it and work your way along Parliament Street and Whitehall to the north, a sea of white stone edifices, monuments to the very offices of government now turned to watchtowers. Pass Downing Street, or rather, the mass of roadblock and security that constitutes David Cameron's literal public face. Then continue, past cabinet offices and more—the functions of government stocked behind a tourist facade that calls into question just how far from the American conception of politics one is. On the right, down the middle of Whitehall, are a row of monuments to Britain's modern military history and its dead, most notably the Cenotaph under which Barbara and her friends from an abandoned future sought brief refuge.

Emerge at last in Trafalgar Square, our final stop in our tour of this lost 2150. Encircled by a seemingly unbroken chain of double decker busses, this square pulls an odd double duty for Ms. Wright. Made strange and hostile in 2150, with Daleks milling about the famous lions, upon her return to London a year later it is one of the destinations in which she and her apparent lover Mr. Chesterton celebrate their return. In this gesture, we see the odd core of London—its abandoned futures and ossified pasts stacking up upon each other until every location has become strange. Even with its unceasing crowds and (at that time) countdown to the London Olympics, seemingly little more than another excuse to shred the city in the name of that ever-withdrawing future, there is the sense of stability here ... four lions anchoring it through all these imagined destinies of London.

Move on, up Charing Cross Road. Here the process Trafalgar Square began is under way in full, with London giving way to its tourist-trap twin. This stretch of road seems a mortuary of former television stars—Diana Rigg headlining *Pygmalion*, and, of course, David Tennant and Catherine Tate holding down *Much Ado About Nothing*. As Charing Cross ends and we depart Westminster, pass the latest film remade as a West End Musical, *Priscilla: Queen of the Desert* shoved, complete with garish high-heeled shoe, into an otherwise innocent theater.

Move on towards Tottenham Court Road, where expat American retailers like TJ Maxx (the second initial incremented by one in the UK) and formerly McDonald's-owned burrito joint Chipotle sit across the street from Foyles, the landmark London bookstore in which I was finally able to acquire a decent set of Iain Sinclair books, the author being maddeningly out of print in the US. Cross Manette Street, complete with helpfully labeled "licensed sex shop" and emerge to the ruins of Tottenham Court Road tube station, now a smoldering pile of "improvement."

Ease slowly around the construction border, around metallic-tinted plaster cast of Freddie Mercury, whose zombified essence now stars in a West End hit musical. At last round to Great Russell Street, turn once, and arrive at Bedford Square, where, in another lost future, the TARDIS added one more distinguished tenant to the ring around this private garden. Here we arrive in the false London of *The War Machines*. Continue down Bayley Street to return to Tottenham Court Road, then cross it and continue into Percy Street. Here we reach a tangle of small streets. The main, Rathbone Street, vents to several pedestrian alleys—Charlotte Place ahead, where the titular War Machines menaced London.

Duck through a small passageway to reach Eastcastle Street, and then the small throughway Berners Mews, which exits out to Goodge Street. Cross it and take Charlotte Street until it becomes Fitzroy Street. Here Doctor Who's false pasts meet its real past, as we are in the immediate vicinity of the famed Fitzroy Tavern, where those portions of fandom not too notorious for their work on the series itself meet monthly for a drink. Stories abound of puzzled fans resplendent in cosplay showing up unsuspecting and wandering the tavern bereft, assuming they have the wrong place. I'd not know, having never been in London on the right day of the month.

Here also we duck around the central set piece of *The War Machines*, the BT Tower, then known as Post Office Tower. This bizarre building—officially a secret until 1990, despite the fact that it looms massively for blocks in every direction—remains a communications hub for London, but casts now, as it did in 1966, a strange aura, its inappropriate architecture another lost future. Designed by Eric Bedford and G.R. Yeats in a striking and visually iconoclastic status, the building had a clear whiff of futurity around it when it was constructed across the early 1960s. But the future aesthetic it augured never arrived. It sits there still, unable now to look either forwards or backwards, left merely to spin madly in place.

By legend, then script editor Gerry Davis asked prospective scientific advisors to the show what menace might lurk in Post Office Tower seeping evil into London, and Kit Pedler proposed a computer which, under the pen of Ian Stuart Black, became WOTAN. Looking at these comfortable pedestrian alleyways, it is difficult to imagine this lost future. The paranoid aversion to the mainframe computer—the only kind known to 1966—seems ridiculous today. I photograph Post Office Tower with my iPhone, itself more powerful than WOTAN could have dreamed of being, then slip it back into my pocket, leave this abandoned future to rot, and make my way down Cleveland Street, the chthonic tower receding behind me.

To the right is a scrawl of graffiti, a brief outbreak of London punk, still a decade out from the era of Doctor Who I'm tracking, reminding me that "If graffiti changed anything, it would be illegal." From this helpful reminder I make my way to the other side of the Tottenham Court Road rubble, past the massive sex store querying why lingerie is so popular if love is blind. I ignore the advertisement offering me an excellent price on a rabbit vibrator and work my way down the alley until my eye is caught by the bizarre Tudor-style gardening hut in the center of Soho Square. Working my way through the square, I wind down Greek Street, sidle up Shaftsbury for a few blocks, and then turn southeast once more to reach Covent Garden.

Here we make our transition away from the lost future of *The War Machines*. The final *War Machines* location is a seemingly minor one—a bustle of morning activity shot at Covent Garden Market prior to the onslaught of computer-controlled death robots. Here we must pause to consider the arc of history and of this walk. The name Covent Garden comes from the Anglo-French, and is synonymous with "convent." The convent in question is the Abbey at Westminster, where first we set foot in the vicissitudes of London's streets, and this space originally formed a garden for that monastery before it was leased out in 1515. In 1552, Edward VI granted the land, seized from Westminster by his father during the process of dissolving the monasteries, to John Russell, 1st Earl of Bedford.

The plot stayed under control of the Russell family, who leased it out for various purposes, until 1918. During these centuries it was, at various times, a posh neighborhood, a red-light district, and an outdoor market. For our purposes, the most notable fact about it is probably the opening of the Church of St. Paul's in a seventeenth-century redesign, creating a through-line from here to our final destination. But for now, let us turn our attention to the stretch of Covent Garden along Floral St.—a row of archways caught on camera in *The War Machines*. This is more or less the furthest reach of WOTAN's malign influence, the last sputtering burst of digital static to pulse from Post Office Tower.

Pushing through the archways, we discover, then, the nail in that future's coffin—an Apple Store. This observation may seem nitpicky. Surely the ubiquity of computerized phones, still responding to the signals of the BT Tower, is in some sense a confirmation of *The War Machines*. But look again—this image of gigantic robots moving by the control of a single computer depends on the idea that these massive machines are extraordinary. Flip open a copy of *The Guardian* to read about the latest US drone strikes in Pakistan, or just look at it on your iPhone, and the idea of a single computer exerting such control becomes mad. The fear, like so much else, has dissolved into the cloud—or, as we see standing here, the iCloud.

From here we need step forward only in time to reach *The Web of Fear* in 1968. Where before we have been tracking the London of spires—Big Ben, Nelson's Column, and the Post Office Tower, here we move from the air to the earth. This is what Neil Gaiman, in his own homage to this mythic city, *Neverwhere*, memorably called London Below. Far below Covent Garden rumble the trains of the Piccadilly Line, carved out in the early days of the twentieth century in an outbreak of unexpected science fiction through the very ground of London.

We must pause here to look at the opening strains of a problem we deferred in *The Web of Fear* essay itself—one that will be a growing concern through the looming Pertwee era. Indeed, here in Covent Garden we must begin to face one of the great thorny continuity problems of Doctor Who: UNIT dating.

I will not spend excessive time tracing out the basic issue here. The crux of it is this—there are at least three completely contradictory accounts of when the UNIT stories take place. The first has them taking place more or less in the year they're transmitted, while the most extreme option, based primarily on dating information in *The Web of Fear*, has *The Invasion* taking place in 1980 and the Pertwee era extending from there. There is (as the next essay will spell out in more detail), no possible way to reconcile the on-screen information into a single timeline. Given this problem, we have a situation where fans have broken in to various camps on the subject of when the UNIT stories "happened."

In 2011, standing in Covent Garden and staring at these abandoned questions, there is a sense of ludicrousness to it. The question of when the UNIT stories happened is, in essence, a matter of dating events that firmly did not happen. When Doctor Who takes place in lost pasts or distant futures, it has a realism it can never have when it takes place in London near the time of broadcast. Whether *The Web of Fear* was meant to happen in 1968, along with its broadcast, or in 1975, some seven years later, in 2011 the real problem is the same: London was never evacuated due to an attack of robotic Yeti.

So when we walk two blocks north to Shelton Street and look at the ground the Yeti did not tread upon, what is it that we see? These monsters, from a different sort of monastery, are not entirely dissonant with this territory of Convent Garden, it's true. But then, what is dissonant with London? A palimpsest of a city, even its spires seem below ground, buried under their contrasting histories. What is there that cannot be found in London?

Walk on towards our final destination. Here the web of symbols and histories begins to crystalize. Down Long Acre until it becomes Great Queen Street, we pass London's Freemason's Hall, advertising a by then long-closed exhibit entitled "Building Solomon's Temple." Reach Kingsway, and Bush House, still for another year the home of the BBC World Service, and turn south, reaching St. Clement Danes. The church as it stands is a seventeenth-century design of Christopher Wren, although the idea of a church in that spot reaches back to the ninth century. Across the way is Australia House, the interior of which serves as Gringott's Bank in the Harry Potter films, and the exterior of which was an establishing shot in *The Invasion* before the Cybermen burst from the sewers.

From here proceed to the Strand, which descends towards Fleet Street, named for the buried River Fleet. This is the sort of city London is—whole rivers lurk below the surface of its present. It is on Fleet Street that another spire makes its appearance on the walk, the peak of the Swiss Re building, another bit of millennial construction replacing the proposed Millennium Tower with the somewhat less ambitious Millennium Cucumber. By and large, however, that awful spire is the outlier here. Fleet Street marks a descent—a sloping downhill incision through the layers of London through increasingly aged buildings.

If London is a palimpsest city, nowhere is that more evident than the crypt that is Fleet Street. Let us enumerate what is entombed here. To start, of course, a river. By tradition, stemming off from the Royal Courts of Justice, Fleet Street is the haven of barristers, and legal bookstores dot its aged storefronts. Past that are the banks, with every major British bank holding an office on Fleet Street, most notably Child & Co Bankers at 1 Fleet Street. Buried deeper than these are the origins of the British printing industry, the name Fleet Street remaining a shorthand for the journalistic profession that is no longer headquartered here. Towards the eastern end of the street is St. Bride's Church, another Christopher Wren design, although the church itself dates back to the seventh century. Exploded by a German bomb in 1940, the layers of palimpsest traumatically peeled back revealing the crypt below, now wrapped in tourist bunting, electrical conduits weaving through the ancient stonework.

St. Bride's, whose Wren-created design is said to be the model of the wedding cake (not Wren's only inadvertent brush with fertility rituals, as we shall see), is known as the Printer's Church by dint of the fact that the first moveable type printing press was brought there by Wynkyn de Worde in 1500. Here also was where Mary Ann Nichols wed printer William Nichols, who later abandoned her to have an affair, leaving her to slip into prostitution and be carved up by Jack the Ripper. This, in turn, points to the last great strand of meaning within Fleet Street, the smell of Mrs. Lovett's pies that wafts from every pub window.

Fleet Street gives way to Ludgate Circus. Here climb Ludgate Hill to reach the highest spire of Christopher Wren's church building—St. Paul's Cathedral. This towering edifice is familiar to anyone who has spent much time in the imagined depths of London, serving as the centerpiece of one of the key scenes of Alan Moore's *From Hell*. In this scene, itself a buried text beneath this one, William Gull, fingered by Moore as the Ripper, completes his own psychogeographic tour of London, tracing a pentagram of symbols around the center point of St. Paul's.

By tradition, a force far stronger than mere history, Ludgate Hill, upon which St. Paul's rests, is named after King Lud, apocryphal namesake of London. Symbolically, then, we are now at the beating heart of London, in the midst of the City of London itself. This small patch of land, metonymic with the financial institutions in whose name David Cameron clumsily wielded his veto power within the European Union, suggests a different sort of symbolic centrality. The similarities between finance and alchemy have been dryly and bitterly noted by others, but even beyond that there is a sense that we are at the true heart of power within Britain.

Strange then, that by tradition it is also on the site of an ancient temple to Diana—a fact which forms the heart of Moore's monologue. Walking through the Cathedral, his claim seems compelling—that something about the lunar cannot be erased, even within this manifestly solar sanctum. On the one hand, the solar nature of the place is screamed out in splashes of gold and vast vaulted domes; the god to whom it is consecrated is, in essence, a solar deity, bound in the familiar structure of death and rebirth that characterizes so many other theologies.

And yet the Cathedral brims with statues a mere breath from the Weeping Angels, cold stone reflecting a dreaming darkness that extends beyond the radiant displays of gold. Moore makes much of the fact that, into the twentieth century, women hugged the pillars of the building as a superstition to evoke fertility, the Dianic myth, like all other lost myths of London, having sunk into the very earth and stone itself.

If this dualism sits in the very heart of London, so too must it be said to sit at the heart of this exploration. Not merely in the rather Dionysian spirit of Troughton's Doctor as a contrast to the Apollonian sprawl embodied here but in a more fundamental dynamism. The solar Cathedral is too easy an ally for the triumphant establishment of the financial district. The very nature of the Cathedral is jarring—an opulent monument to deity with an overt hostility to opulence. The gold of the Cathedral is, let's face it, as perfect a metaphor for the triumph of capitalism as can be mustered.

And yet equally it is here that the four and a half month occupation of London by anti-capitalist protesters took place, kicking off some four months after the first draft of this piece was composed. The Occupy movement, informed by a resurgent interest in Situationist thought, marked a weird recurrence of the late '60s. Perhaps nothing so much as a new '68, a last gasp of counterculture resistance before the truncheons are warmed up, it is nevertheless oddly appropriate that the St. Paul's grounds should have been the last major Occupy site to remain, and should have drawn such unexpected blood from the management of the Cathedral. Certainly there can be little ambiguity which side of the debate Troughton's Doctor would have found himself on.

(This dualism extends into the ground itself. The crypt of St. Paul's contains a memorial to William Blake, the visionary poet whose work more loyal readers will know underpins my essay on the next Troughton/UNIT story. Blake—as far from a solar or establishment figure as it is possible to be—is an odd fit for the church, and yet despite no particular opulence to his memorial it merits a mark on the official map and an entry in the audio guide issued with admission. The guide, of course, butchers things, conflating Blake's massive epic poem *Jerusalem* with a section from the preface of *Milton: A Prophecy* that was set to music in 1916 and became the well-known hymn "Jerusalem.")

Raze London a thousand times yet—and have little doubt that, given time, this will happen—and Diana will always live upon this hill. Or does she rise up separately. Does this hill dream endlessly of a lunar goddess? Or was the lunar goddess—perhaps the moon itself—nothing more than the idle dream of Ludgate Hill?

Depart, down St. Peter's Steps towards the Millennium Bridge, then turn to see the ground the Cybermen stormed down. Let us pause to consider the basic spectacle here—the very idea of Cybermen in London. If London is a palimpsest of a city, then there are perhaps no monsters more suited to its streets than the Cybermen, themselves endlessly reinvented and reconceptualized. And likewise, if the lunar glow of Diana cannot quite be erased from the heart of London, leaving the city eternally a land of dreams and imagination, then the Qlippothic terror at the heart of the Cybermen too cannot be erased.

Miles and Wood suggest that the real point of *The Invasion* is to relaunch the program, with the Cybermen just being thrown in to spice things up a bit. But it is more than that. The Cybermen, from the start, have been agents of strange and alien change. This is in the very idea of them, as much as Diana is in the very idea of St. Paul's, or the buried river is in the very idea of Fleet Street. As much as tearing London down is in the very idea of London.

Is this, then, the key to UNIT dating? Had the UNIT stories emerged with any setup other than the invasions of London it might be different. Instead we are faced with impossible monsters whose very setup—a non-existent invasion in 1968—marks them as a lost future, invading a city whose very nature is that no version of itself is truly lost, merely buried, waiting to be dug up and gutted anew. A city where nothing lasts and everything remains.

The true strangeness of the UNIT dating controversy is this—to anyone who came at the stories after all possible dates they could have happened—someone, in other words, of my generation—it is transparently obvious when they happened. The Brigadier's line about the length of time from *The Web of Fear* to *The Invasion* notwithstanding, it is clear that both are set in 1968. A lost future belongs nowhere but the time it was dreamed of. And *The Invasion*'s future was lost within weeks of transmission. Its first episode includes a shot of the far side of the moon, a vista whose true face was revealed for the first time only a few weeks later by Apollo 8, which was launched the same day the final episode of *The Invasion* aired.

To put it another way, it does not, in the end, matter when the UNIT stories happened. It is enough that the place where they never actually happened is some imagined London, buried underground like everything else, and thus as real as anything that actually happened in London. The stories themselves are about the years they were transmitted, and their fears and terrors are fears of their audience. It does not matter if they never happened in the year they were broadcast or if they never happened in some future year that itself never really happened. The truth is this: they never happened in London, and thus live forever in its stones.

The Invasion Redux

Since I did, in some ways, sidestep the actual story with my psychogeographic take on *The Invasion*, it seemed only right to set things at least partially right and toss in a side essay about, you know, the actual story. This is harder than it might appear. *The Invasion* is an oddity in that it loses definition to both the future and the past. On the one hand it is unabashedly a remake of *The Web of Fear* that's been souped-up a bit. On the other it's consciously a backdoor pilot for the UNIT era. This leads some people to think that *The Web of Fear* and the UNIT era are equivalent. We've seen how that misrepresents *The Web of Fear* already, but it in many ways poses a larger problem for this story, which, looking as it does like two other things, has precious little ability to speak for itself.

On top of this, it's one of the handful of Troughton stories we have the majority of. With only two episodes missing, both of which have been animated—and quite well to boot—this story represents fifteen percent of our existing episodes of Troughton. All of this is, quite frankly, a bit too much for the poor story to handle. While *The Invasion* is a hefty story, serving as the stand-in for the much-desired *Web of Fear*, as the pilot to the entire Pertwee era, and as a major representative of the Troughton era is more weight than it can bear.

In truth the story isn't quite any of these things. That it was not meant to be one of the few surviving stories of the Troughton era is obvious. The other two are less so. The success of *The Web of Fear* led the show to try again, it's true, but the differences between the stories are significant. *The Web of Fear* is a story about mistrusting everybody and increasing paranoia. *The Invasion* consciously brings back a character from *The Web of Fear* in order to build a significant body of clearly trustworthy characters. *The Invasion* hinges on the fact that it's obvious from the start who the villain is—an almost complete inversion of how *The Web of Fear* works.

Meanwhile, even as the Pertwee era looms in the future the degree to which this serves as a pilot is incidental. Yes, it introduces the UNIT crew, but the Brigadier is incidental to this—indeed, it's during this story that the idea of having him be a regular occurs to anyone. So it's less that this story was a trial of the new setup as that the setup of this story looked good and got adapted. But even then the Brigadier underwent a fairly substantial revision between this and *Spearhead from Space*.

But the more important thing to point out about the Brigadier is that he's a relatively minor character in this story. His main role is to tell us about the very impressive things people are doing off-camera to deal with the threats in the story. A story like this needs someone like him—the series in 1968 was never going to manage to have the bulk of the military and cultural response to an invasion by Cybermen happen on screen. We're lucky we got St. Paul's, frankly. And so a character like the Brigadier who can nip off screen for a bit then come back and tell the Doctor what's happened is important.

No, the real content of this story is the opposition between the Doctor and Tobias Vaughn. This isn't something Troughton gets to do all that often—there's really only a few stories in which Troughton gets a human counterpart to deal with as the primary villain. This is not entirely surprising—Troughton is a hard actor to be paired against. Joseph Furst—no slouch as an actor himself—was left with little to do but gnaw furiously upon all available scenery. Actors like Emrys Jones are almost completely out to sea. Edward Brayshaw and Philip Madoc will eventually manage in *The War Games*, but it's worth noting that the only person to manage to stand up as a human villain opposite Patrick Troughton prior to this story is, in fact, Patrick Troughton himself.

But here Kevin Stoney, previously sublime as Mavic Chen in *The Daleks' Master Plan*, shows himself up to the task. Vaughn is superlative as a villain, leering majestically over the proceedings. The bulk of the plot constitutes his slow chess match with the Doctor over the backdrop of a Cybermen invasion and Vaughn's increasingly desperate attempts to keep control of the situation.

In this regard we get to see a slow motion and character-based version of the Doctor's usual tearing down of society. Vaughn is an arch-industrialist—a paragon of the capitalist, consumerist order of the world. And the Doctor brings him down gradually, over eight whole episodes. Instead of simply watching him undermine the social order, then, we get to see it happen to one specific person, and at a gradual enough speed as to not just be lightweight fun. This is the most direct critique that the series makes of Troughton's Doctor and of the nature of his anarchism prior to *The War Games*, and in that regard the way in which it sets up the status quo for the era that follows is wholly apropos.

But none of that has to do with the bits of the story everyone focuses on—its "aliens attack London only bigger" is, well, exactly what you do after aliens attack London. The fact that Nicholas Courtney was very good at standing in for an actual budget made him a sensible hire for the future. But what this story is really about is finding an excuse to take two great actors—Troughton and Stoney—and put them in a bunch of scenes together. It performs that job admirably.

A Mineral Slime (*The Krotons*)

It's December 28, 1968. The Scaffold still have number one with "Lilly the Pink," with The Foundations in number two with "Build Me Up Buttercup." Just that kind of week, I suppose. A week later Marmalade, the first Scottish group ever to hit number one, does so with a cover of The Beatles's "Ob-La-Di Ob-La-Da." They proceed to trade back and forth with The Scaffold for the rest of the story. Fleetwood Mac, The Foundations's version of "Build Me Up Buttercup," Stevie Wonder, Herman's Hermits, and Dusty Springfield also chart, the latter with "Son of a Preacher Man."

Out of the charts, the first photos of the far side of the moon are taken by Apollo 8, Rupert Murdoch makes his entry into the British press by buying *News of the World*, The Troubles get more troublesome, and the Waverly Line is abandoned for good. So really, not a great month for Britain, with continued echoes of 1968 ricocheting through the culture. Though again, as awful as Rupert Murdoch is, it's tough, in historical terms, to view his entry into the British press as anything other than a pale echo of Richard Nixon's re-entry into American politics. As I've said previously, Britain had a pretty good 1968 as 1968s go.

So *The Krotons*, then. This story has an odd reputation not helped by the fact that it was the Patrick Troughton story picked for the 1981 Five Faces of Doctor Who string of reruns. The importance of these reruns can't be overstated—in 1981, a whole generation of Doctor Who fans existed who had never seen Troughton. Not that they were unaware of Troughton—the existence of the Target novelizations and a genuine working memory of the show ensured that. But there were simply no opportunities for people to see him. And so for a while Troughton was known entirely by reputation. And the reputation was largely the "base under siege" reputation—for years the only four Troughton stories to be novelized were *The Abominable Snowmen*, *The Moonbase*, *The Ice Warriors*, and *The Web of Fear*, with *The War Games* joining the list in 1980 and, somewhat puzzlingly, *Enemy of the World* in 1981. And so people had a fairly solid idea of the Troughton era. But that idea was definitely not *The Krotons*, a story that would have left most viewers saying "the whats?" (It was picked for the simple reason that the Five Faces repeats ran Mondays through Thursdays, and in 1981 it was the only four-part Troughton story that existed.)

So the initial reaction to this one—and we've discussed enough times how initial reactions from the '80s and '90s colored fan reactions for decades to come—was puzzlement, and, predictably, that has endured with the general reaction to *The Krotons* still being puzzlement in 2011. Miles and Wood suggest that the root problem is that it doesn't quite fit with anyone's memory of what the Troughton era should be. But having endured the classic "monster" season and found it somewhat wanting, one struggles to, watching it in sequence, get particularly upset about the fact that it's not the bog-standard monster runaround everyone expects a Troughton story to be. The question is what sort of story it is.

Were this from the other end of the "monster" season—i.e. a Season Four yarn—and if it were a missing story its reputation would probably be right around that of *The Faceless Ones* or *The Macra Terror*, or, from a bit earlier, *The Savages*—reasonably well-regarded non-classics. Except that there's a confidence to the program in Season Six that it didn't have two years earlier, and this shines through in *The Krotons*. (Two years earlier, for reference, are *The Highlanders* and *The Underwater Menace*.) The result is that *The Krotons* has a composure and intelligence to its construction, even if the overall product seems ever so slightly out of step with what we expect Doctor Who to be heading into 1969.

Which is a strange thing to be saying about the debut of Robert Holmes, who will go on to write for the program through to 1986 and become its most prolific and acclaimed writer. But the fact of the matter is, Holmes handed in a script that feels distinctly like Doctor Who of old—it's just that at this point in the series history, Doctor Who of old feels oddly fresh. Which is worth remarking on. It's worth specifically noting that Doctor Who, in its first six seasons, was making forty or more episodes a year, as compared to the roughly twenty-six it will settle on as the norm from Seasons Seven through Twenty-Two. The fourth episode of *The Krotons* is the 230th episode of the series. By comparison, if you start from *Spearhead from Space* the 230th episode is the fourth part of *The Ribos Operation*. In other words, even though it looks from a modern perspective like we're still very early in the history of Doctor Who, the Doctor Who of *The Krotons* is not a young show by any measure. We're at a point where "this is an updating of a story style from a previous era of the show" can't be treated as a problem. At this point, showing off what the show has learned by redoing old classics is part of what the show should be doing, both to show its own growth and because we're at a point where people probably haven't seen the classics and you can get away with doing them anew.

So let's look at what *The Krotons* does that moves things forward. I mean, it's not that it doesn't have silly problems as well. I'm pretty sure the acting in this one is what Steven Moffat had in mind when he famously snarked that some of the actors in the Troughton era should never have gotten their Equity cards. Both Hines and Padbury are off their game here, but worse is the supporting cast, almost all of which is, in this story, barely watchable. On top of that, the monster design is … well, actually, it's quite good until you run into the problem that the costumes were made way too short and had rubber skirts tacked onto their bottoms to actually cover the actors.

(Maloney does a heroic job trying to hide this, managing to make it until the fourth episode before it becomes clear that the monsters are rubbish.)

But past that, there are some things here that make *The Krotons*, if not a revolutionary moment where Doctor Who steps forward, at least one where one can see that there is forward momentum in the show. For one thing, Robert Holmes can actually be bothered to create a world in which things happen instead of slapping together some base commanders and a monster and calling it a day. *The Krotons* doesn't satisfy the concerns I raised back in *The Ice Warriors* and *The Enemy of the World* by any stretch of the imagination—it's impossible to come up with any sense of what the Gonds did in a normal day before the Doctor arrived. They seem completely ill-suited to normal day-to-day life.

But on the other hand, the story is actually about them. The Doctor, Jamie, and Zoe are external forces that intersect with this world and throw it into chaos. Yes, the idea of the world before they showed up is painfully underdeveloped, but that overlooks something really unusual for a Troughton-era story—the characters here have traits that are not directly related to their competence in dealing with monsters. Compare that to any of the bases under siege, where any given character has basically no traits that don't directly relate to how they're going to handle being under an invasion, and *The Krotons* stands in sharp and satisfying relief—its characters have distinct approaches and worldviews that come in conflict. When Eelek and Selris come into conflict over how to deal with the Krotons, it's not that Selris is a better leader and Eelek is a spineless incompetent—it's that they have two very different views of how to handle the situation.

Part of this comes down to a subtle but interesting thing. If you want to do a story in which evil aliens menace people, there are two basic approaches—either the aliens invade within the story, or they've already invaded and the story is about liberating people from them. Base under siege stories are, generally speaking, invasion stories—a defined territory is penetrated by aliens that must be repelled. But this is the opposite—Gond society has already been taken over by the Krotons. By definition, that means that the story is about the world that the monsters have created as opposed to just about fighting the monsters off. This is, in most cases, a more interesting take, in that it requires the show have an idea beyond a cool costume for a nasty. (This observation, unfortunately, has some unfortunate implications for the Pertwee era.)

The second big thing that Holmes manages here is to use the Doctor and his companions' character traits in interesting ways that get the characters to do things that are more complex rather than just pragmatic. As good as Hines and Troughton are together (and they are a quite good comedic double act), they've never really had a scene as good as the one in which the Doctor and Zoe get progressively irritated at each other as they try to pass the Krotons' tests, with the Doctor snapping at Zoe "Now go away and don't fuss me ... no, come back, what's this? ... It's all right, I know," and Zoe insisting that the Doctor is "almost as clever as I am" and pouting that the Doctor only got a higher score because he answered more questions than she did.

What's interesting about this scene is that it's a character-based comedy of a sort we haven't really seen from Doctor Who before. The companions aren't just there to fulfill the plot functions of being menaced or beating things up here—they're actually people who act in a particular way, and do so for more than just one-liners. In the past, this sort of thing has been confined to the TARDIS scenes at the beginning or end of a story, with generic comedic banter that was, if anything, based on the endless "Jamie is thick" jokes. That's distinctly different from Zoe and the Doctor having an extended scene in which how they act in a given set of circumstances is defined by who they are. The scene isn't about the Doctor and Zoe, it's about trying to sneak into the Kroton ship. But everything that happens in it is defined purely by the sorts of people Zoe and the Doctor are. And it's clear Troughton relishes it—he's having as much fun as he's had on the series in ages in this story, to the point where one imagines that if it had come where *The Dominators* did in the run we might have had a Troughton season in color.

We also have, with this story, one of the clearest moments of the embrace of psychedelia in Doctor Who. The Doctor teaches the Gonds to mix up acid and overthrow their bland and cruel masters who fill them with a head full of useless facts and don't prepare them for the real world. It's such a perfect resolution to a story for Troughton's Doctor that it's easy to forget that psychedelic anarchism isn't actually business as usual for his era.

My point is not that *The Krotons* is some work of profound genius. It's not. But on the other hand, those who first saw it in 1981 with the strange sense that this was not what the Troughton era was supposed to be like were wrong. This is, above everything else, a strange and intriguing tease of what the Troughton era could have been. And indeed, all things considered, what it should have been. It's a pity, really, that it comes so close at the end of it.

Time Can Be Rewritten: *The Prison in Space*

The idea of lost stories is interesting. Not missing episodes—those are also interesting, and dealt with in a few essays' time—but stories that were abandoned before being made. Ones that never happened. For we fans, of course, they provide a tantalizing allure. Not only are they potential additions to the existing body of Doctor Who stories, they crackle with both an authenticity (they're actually products of their eras) and with the mysterious glamour of what might have been. It's no wonder, then, that the efforts of Big Finish to produce the unmade scripts of Doctor Who are treasured—especially things like *The Song of Megaptera* or *Paradise Five* that offer the opportunity to see how respected writers like Pat Mills or P.J. Hammond would have approached Doctor Who.

On the other hand, sometimes there's a reason why something was left unmade. Case in point, Dick Sharples's *The Prison in Space*, a story that was left unmade for the relatively straightforward reason that it was an appallingly sexist and offensive piece of garbage that should never have been commissioned in the first place. What, then, are we supposed to make of its resuscitation some forty years later as an audio narrated by Frazer Hines and Wendy Padbury?

From a historical or scholarly perspective the question is tricky. On the one hand, there is a genuine amount of information to be gained from it. Especially given that there are so many issues with sexism and the 1960s series (and the 1970s series, and the 1980s ...) it's interesting to see exactly what constituted a story so sexist that they wouldn't make it. Archival scholars have a certain consistency on this point. You're hard-pressed to find a film scholar who agrees that Disney's *Song of the South* should never be re-released, for instance, or who doesn't want to see a cut of *Fantasia* with Sunflower, the minstrel stereotype centaur, reinserted so they can see what the film was like in the 1940s.

On the other hand, this is different. *Song of the South* and *Fantasia* happened. They were real films that got made, sent to theaters, and were watched by millions of people. To want to see them is to want to learn more about an actual historical event. The films already exist. Whereas *The Prison in Space* didn't exist prior to 2009. To make this story into something more than just a discarded concept required, in other words, active effort to make a story that was previously considered too sexist to make.

The first question, of course, is whether that judgment was correct. This is not a hard question. That judgment is absolutely correct. The premise of this story is that the Earth has had its government overthrown by women, led by a woman called Chairman Babs, who have abolished war and violence but who have also, it turns out, created a fascistic state where men are oppressed as "inferiors" and routinely carted off to the eponymous prison in space. The Doctor, Jamie, and Zoe show up and eventually restore order, but not before we have a lot of horrific sequences of Chairman Babs—explicitly portrayed as an overweight "toad" of a woman—mooning over the Doctor as a perfect man and falling deliriously in love with him. And of Zoe being brainwashed by the "silver maiden" into being a man-hating feminist and only being brought back to reality when Jamie spanks her at the end. It is, in other words, impossible to read as anything other than a story about how feminism is evil and needs to be stopped.

Let's square away a possible objection here, if only to clean up an old point from the previous volume about *The Savages*. The idea of *The Savages* is that the elders—who are played blacked up—are oppressing the savages in the wilderness outside, who are white. The original title, in fact, was *The White Savages*. And several people, when citing my sharp criticisms of *The Celestial Toymaker* and *The Ark* on racial grounds have pointed to *The Savages* as a third example of horrific racism in the third season.

Respectfully, I disagree. *The Savages* is a straightforward piece of racial inversion—a story that is plainly about showing the absurdity of racism by simply reversing the colors. Notably the elders do not display the stereotypical traits of Africans. It's a complete reversal of the entire stereotype—the white people are the uneducated savages and the black people are the civilized scientists. The only thing that is reversed from the colonial order of things that the story is critiquing is what color each side is.

But this logic can't be used to defend *The Prison in Space* as a story that exposes the absurdity of sexism by showing how wrong it would be to oppress men like that. Because *The Prison in Space* both explicitly aligns the domineering women with feminism and takes explicit swipes at their gender. The fact that the rise of Chairman Babs is explicitly linked with progressive causes like pacifism makes it impossible to treat it as a straight role reversal. The story is unambiguously a dystopia about what would happen if those feminist hippies won.

And similarly, the portrayal of women in the story goes out of its way to make them dislikable for reasons that connect to existing threads of misogyny. It's not just the idea that even a hard-nosed and powerful woman like Chairman Babs is vulnerable to her sexual desire for men. It's the fact that Chairman Babs is shown to be attracted to men after all, when otherwise she'd be clearly read as a lesbian, and the appalling heteronormativity implied by it. It's the fact that the contrast between her age and unattractiveness and her fawning desire is played for laughs where the joke is clearly that the Doctor would never have any feelings for such a woman (and indeed runs in terror from her, because there's nothing scarier than being tied down by a woman). It's the fact that the script repeatedly stresses the tight-fitting black outfits of the women, making it clear that even when the women are in charge they're meant to be nothing but sex objects. It's the fact that it's made explicit that before the women of the world could reject Chairman Babs they had to be inspired by the Doctor, because of course women can only do the right thing with a man to lead them. And it's the fact that Jamie, who spends the whole story talking about how women should know their place, ultimately gets to win out over Zoe and spank away her feminism.

So the decision to spike this story at the last moment and replace it with *The Krotons* was straightforward. This story was indefensible. But what do we do with its recreation forty years later? It is, after all, at least somewhat interesting to see what this story was and to get a sense of the full extent of the horror. But the horror is, in the end, all there is. There's very little to this script beyond a pile of horrifically sexist jokes. The description we had to go on for years—that it was a misogynistic story that ended with Jamie literally smacking the feminism out of Zoe—turns out to have been completely accurate.

And so it's difficult to find much to like in the resulting recording. Frazer Hines does a reasonably good imitation of Patrick Troughton that captures his diction well, even if it is a bit flat and subdued compared to Troughton's actual performance. (Hines's Troughton tends to growl and grumble, losing the manic eagerness of Troughton himself.) But this is two and a half hours of unfunny sexist humor for twenty-five quid. And there's something unsettling about the fact that effort went into making a recording of this script exist—and particularly that Wendy Padbury, who had previously been spared having to record having the feminism beaten out of her, got the dubious honor of being a part of it. Certainly it's a waste of the talent of Simon Guerrier, who adapted the script to be suitable for audio, and who could surely have been doing something less contemptible than this.

It's perhaps worth comparing this to the other version of *The Prison in Space* that exists—a scriptbook published by *Nothing at the End of the Lane*, a fanzine dedicated to historical research of Doctor Who that attempts to find missing material, both recorded episodes and scripts. That book approaches the matter from a purely historical perspective, treating the script as an odd and admittedly troubling artifact from the 1960s.

But this is different. Big Finish doesn't just invite us to learn about the unmade story, it invites us to enjoy it and take pleasure in it. Despite the fact that it was rightly spiked for being a nasty little thing. And there is something genuinely wrong with that. It's wholly appropriate to be troubled by the invitation to enjoy misogyny.

And this gets at something important when dealing with the bigotries of the past when they apply to something like Doctor Who. The desire to learn more about the series' history too often becomes a convenient cloak to hide the judgment that a bit of misogyny or racism can be excused in the name of seeing more Doctor Who. Yes, plenty of film scholars would be fascinated by the opportunity to see a cut of *Fantasia* with Sunflower, and a number of scholars would have a much easier time with their research if there were legal copies of *Song of the South* circulating. But nobody in their right mind wants Sunflower reinstated in the normal home video release, and it's hard to seriously argue that *Song of the South* should just be slapped on DVD and released to the mass market as opposed to made available as part of one of Disney's explicitly archival lines of DVDs.

Similarly, as interesting as it is to know exactly what the production team of 1968 thought was too sexist, this isn't a story like *Evil of the Daleks* that's both good and offensive. This is a story whose only ideas are morally reprehensible and that exists to do nothing but demean and belittle women. The fact that it's a Doctor Who story doesn't make that OK, and wanting to experience it and enjoy it because it's a Doctor Who story means willfully overlooking its ethical failings for no reason other than that it's called Doctor Who.

It is difficult to seriously argue in favor of this. And it's difficult to say that the world was in any way improved by *The Prison in Space* finally getting made. An unmade story always has a reason why it wasn't made. When that reason is that a season only has room for six stories and this was the seventh best script submitted, that's one thing. When it's that the script submitted was ethically bankrupt, well, sometimes there's a good reason why something wasn't made. And in this case, now there's a bad reason why it was made as well.

Elizabeth Sandifer

Pop Between Realities, Home in Time for Tea: *2001: A Space Odyssey*, *Star Trek*, Moon Landing

In the White Wolf roleplaying game *Changeling: The Dreaming*, the point in the '60s that is flagged as being the zenith of hope and dreams and beauty is the moon landing. What utter rubbish.

For one thing, as we've already seen, the idealistic aspects of '60s culture were inexorably tied to a form of left-wing radicalism, to an extent that Doctor Who, by embracing a psychedelic aesthetic, lodged a radically leftist approach at the heart of what it does. It is in no way the case that this approach, or, for that matter left-wing politics in general, ended in 1968, but the fundamental shift described in this entry was that political liberalism shifted from being in the ascendency to being on the defensive. Which means that the idea that any culminating event in the realm of hope and utopian ideology happening in 1969 and from the Nixon administration is fundamentally ludicrous.

The moon landing, in many ways, is a perfect way into just how complex leftist politics of the 1960s were. On the one hand, even if it was Nixon who was President when the moon landing took place, the Apollo program was largely a product of the New Frontier style of liberalism espoused by Kennedy. Kennedy's youthfulness is, in the popular imagination, tied inexorably to the youth culture from which the radical current of the 1960s arose, but the fact of the matter is that the moon landing (and the Kennedy administration as it actually existed)

259

was no darling of the radical left, with the usual refrain being some observation about throwing money away in space when there are so many problems here on Earth.

So what was the moon landing, if not one of the high points of the utopian '60s? By and large, it was a dead end. The reality turned out to be that space is enormously expensive and lacking in all practical value. The moon wasn't our first step into space—it was our last one, with no realistic plan in existence over forty years later to even return there, little yet to push on to Mars or elsewhere. Why? Mainly because there's no visible point. No cost-efficient way of gathering any materials from foreign worlds exists or appears to exist. No life or habitability appears to exist. And once we get out past Mars we rapidly reach a point where we are putting people in capsules for obscenely long amounts of time so that they can walk on rocks no more habitable than the last uninhabitable rock they walked on.

In other words, all visible evidence regarding any point in space that we can get to suggests that we are alone and would be spending massive amounts of money for nothing other than the sake of getting there. As long as this remains the case—and there's no particular reason to think it's changing at any point in the near future—space travel will never be a major priority of any organization with the money to accomplish it. In this regard, then, the real question is why we were even doing it in the '50s and '60s. And the truth of the matter is that the moon landing was really just a victory in the Cold War.

Let's rewind, actually, and look at how we got to the moon. Mostly, it's Hitler's fault. In all seriousness, the use of rockets for space travel mostly comes down to the fact that Hitler was oddly obsessed with the things and happened to have (before he destroyed it by driving all the Jews out) more or less the best science program in the world. And so rocket technology advanced considerably in Nazi Germany. And perhaps more importantly, once the war ended, there were an awful lot of unemployed German rocket scientists.

Thankfully, rockets were handy things to strap atomic weapons to. If you happened to have, as the US and USSR both did, obscenely deadly weapons of mass destruction that you really didn't want to be near when they blew up, suddenly hiring a few rocket scientists—particularly when they were readily available—became tempting. Since accuracy is not a massive issue with a hydrogen bomb, the fact that the rockets were crap at accuracy was no particular barrier. And since the US and USSR were both decked out with high quality Nazi scientists who were, by dint of their last projects, all very good at rockets, they developed rockets. Indeed, Eisenhower is supposed to have remarked, when asked why the USSR was ahead of the US in the space race, "their German scientists are better than our German scientists."

So why space? Here's the thing. It's not very nice to show off your rocket technology by nuking people. And so the US and USSR had to, in order to thump their chests and proclaim their superior ability to blow things up, find something that quietly implied their blowing-up ability while not actually engaging in unfortunate and likely apocalypse—producing acts such as annihilating major metropolitan areas in horrific nuclear holocausts. The obvious choice was space travel. And so to the moon we went in what was basically a nice, sanitized PR proxy for the arms race.

In practice, that's all the space race was: a high profile public relations front for the business of preparing for the slaughtering of millions of civilians in the Cold War, dressed up in patriotic bunting. And once the agreed upon goal had been reached and the US reached the moon, that was basically it for the space race. After that, space served precious little purpose. We went through the motions of Mir and Skylab, Soyuz and Shuttle, but it was by that point something else, and it's hard to be surprised now as manned spaceflight steadily peters out. Even in its current form, where private spaceflight seems more promising—indeed, even if we return to the moon or make it to Mars—the fact of the matter is that space travel has no visible future except as a richer and more eccentric version of climbing Mount Everest—something people with a lot of money do to satisfy their thrill-seeker urges.

Which brings us to the other key aspect of the space race. The thing that was not so much what was happening as what a particular segment of the population—namely those interested in science fiction—imagined was happening. There was the space race we had—a damp squib—and the space race we dreamed of. And it is, in many ways, the latter one that has had the most impact. For where we are at this point in history, there are two key texts: *Star Trek* and *2001: A Space Odyssey*.

Let's start there, actually. Stanley Kubrick's film version of Arthur C. Clarke's *2001: A Space Odyssey* is odd largely because of its strange fusion of an extremely hard SF attitude with an exceedingly wide-eyed mysticism. In some ways it's hard to see how these were meant to fuse, though as with so much of 1960s science fiction, hindsight is our enemy here. In hindsight, we know that Arthur C. Clarke was a part of the classic golden age of science fiction in the US. This is the John W. Campbell-assembled school of writers who made their name in the American science fiction magazine *Astounding Science Fiction*—Isaac Asimov, Robert Heinlein, and the like.

The thing about this movement is that there was a juxtaposition to it. These were mostly (though not entirely) writers who were very serious about science. The sorts of people who these days would post on *Less Wrong* and talk very passionately about secular humanism. But in the 1940s and 1950s when they were writing, there was, if you will, a much more spiritual dimension to rationalism than is normal today. Science was viewed as an ideology that could bring about productive social change so that, if we organized the world around scientific principles, it would be a better, more rewarding place. And nowhere is that clearer than Arthur C. Clarke, who tended to combine hard SF, a detached, emotionless writing style, and a continual sense of mysticism. This was not a contrast, but rather a logical combination. Science was depicted as mystical because science was where we would find the enduring truths that would save humanity.

(You can see echoes of this all over early Doctor Who, where the usual shorthand for "this is a sensible person that the Doctor can attempt to reason with" is that the Doctor and the person in question recognize each other as scientists. Even as late as *The Underwater Menace*, this is the operating assumption when the Doctor meets a scientist—we're meant to be surprised that Zaroff is off his rocker there, because he's a brilliant scientist and brilliant scientists are supposed to be sane, reliable people.)

Under Kubrick's direction, the mystical elements of *2001* were boosted considerably. Lengthy sections of what we now sarcastically refer to as "space porn," in which spaceships move with languid beauty through the stars served, in this film, to stress the degree to which the machinery itself was an object of sublime awe. But this is nothing compared to the twenty-minute dialogue-free opening sequence featuring a bunch of monkeys experiencing a great leap forward because of a mysterious black obelisk from space. Nor to the equally bizarre space-acid trip at the end of the film (a sequence that is the direct inspiration for the title sequence of Doctor Who featured in the bulk of the Tom Baker era).

It's worth being specific here. It's not just that *2001* pushes the idea of a spiritual dimension of science. It's pushing the specific idea of a spiritual dimension to space. This isn't entirely surprising. As the famed piece of dialogue from our other main text says, space is the final frontier—the only place that is left for mankind to go. If spiritual fulfillment has not been found on Earth, it must come from the stars. And so we got the image of the Star Child, already discussed in relationship to Vicki last volume, and persistent all the way through the early glam rock days of David Bowie in the Pertwee era.

The other myth of space, of course, is *Star Trek*. Perpetually the comparison point for Doctor Who, the first thing we should say about *Star Trek* is that at the time in Doctor Who we're writing about, nobody on either show had ever heard of the other. *Star Trek* made its UK debut in the gap between Seasons Six and Seven of Doctor Who, and Doctor Who didn't make it over to the States until long after the show ended. Once we get into the Pertwee era of Doctor Who and into the Next Generation era of *Star Trek*, the influences between them fly fast and furious, but right now the shows are actually completely independently developed science fiction shows. So when we make comparisons between 1960s Doctor Who and the original series of *Star Trek*, we're making raw comparisons between the iconic sci-fi television series of the US and UK.

I say comparisons, but actually, there aren't very many. For all that *Star Trek* features a similar premise of "the ship arrives somewhere and there's trouble," the shows are diametric opposites for the most part. The biggest difference, of course, is their relationship with military power and colonialism. At the end of the day, Starfleet is unambiguously a military organization, and the mission of the Federation is unambiguously a twenty-third-century version of empire building. Sure, the Federation is enlightened, scientific, and democratic, but then again, so was the British Empire—a pinnacle of reason bringing enlightenment and civilization to the darkest corners of the world. Which is to say, no empire is built by people who are short on self-belief.

At the end of the day, the basic structure of *Star Trek* is not, as it was pitched, *Wagon Trail* to the stars, but rather *Master and Commander* in space. It is a show about loyalty, valor, and the chain of command. And if we're being honest, *Star Trek* is an embodiment of a particular American anxiety following World War II—the realization that they missed their chance to be a global empire and were going to have to be a different flavor of world superpower. And so in *Star Trek* an international crew in which Americans are firmly in charge discovers that there's no end of new planets to explore, and that America can finally have its vast empire in space.

(Again, in contrast, pretty much whenever Doctor Who gets into galactic empire territory, the empire is shown to be a trainwreck. More or less every single empire we ever see humanity have goes completely wrong. This is because Doctor Who was written in a country that had an empire and watched it go completely wrong, whereas *Star Trek* was written in a country that never had a proper one and was frankly a bit jealous over it.)

The place this is clearest is probably in Harlan Ellison's classic episode "The City on the Edge of Forever." Acknowledging that Harlan Ellison disliked the version of that episode that actually aired, and that his complaints were specifically about its treatment of pacifism, the most significant thing to note about "The City on the Edge of Forever" is that its end message is very obviously that the anti-war movement risked destroying the planet. Putting, as it did, a story in which a vaguely hippie pacifist living during the World War II era nearly destroys the entire future by letting Hitler win out during the Vietnam War protests, leaves very little room for ambiguity. Ellison was, as I said, furious about this change, but let's be honest—what did he expect? He was writing military science fiction. Of course it turned anti-pacifist. What else could it possibly do?

The space race, outside of its militaristic dimensions, largely fell between these two stools of spiritual enlightenment and empire building. The latter of these, of course, was a better fit for the militarist dimensions of the space race, but on the other hand, for any country that wasn't the US, the idea of the American empire in space was a bit of a non-starter.

But in practice, as I said, space was empty. And continues to seem so. Neither narrative was right. And the period of Doctor Who we're looking at was, in many ways, the last time it was possible to be optimistic about space without seeming just a bit silly. Once the moon landing goes off, all that's left is the slow, decades-long deflation of a particular dream of science fiction.

Not that space ever leaves science fiction—or Doctor Who for that matter. But over time those images have stopped being images of the future and become images of themselves— images that, like the archetypes of Tolkien-esque fantasy, resonate more as tropes of a genre than they do as images of what we might someday become. (And of course eventually we'll deal with the film that ensured this transition, *Star Wars*.)

The end point is summed up by one of my favorite moments of Joss Whedon's science fiction series *Firefly*, in which one character expresses skepticism of the existence of psychic powers, calling them "science fiction stuff." At which point his wife remarks, "Honey, you live on a spaceship." Some people objected to this joke, viewing it as anachronistic. And perhaps it was. But on the other hand, it's a surprisingly cogent comment on the nature of our futures. Space travel, even in a world where it exists, seems more like science fiction than reality.

Skulking about the Galaxy in an Ancient Spaceship (*The Seeds of Death*)

It's January 25, 1969. Marmalade are still at number one with their cover of "Ob-La-Di, Ob-La-Da," but after one week are overtaken by Fleetwood Mac, who are here seen in their early stage, i.e. not the one anyone recognizes as Fleetwood Mac, in that Christine McVie, Lindsey Buckingham, and Stevie Nicks were not yet in the band. From there it's The Move with "Blackberry Way," a bleak and dour song from a band previously known for cheery psychedelia. Welcome to 1969. From there it's two weeks of Amen Corner's "(If Paradise Is) Half as Nice," then, for the last week of this story, Peter Sarstedt's "Where Do You Go To (My Lovely)," which readers of my blog chastised me for never having heard, making me glad that books are far less interactive. Diana Ross and the Supremes and the Temptations, Simon and Garfunkel, and Engelbert Humperdinck also chart.

In other news, Ian Paisley is arrested for political demonstrations in Northern Ireland and jailed for three months, one of the more radical moments in his long political career. There's some vandalism of art at the New York Metropolitan Museum of Art, Yasser Arafat is elected leader of the PLO, and, ironically, St. Valentine is stricken from the Roman calendar of saints on Valentine's Day. But perhaps most importantly, The Beatles give their last public performance, an impromptu rooftop concert broken up by the police, another step in the slow and painful deflation of the 1960s.

The elegiac feel of this concert mirrors an elegiac feel to *The Seeds of Death* that has been remarked upon by more than one commentator. This makes sense—especially through the lens of history. This is the last time Troughton appeared in a straightforward rendition what was by and large his archetypal mode of story—the base under siege. It was the last time Troughton met one of the "big monsters." And on top of this litany of lasts, Troughton's departure was announced during this story's filming. The sense of an era coming to an end is unavoidable.

These, however, are elegiac only for a viewer with knowledge of the larger context of Doctor Who. Even if you don't know Troughton is on his way out, this story feels like a wake. And the most elegiac aspect of it seems positively audacious for the time: space travel is portrayed as an outdated and abandoned technology. Miles and Wood relate this to the common news story of the day—of train lines running their last service. It's a sharp observation, and it gets at the heart of what's clever about *The Seeds of Death*; it takes the hottest and most advanced form of transportation technology of 1969 and treats it like the one that's going obsolete.

From our post-space vantage, this seems oddly prescient. Even if space rockets were rendered obsolete not by teleporters but by, essentially, their own lack of relevance, the image of an old man in a museum full of rockets mourning the abandonment of space is a crushingly familiar one in 2012 as the US has functionally abandoned human spaceflight with no serious plans to return in the foreseeable future. Private spaceflight is still a decade away from catching up to where NASA was when it largely quit the human spaceflight game. *The Seeds of Death* is, in many ways, the closest thing to a realistic portrayal of the twenty-first century that Doctor Who ever managed during the twentieth.

I suspect in many ways that my generation is the last one to really feel this sense of loss. Certainly when I grew up there was still the sense of space as something that humans were going to figure out. The idea of a Mars colony in my lifetime seemed plausible, even inevitable, and concepts like terraforming seemed important. Individual Shuttle flights were not usually a big deal, but space as a whole was still assumed to be a part of the future. In hindsight this seems silly—it should have been obvious by the time I was born that the Shuttle was an ill-conceived mess that had effectively set the space program back by decades. But more than that, it should have been clear that space travel was not going to be useful without massive technological breakthroughs that showed no signs of coming.

But for whatever reason—perhaps out of the sheer momentum of 1969 (only thirteen years ago when I was born; there were still teenagers who remembered the moon landing then) or out of the fact that black holes, wormholes, and other things that might render real, proper interstellar travel possible were trendy—space was not dead when I was born. Nearly twenty-nine years later, however, it seems to compare unfavorably with doornails.

And so there is an oddly prescient power in the image of a discarded future here, especially given how often Doctor Who in the '60s appears itself to be a discarded future overwritten by the rise of portable digital technology and global communications. It's not just (or even really at all) that the future seen in *The Seeds of Death* seems more accurate and plausible in 2011 than most 1960s Doctor Who futures. It is that *The Seeds of Death* is, unusually for science fiction, more interested in questions of obsolescence than of possibility, and in taking that angle ends up far closer to the actual future than anything else in its era. Guessing what people will invent in the future is nearly impossible. Guessing that most of what we know will be relegated to the scrap heap is, on the other hand, almost certainly accurate.

More than that, there are numerous ways in which the tone of *The Seeds of Death* is more on target for the future than much of what we've seen. Even *The Enemy of the World*, the Troughton story most immediately concerned with providing a glimpse of how the world might change in the near-future (as opposed to *The Invasion*, which, while clearly near-futuristic, takes as one of its central premises that no essential changes to day-to-day life have occurred), does not seem quite as on-target. The tone of that story gestures towards a world government, which is another fast-receding bit of futurism, especially after a year of watching the EU go through a slow-motion suicide.

The Seeds of Death, on the other hand, largely presents T-Mat as a business venture. One does not get the sense that T-Mat is a government operation so much as that it's a multi-national company, possibly with lots of government contracts. This is a world where mass starvation happens because a company gets stuck with some shipping delays. This seems almost inevitably to be a much more believable future.

But look further and the underlying strangeness starts to become a bit clearer. We're clearly supposed to sympathize with Professor Eldred when he sighs that the moon was "far enough" for humanity, and to mourn the lost future of space. But that requires that we figure out which ideology of space is being mourned. Which brings us back to the previous post and the issue of New Frontier liberalism vs. the radical strain of the late '60s.

Political liberalism (used in its American sense of being a synonym for leftism) cannot be collapsed into the radical tradition of the 1960s. After all, in America at least, that tradition turned viciously on LBJ for his failings in Vietnam, forcing him out of contention for the 1968 Democratic nomination. The LBJ/JFK tradition of liberalism did exist. And the space program owed huge debts to it. But that doesn't in any real way undercut my observations about the space program as a military proxy program. Because New Frontier liberalism was essentially just a kinder, gentler militarism. Although to a later generation of American liberals the ousting of the most effective anti-poverty President since FDR over the Vietnam War seems like a bit of a poor move, the fact of the matter is that it is not as though the Vietnam War was an anomalous data point in the Johnson Presidency. His vision of what America was held that American ingenuity and spirit provided the humane counter-narrative to the Communist ideology of the Soviet Union, and that America was obliged to spend its military might spreading these cultural values.

But equally crucially, this flavor of New Frontier liberalism was the underpinning of *Star Trek*. Which brings me to a point about the last essay to which some of readers objected at the time: my claim that *Star Trek* represented a sort of deferred fantasy of American imperialism, which several people pointed out seemed to ignore things like Manifest Destiny.

Simply put, I think this misunderstands the nature of the imperialism that lies at the heart of the *Star Trek* fantasy. And while I'm skeptical that *Star Trek* itself had any influence on Doctor Who, the cultural fantasy that animated *Star Trek* undoubtedly did. My comment that *Star Trek* is in part about a lost opportunity at empire is not intended to ignore the systematic destruction of numerous cultures and the wholesale genocides committed by Americans in the Indian Wars—genocides that were unsuccessful more because America is prone to weak follow-through on such things than because there was some redemptive "nice side" to our massacres. My point isn't that American history was lacking in chilling historical atrocities. It's just that there's more than one kind of imperialist tendency. The one that was on display in Manifest Destiny was primarily a local, backyard land grab—an attempt to annex nearby territory. Every country goes through that, generally to their shame. In the United Kingdom's case, this is the imperialism that led to the formation of, well, the United Kingdom instead of just England.

But that's not the sort of imperialism on display in *Star Trek*. Nor is it the type of imperialism most associated with the British Empire, whose imperialist tendencies had a bizarre moral foundation behind them. Take a tour of Rudyard Kipling and chill at something like "The White Man's Burden" and you can see the bizarre moral logic of British imperialism, which was founded not on the nationalistic desire for power but on a sort of messianic altruism grounded in systematic racism.

In practice, of course, the British Empire was based on economic exploitation as well. But the fantasy of the British Empire—which was at least as important as the actual empire (upon which the sun eventually did set, whereas the fantasy lives on)—was about bringing culture to the savages. The nationalism came in the form of the genuine belief that British culture was superior to all others and thus the culture most needed by the savages.

This is what *Star Trek* was about, and it's what New Frontier liberalism was about. It's also what the American nationalist myth about rescuing Britain in World War II (despite the fact that Britain had already successfully repelled the German attack by the time the US entered the war, and that Germany had moved on to Russia) is about: the idea that following World War II, since we'd saved Britain and Europe, we had supplanted them and it was our turn to form a cultural empire across the world. Or, as that started to run aground into the reality of the Cold War, across the stars.

What's oddly dissonant about *The Seeds of Death*, then, is that Eldred is visibly mourning for this more or less American vision of space. Look closely at what it is he regrets. He wants to explore Space. He's positioned, in other words, as a version of the pith-helmeted Victorian explorer. Interestingly, although his ideology is clearly Victorian explorer, his demeanor is Victorian scientist—which is why he's so able to connect with the Doctor, who always derived from the Victorian-scientist archetype. It's easy, when you look at him between Hartnell and Pertwee, to imagine that Troughton dropped this aspect of the character, but here we see that what he actually did was much more complex. He didn't drop it so much as rebel against it, playing the Victorian scientist who had dropped acid and become enlightened. (See also *The Mind Robber.*) But it's interesting the way that these two Victorian archetypes are shown here to be adjacent, with a real slippage between them. (In a story with more radical leanings, this equation of Victorian science and imperialism would be a fascinating point of departure. I say this because, many seasons from now, we'll actually see that story in *Ghost Light*.)

In terms of *The Seeds of Death*, all of this becomes problematic with the Ice Warriors. Although their plans are solidly in the category of "genocidal," it is worth stopping and looking at what they're actually doing. Hailing from a dying world, they are desperate to ensure their own survival. And so they are attempting to colonize Earth, and specifically to terraform it to their liking. This will, of course, result in the extinction of humanity. But remember, earlier in the thread I talked about terraforming as something that was an expected outcome of the future when I was growing up. This was something we fully expected to do to other planets.

We might duck and cover behind the idea that we would surely not have done it to populated planets, but saying that requires us to ignore the reality of imperialism at every stage of human history. Both manifest destiny-style imperialism and Victorian imperialism led to massive deaths among the conquered, generally with little fanfare or worry on the part of the empire. The reality is that if we got in the habit of terraforming planets, everything about our history says we'd terraform inhabited worlds too.

In other words, *The Seeds of Death* on the one hand romanticizes the pioneering spirit of imperialism and, on the other, creates villains who are evil because they act like imperialists act. In just four stories we'll encounter a story that takes the question of an indigenous population rebelling against an occupying force much more seriously, but for now the real problem here is that the Doctor is so ruthlessly unsympathetic to the Ice Warriors. We're miles here from the mad self-sacrificing Doctor in something like *The Sontaran Strategem/The Poison Sky* who can't destroy an invading alien force without giving them a choice first. Instead the Doctor casually dumps an entire fleet of Martians into the sun, runs around with what amounts to a solar gun shooting down Ice Warriors, and generally shows no problem whatsoever with all of this.

But in an odd way, this all becomes part of the vaguely mournful feel of the story. The series, squeezed by budgets, suffering declining ratings, and seemingly on the brink of cancellation was saved (according to the production team) less because of their clever Earth-based reinvention to come but rather by the BBC not having any better ideas, and so settling on a massive revamp of Doctor Who. We saw in the last story an alternate version of the Troughton years. But here, in *The Seeds of Death*, we see, albeit inadvertently, as clear an argument for the obsolescence of this version. The elegy for the inevitably doomed era of human spaceflight necessarily doubles as an elegy for the inevitably doomed era of science fiction concerned with it.

I've displayed a marked lack of patience with base under siege stories over the course of the Troughton era. *The Seeds of Death* essentially shows why. The central tension of the base under siege is that "they" are on the outside and trying to get in to hurt "us." Sometimes—even most of the time—the show is able to dance around the immediate xenophobia of this. When the base is under siege from the Cybermen, well, they're very consciously our own shadows. When it's the Yeti, well, they're robots. When it's seaweed, that's hardly a big deal. But all of this in aggregate starts to become xenophobic. Sure, there are terrible things bred in corners of the universe, but surely not everything that isn't human is a faceless evil. Surely not every corner that isn't Earth breeds the most terrible things. The base under siege itself is fine, but as a mode of being for the series, it's maddening in its overall portrayal of the alien.

And in *The Seeds of Death*, that really becomes clear, because the argument for why the Ice Warriors should be treated as generic evils to be slaughtered is so very weak. And suddenly we can see the whole flawed structure of this era. For all that Troughton's Doctor was an anarchic source of enlightenment, the series never quite worked up the strength to turn his anarchic tendencies against the Victorian imperialist values that still, to a great extent, underpinned the series. Consider, after all, that when the Doctor was traveling with two companions from Earth's past, one of them—the Scotsman—is the primitive idiot, while the other—the Victorian girl—is never rendered as a comically thick character, but is instead treated as the fetishized and perfect body-in-peril, the adoring object of the male gaze. The era has been wearing its prejudices on its sleeve the whole time.

And so it comes to this story, in which the Doctor praises neo-Victorian adventuring imperialism with one hand while gunning down imperialists with the other, the only difference seeming to be that one set of imperialists is human and British and the other is green. The Troughton era's one catastrophic blind spot stands revealed—for all of its anarchic and psychedelic charm, it could never bring itself to hurl the brick through its own window. And as the psychedelic spaceship crashes back to Earth, this contradiction becomes fatal. There is no way past it without completely altering the entire structure of the show.

This is the real elegiac content of *The Seeds of Death*. It, more than almost any Troughton story, explains why the Pertwee era was necessary. Because before the Doctor can fight aliens in space again, he's going to have to be forced to throw the brick through the window of the culture that made him—mainstream contemporary Britain.

Time Can Be Rewritten (*The Wheel of Ice*)

Stephen Baxter's 2012 novel *The Wheel of Ice* was released so recently that it seems almost absurd to historicize it in the past tense. This is in some ways a pity, as it marks a distinct change in the relationship contemporary Doctor Who has with its 1963–'89 iteration. The launch of the new series in 2005 brought about the end of the BBC Books Past Doctor Adventures line, with the last title being Andrew Cartmel's *Atom Bomb Blues*, featuring the Seventh Doctor. This wasn't the end of adventures featuring classic series Doctors—Big Finish continued their audio series, which, through the Companion Chronicles and Lost Stories lines, have expanded since 2005 to encompass all of the first eight Doctors. But it was the end of official BBC releases of stories featuring pre-Eccleston Doctors.

It's absurd, of course, to suggest that the BBC had simply abandoned the classic series. DVD releases continue apace. But there is something of a line drawn between the two series. The DVDs only occasionally feature personnel from the new series on their special features, and maintain their own distinct packaging and, most tellingly, a completely different logo to that of the new series: the one designed for the Paul McGann TV Movie, itself based on the logo used for the first four years of the Pertwee era. This is a mixed blessing. On the one hand there is something nice about this. It would be easy to treat the classic series as nothing more than a lead-in to the far more popular and commercially viable new series. The focus on foregrounding the people who made the classic series and the use of a distinct logo makes the classic series its own thing, to be valued on its own merits.

On the other hand, the disconnect between the classic and the new series inherently marginalizes the classic series, treating the new series not as its continuation but as its replacement. This is what fans rebel against when they insist on calling the season starring Christopher Eccleston "Season Twenty-Seven," and it's a fair point. By and large the classic series is treated as something to be respected, commemorated, and, ultimately, buried in favor of the new series. It gets beautiful and well-made DVD releases, but these are firmly releases that celebrate a concluded past. And in line with this the BBC did not release any new material featuring the classic series Doctors.

Slowly but surely this line began to blur, however. First came a reprint series of various classics from the Target Books line, which set up Gareth Roberts's novelization of the unfinished Douglas Adams serial *Shada*. This wasn't technically a new story featuring a past Doctor, but it was closer than had been seen in some years. And this, in turn, led to Stephen Baxter's *The Wheel of Ice*, an all-new novel featuring Patrick Troughon's Doctor.

The question of why the BBC would return to new material featuring old Doctors is, perhaps, less complex than it sounds on the surface. Stephen Baxter is a big name and a big get for the BBC, and if his condition in writing a Doctor Who book was that he wanted to write the Season Six TARDIS crew, well, that's probably worth accepting. But it creates an interesting situation. The same logic that says that letting Baxter write whatever Doctor Who book he's interested in writing also means that the BBC is put in the position not just of having a new story set in Doctor Who's past, they're put in the position of having that be a major release. This isn't just a case of pandering to the few die-hards who still love the classic series and will buy stuff closely related to it. Stephen Baxter brings his own fan base that is not coextensive with the Doctor Who fanbase. People will buy this book who would not, in normal circumstances, buy a Doctor Who book. And what they'll get isn't a taste of the current series. Instead they get something that ties into an era where the overwhelming majority of episodes don't even exist anymore.

And so whether part of a conscious plan to develop the role of the classic series in the larger franchise of Doctor Who or not, *The Wheel of Ice* still marks a real transition in how the past of the series interacts with its present. And it's clear, within the book, that something has changed from the old Past Doctor Adventures. On the book's first page it breaks the old tradition of not mentioning the Time Lords or Gallifrey by name in a pre-Pertwee adventure. It doesn't introduce "continuity errors" or anything—the Doctor doesn't talk about them to Zoe or Jamie or anything. But the first full sentence of the book begins, "One day, in the dusty libraries of Gallifrey, she would be given a name."

On the other hand, the book has a number of continuity references that would, from any writer without Baxter's preexisting pedigree, be called fanwank. There are references to *The Daleks' Masterplan, The Tenth Planet, Evil of the Daleks, The Wheel in Space, The Mind Robber, The Seeds of Death, The Silurians, The Talons of Weng-Chiang,* and *Black Orchid,* and those are just the ones I caught and noted off-hand. It's obvious both that Baxter is a huge Doctor Who fan, and that it matters to him that he shows his credentials, so to speak. Again, this isn't hard to understand—the density of references makes it clear that his writing for Doctor Who is not a case of some big-name writer carpetbagging in the Doctor Who sandbox, nor a case of a writer looking down his nose as he writes a licensed property.

But there's something going on in this novel that hadn't really been the case in most of the Past Doctor Adventures. This is, in many ways, what the books during the sixteen years in which Doctor Who's primary medium was novels all too often wished desperately that they had been: serious attempts at science fiction that happen to be Doctor Who stories. Even when the novel series were good or great—and they often were both—their writers were mostly Doctor Who fans who established themselves as writers on Doctor Who novels. Many were phenomenal, but their Doctor Who work is usually some of their earliest work, and a springboard for a later career. They're talented fans. Baxter, although clearly a fan, isn't approaching the task of writing Doctor Who from within fandom.

The result is a book that actually has to be done as a Troughton novel. Troughton's Doctor has a reputation for being hard to capture in prose. This makes sense, given that he, more than almost any other Doctor, is defined heavily by the actor himself and by the physical aspects of his persona. Many novels featuring Troughton's Doctor suffer from being books with a very generic Doctor, while others fall prey to the illusory fan memory of Troughton's Doctor as "the clown Doctor." Baxter resists both temptations. On the one hand, his take on Troughton's Doctor is thoroughly non-clownish, with essentially no comedy scenes.

Equally, he's not a generic Doctor either. Indeed, the entire structure and thrust of the adventure depends on the fact that the Doctor acts as he did in Troughton's era instead of in the more modern approach. These days the Doctor is defined primarily by the amount that he already knows. The Doctor has become a sort of walking compendium of knowledge about the universe. This contrasts sharply with standard operating procedure in the Troughton era, where the Doctor was defined more by his ability to figure things out and come up with clever solutions than he was by how much he already knew.

Baxter, in other words, writes something that is thoroughly recognizable as a Patrick Troughton story. This is true even to the details of its interests—it's a near-future space story. It's not quite specific about its time period, but it's clearly set in the twenty-first century, with events that are explicitly related to those of *The Wheel in Space* and *The Seeds of Death*, tying the novel in with the Troughton era's larger concern with the near future. This is in some ways anachronistic. The most reasonable date for the novel is about 2050. The prospect of a permanent base near a Saturnian moon in forty years is slim at best, as is the prospect of artificial intelligence anywhere near as advanced as what Baxter casually drops into his world.

But this isn't some nostalgic '60s revivalism either. Baxter's reputation is as a hard science fiction writer, and though he avoids tedious and discursive bits of science jargon there's a vividness and texture to the Wheel that never existed in the Troughton era itself. This doesn't feel like an idle 1960s dream of the future, but rather like a bit of futurism that's thoroughly thought through. That doesn't mean it's anything short of fantastic—there is, after all, a creature hundreds of millions of years old living at the center of a Saturnian moon. But it's a fantastic possibility grounded in levels of complex research about space unthinkable in a pre-Apollo 11 world.

There are also scattered mentions of themes that ground the novel firmly in 2012. The 2050 date I proposed is based on a section of the novel that traces the progress of an alien artifact as it passes from generation to generation within a family, with stops at 1930, 1970, and a roughly present-day one that talks about the economic downturn. There is also a section in which the corporate supervisor running the Wheel talks about "kettling" a bunch of young protesters who are actively described as rioters, to which the Doctor responds with an accusation that "you people are turning on your own children." It's impossible not to connect this image with that of the 2011 London riots and the Occupy movement.

There's something phenomenally wonderful about any story that gives us the opportunity to see Troughton's Doctor, however symbolically, meet the Occupy movement. The movement itself is an unexpected late revival of the mercurial, Situationist anarchism that characterized the 1960s and, more substantively, Troughton's Doctor. If there's a reason to do a Troughton story in 2012 it's surely to allow Troughton to meet his own cultural descendants.

The balance here is incredibly difficult to pull off, and in many ways Baxter is the first one to do it. The book is simultaneously firmly a Troughton story and firmly of 2012. And it provides a significant rejoinder to those of us who favor historically focused approaches to the Troughton era. In just a few essays I'm going to argue for why the Troughton era was ready to end in 1969, and I stand by that—the era required a conclusion, and it got a good one in *The War Games*. But the fact that the '60s ended and that the Troughton era, which was so grounded in them, ended alongside them doesn't mean that they had no future.

Just as the Occupy movement that the book implicitly cites took the ideology and approaches of the 1960s and repurposed them for a new time, showing that they still have relevance, *The Wheel of Ice* is a Patrick Troughton story for 2012 that shows that, as good as Doctor Who in 2012 is, it doesn't need to treat its past as nothing more than a respected antecedent. It's a novel that shows that the Doctor Who of the 1960s, although over, still has much to say to the present. It's not that the Troughton era is as good as the present day series: truth be told, very little of it is. Rather, it's that the approach and concept of the Troughton era still works. And that's what Baxter's novel is: a love letter to the past based not in nostalgia but in a profound love of what that past really was. That it also manages to show what past Doctor novels should always have been is almost incidental.

If We Don't Do Something Quickly (*The Space Pirates*)

It's March 8, 1969. Peter Sarstedt is still at number one with "Where Do You Go To (My Lovely)." The rest of the charts are relatively uninspiring: Cilla Black, Dean Martin, Engelbert Humperdinck, Glen Campbell … we're not exactly dealing with pioneering music that advanced the art. I mean, all lovely stuff, and the Bee Gees and Marvin Gaye are nice touches, especially when "I Heard it Through the Grapevine" unseats Sarstedt. It's almost enough not to notice the UK's 1969 Eurovision entry in number two, Lulu's "Boom Bang-a-Bang." Almost. (And Lulu co-wins that year, I regret to inform you.)

While in real news, Apollo 9 returns safely to Earth. A small dustup in the colony of Anguilla results in British troops being quasi-peaceably deployed there, and the TV mast at Emley Moore collapses due to ice buildup. In other countries' news, former US President Dwight Eisenhower dies, Golda Meir becomes Prime Minister of Israel, and James Earl Ray pleads guilty to the Martin Luther King assassination, which, gives you an idea just how much was going on in 1968 I really missed covering in any detail because I was too busy doing Enoch Powell's "Rivers of Blood" speech. Oh, and if you want to be technical about it, *The Impossible Astronaut* takes place between the transmission of the fifth and sixth episode of this story, which I point out because it's one of two times that Doctor Who has overtly set a story on Earth during a time when the series was on the air (other than the present). (*Mawdryn Undead* being the other.)

So this story. Another entry into the bottom ten of all time; in fact, this is apparently the worst Troughton story ever. It has a seriously bad reputation—largely due to the "one surviving episode" problem we've mentioned as afflicting *The Underwater Menace*. But this lets us segue into something else that's really important about this story—it's a missing story.

We've evaded talking about this phenomenon at any great length, and now we're at the last missing episodes of Doctor Who (although some colorization gaps exist in the Pertwee era, everything from that era exists at least in black-and-white), so I suppose we'd better. The idea of missing stories is a strange one to people. Inevitably a new fan of Doctor Who, high on the fumes of Matt Smith and Karen Gillan, will declare that they want to watch the whole classic series, and one of us old-timers will have to gently explain to a baffled twenty-first-century television viewer that, actually, you can't do that. This is very strange to them. And understandably—as Miles and Wood point out, it's difficult to imagine fifteen percent of *Buffy the Vampire Slayer* simply not existing in any form. The very fact of the wipings is profoundly strange.

Historically, what happened basically comes down to "The BBC didn't make preservation a priority." Miles and Wood have an excellent essay in the first volume of *About Time* which covers this, in which they talk compellingly about how the BBC's vision of televised plays was so rooted in the logic of transmission as live performance that nobody at the BBC thought about preservation. For the bulk of Doctor Who's original run, past episodes were things that had happened and were gone. You moved on. There's a reason why 1981's *Five Faces of Doctor Who* repeats, which we mentioned back in *The Krotons*, was so important—it was actually the first time old Doctors had reappeared since *The Three Doctors* in 1973. It wasn't until the early '80s and the home video market that the idea of a past story being available existed, and until you have that idea you really don't have the cultural context needed to realize that the recordings are something to keep. And both the end of the wipings and the beginning of the search for missing episodes, not coincidentally, coincided perfectly with the invention of the VCR.

And so, between recycling videotapes for future use, purges of film libraries for storage space, and sloppy record keeping, 106 episodes of Doctor Who are simply gone. This is actually down quite a bit from the original tally when the junkings were stopped, in a great part due to the intervention of both Sue Malden, the BBC's incoming Archive Selector in 1978. Malden, upon taking the job, grew concerned about the junkings and happened to pick Doctor Who as her case study to see what was going on.

Since then, thirty-three episodes of Doctor Who have been recovered, both from relatively expected sources—often overseas television networks that hadn't complied with orders to destroy them, or from private film collectors who had nicked them from inside sources who were happy to, for a small payoff, inadvertently confuse the furnace door with their mate's car door. Others came from borderline surreal sources—the cellar of a Mormon church that used to be a BBC property, and that turned out to have two episodes of *The Daleks' Masterplan* being the most notable. As mentioned, 106 are still missing. Realistically, there is no chance that all of them exist, and the chances that any of them exist, even with the recent good fortune of finding two episodes in late 2011, are quickly diminishing.

In truth, although Doctor Who fans look at the junkings as a particular travesty, Doctor Who is actually extremely lucky as 1960s BBC programs go. The fact that Sue Walden used it as her test case and that Ian Levine raised as much of a stink as he did preserved large swaths of the show, putting it in far better shape than a lot of other programs. Countless major moments of British TV history are lost—the earliest episodes of *The Avengers*, swaths of *Adam Adamant Lives!*, much of *Z-Cars*, early work from the members of Monty Python, chunks of Spike Milligan's work, the coverage of the moon landing—all gone. Doctor Who has 106 missing episodes from its first six years, which sucks, but the more remarkable fact is that Doctor Who has 145 existent ones.

This is the glass half full/half empty debate. On the one hand, Doctor Who's history is wildly impoverished compared to that of other major science fiction shows. On the other hand, it is in wildly better shape than any of its BBC stablemates. On top of that, due to a global network of fans, audio exists for every single one of the missing stories, and many of them also exist in the form of telesnaps, a product sold by a man named John Cura where he would point a camera at his television and take repeated photos of a TV program to sell to the producers in order to have a visual record of what they did.

Unfortunately, Cura died in early 1969, and *The Space Pirates* is not one of those blessed with telesnaps. Other telesnapless stories like *The Daleks' Master Plan* and *The Massacre* do fine for themselves in reconstructions, but *The Space Pirates* turns out to be a heavily visual story, which means that the reconstructions of it are more dubious than most—a lot of repeated use of publicity photos and stills from other episodes, and, in a first for Doctor Who reconstructions, the folks at Loose Cannon sometimes had to just throw up their hands and put up a text card explaining what was happening.

Which is sad. Reconstructions are usually pretty watchable, but the fact of the matter is, *The Space Pirates* is kind of brutal. This hasn't helped its reputation any, obviously, but that's a bit unfair. Simply put, the bits where "nothing happens" on the audio are bits where things are happening visually that we just can't see. And judging the story based on the fact that it doesn't work as an audio is inaccurate.

But a flip side of that is that, very often, particularly when you're someone who has done a big marathon of reconstructions like Season Five, you start to assume that the reconstructions are up to the task of showing what the episode would have been like. Often they seem to be—among my favorite stories are reconstructions such as *The Enemy of the World* and *The Power of the Daleks*. But not always. And at the end of the day, we may just have to admit that *The Space Pirates* is a missing story—one we can't see, and can only guess at what might have been.

Because other than the fact that the surviving episode is a bizarre bit of men in comedy accents arguing, and the fact that the audios are an utter mess, everything about *The Space Pirates* looks pretty good. Certainly it has a strong creative pedigree, with Robert Holmes writing. So instead of trying to watch a story that can no longer be watched, let's try to approach the story archeologically—to try to see what it must have been like. Doing so, we discover some interesting things.

First of all, let's admit that the ratings were poor. The audience appreciation figures were average. But there's not the sense that this was hated. Unlike *The Gunfighters*, a story that was clearly despised at the time but has had its reputation redeemed in later years, *The Space Pirates* was perfectly enjoyable at the time—essentially indistinguishable from the two stories before it, save for a dip at the second episode which is, to be fair, the episode everyone judges it poorly on today as well.

Why was this seeming mess popular? A lot has to do with the fact that this took place right at the height of space mania. This was a mania every bit as much as Beatlemania or Dalekmania. The culture, understandably for the time, was mad for space. And, as Miles and Wood point out (in *About Time: Volume 2*), this is actually structured much like the news coverage of space flight, with anticipation and waiting serving as a fundamental part of the narrative. More than almost anything else in 1960s Doctor Who, this is a story that is in part about expectation—about setting up a confrontation and then making us wait to actually see it play out. It's a structure we've seen used successfully before; *The Enemy of the World* and *The Power of the Daleks* both depend on this sort of delay structure. (In fact, Whitaker is arguably the master of this structure.) Holmes uses it here as a structure wrapped around the set pieces of model work, spacewalks, and other payoffs for the space mania crowd—basically the machine waltzes of *2001*. All of which is gone now, so we really can't say anything about it one way or the other.

But if we're being honest, that's probably still too flat to appeal to people. So Holmes goes a step further. Here one gets the sense that he's making lemons out of lemonade. His original pitch was apparently "space realism with a Wild West tone," and he got asked to stretch it to six episodes. This stretching explains why he adopted the space launch structure of delays and anticipation—because it would pad the story out without adding running-in-place episodes while still giving it a structure that would still feel fresh and exciting for the audience (and again, for the audience of 1969, this would have worked). But the story he's telling isn't just space porn. He's got a complex thing going on under that.

Calling a story "*The Space Pirates*" makes its genre relatively clear. We know what pirate stories look like. The British know this doubly so—it was a core adventure genre there for some time. And one of the archetypes of that genre is the story where a ship of good guys—usually led by a bland but fairly competent British military type—chases a ship of bad guys who are, inevitably, much more fun and charismatic. This is the basic frisson of the pirate story—the good guys win, but the bad guys are more fun, so we get a sort of structured enjoyment of the taboo by quietly rooting for the wrong side even as we get to pretend that we're watching good, wholesome fare. And for the first episode of *The Space Pirates*, this is what we get—indeed, as is often remarked, Holmes all but leaves the Doctor out of the first episode, instead taking the bulk of the episode to set up a very traditional pirate yarn.

This is often taken as a criticism, but it really shouldn't be. Holmes actually needs most of the first episode to set up the pirate yarn, because in the second episode, he blows a hole in the setup by introducing Milo Clancy, a character who clearly is not supposed to exist in a pirate yarn. Clancy, you see, is a cowboy. Miles and Wood make much of the adjacency of the British pirate genre and the American Western, but while they may have been similar genres, this ignores the fact that they're still different genres with radically different iconography. This, in fact, is why Holmes's trick works—the cowboy is close enough to pirates to function in the narrative, but looks so out of place as to be striking. This is Holmes's central brilliance in this story—he creates a standard pirate story in space, then drops a cowboy into it and watches the sparks fly.

If there are two seeming weak spots, they are these. First, it's not clear the actors understood what Holmes was doing, layering comedy voices over his script that in no way help or improve what's going on. The script relies on the juxtapositions of the genre tropes, and when the actors play comedy voices over it, we can't take the genres seriously enough to see their interplay as anything other than a high concept "Look! Pirates vs. Cowboys!" joke that gets old long before the sixth episode. It is, for the most part, a classic case of a joke being spoiled when the actors actually try to play it as funny.

Second, Holmes makes the mistake here of forgetting about the Doctor, getting too wrapped up in his pirates and cowboys idea to quite fit him into the plot. Troughton is left with the task of holding yet another script together based on the Doctor's charisma instead of on the idea that the Doctor should be doing something interesting. Unlike the myriad of times he's been given this job in the past, however, he's sick of it, and declines to do it, playing the Doctor with the grim seriousness that everyone else in the story lacks. On the one hand, this means that Troughton is playing the story correctly, but as the only one who is he's at odds with everything else going on. With the guest stars stealing his comic ground and the script stealing his serious ground, we're left with a script Troughton visibly wants out of.

He still gets some good scenes. By playing his failed attempt to use magnets to pilot the fragment of the beacon that he's stuck on completely straight and visibly kicking himself for his own arrogant stupidity when he makes the problem worse, he manages a real sense of danger and vulnerability. But mostly he's left without a way into the episode, visibly counting the days until he gets to go home.

But none of this erases the fact that Holmes has what's actually a pretty interesting idea here: Pirates vs. Cowboys paced like a space launch. If we're being honest, it's probably not an idea that would play well post-space in 2011. If, incredibly, these episodes were to turn up, *The Space Pirates* would still be, in some sense, missing, because it's simply of a time that doesn't exist anymore—a moment of television so dependent on the particulars of its transmission that it cannot exist any time outside of the spring of 1969.

But that's not a fault. If anything, it's to the story's credit, and certainly to Robert Holmes's. One of the things that's always tough with Holmes is dealing with the outsized nature of his reputation. But it's largely a deserved reputation. Not because his stories were all timeless classics—many weren't. But because he understood the language of television well enough to, in three different decades, write compelling Doctor Who stories. Porting the narrative logic of a space launch to Doctor Who in order to collide two pre-space genres is a brilliant move that could only be made by someone who gets how to do television.

But part of television in 1969 was that it was a one-time occasion. Holmes was writing television plays to be acted once, amuse the crowd, and then be forgotten. He did them extremely well, but, like all of television, did them for their own time and nothing else. In this regard, it's hard to say seriously that a story like *The Gunfighters*—a failure in its time that we happen to appreciate later—has anything on *The Space Pirates*, a success in its time that we can't appreciate now.

But what's truly strange is that the attitude that got it destroyed—that television was a live event that happened and was gone—was also the attitude that justified why it was good. *The Space Pirates* is missing. But in a way, it has to be. These gaps are as much a part of what Doctor Who is as the TARDIS or the Daleks—something that is not just a DVD set for obsessive twenty-first-century fans, but that has been a living, breathing part of every year since 1963. Without stories like *The*

Space Pirates that flicker on in an imagined 1969 we can never reach, a vital part of the show's magic would be lost.

What Ought Be Found?

Most of the time, when we think about missing episodes, the thought goes entirely to what stories we wish we could watch as fans. Accordingly *The Web of Fear* topped an overwhelmingly large number of wish lists and was the subject of by far the most spurious rumors of recovery right up until one of them wasn't spurious. And fair enough, it's a story of a type that a lot of people quite like (even if I do think the consensus view of it is somewhat unrelated to the actual episodes). On the other hand, enjoying a reconstruction is perfectly doable—*The Power of the Daleks* remains one of my absolute favorite stories even as a reconstruction. To say that an episode has to be found to be enjoyed isn't quite true. And while they're clearly more fun to watch as actual episodes, I'm morally opposed to fun. But what is true is that there are things we can't understand about some stories without seeing them. What follows, then, is not a list of the best stories to be missing, but of the biggest gaps in our knowledge left by the ninty-seven missing episodes.

Marco Polo: Episodes One–Three

Over the course of these episodes the Doctor disappears from the plot for a while and emerges as an altogether friendlier character—the one we know from the rest of the Hartnell era. On audio the transition seems abrupt, but Hartnell's portrayal was always more visual than people gave him credit for. (His fussy use of his hands being, as Peter Purves has explained, a case of him understanding the small screen of television and of what physical acting means within it.) This is the story where the Doctor goes from being a not-entirely trustworthy figure to being the heroic protagonist we know and love. And we can't see him do it.

The Massacre: Episodes Two–Three

The entire ending of this story hinges on the question of whether or not Steven should have known that the Ambrose and the Doctor are two different people. But to come up with an answer to that would require us to see Hartnell's performance as the Ambrose and just how different it is from his Doctor. On top of that ambiguity, there's the matter of Hartnell's faltering abilities as the series wore on. Hartnell's post-Doctor Who acting career was minimal, meaning that the Ambrose was one of the last characters he portrayed. This alone makes it interesting to know what he did with it.

Any of The Savages

We know that there's some major issues with race in this story. It was originally to be called The White Savages, and we know the elders are played blacked up. But telesnaps and audios don't tell us everything about how these racial politics played out. Ian Stuart Black was an intelligent writer, and it's entirely possible this story had some interesting things to say. It's also entirely possible that it was troublingly racist. We don't know right now.

The Tenth Planet: Episode Four; Power of the Daleks: Episode One

Although the later episodes of Power of the Daleks are where the script really starts to shine, both of these have obvious value in showing us the particulars of how the actor change was presented to the audience. From audio it's difficult to tell how foreshadowed or explicable Hartnell's collapse is, and it's obvious that Troughton is playing a complex game with the audience's patience and willingness to accept his character through his first episodes, but it's impossible to see the particulars of this game. In many ways this is the biggest gap in knowledge about the series. The ability to change actors is a fundamental part of why it's still on the air, and we don't really understand how that ability was introduced to the audience.

The Macra Terror

One of the strangest and most surreal episodes of Doctor Who ever to air, this is one where it's hard to even tell what we don't know about it. I mean, we don't have a very good idea of what the Macra themselves looked like, so that'd be interesting, not least as they're a centerpiece of Jack Graham's fascinating analyses of the weird in Doctor Who. But it's really the whole holiday camp/Soviet paranoia feel of this story that's hard to quite get a handle on from stills. This is one where the entire tone of the story rests in the visuals, and periodic stills don't really cut it.

The Space Pirates

Even if it's impossible to see in the context that it aired, the fact of the matter is that this is an extremely visual story by a writer who is otherwise very, very good. For the most part we can take a pretty good guess of whether a missing story was good or bad. We can't know if it came off, but we can get a solid idea of what it was doing. Here, though, it's not even clear what the story was doing, little yet how well it accomplished its goals. With a writer as capable of surprises as Robert Holmes, that's an awfully big question mark.

You Were Expecting Someone Else: *TV Comic*

Back in the Hartnell volume I have an essay regarding the World Distributors Doctor Who annuals. Consider this, then, the companion piece looking at the other major piece of non-televised Doctor Who merchandise of the 1960s, the Polystyle *TV Comic* strips.

What's funny, though, is that despite being a completely different company and publication, it's tough to make too much out of the differences between the World Distributors comics and the Polystyle ones. This might not seem surprising given that they are both telling Doctor Who stories, and thus presumably have some unifying influence. Except that both are so wildly different from the television series that it's mildly surprising to watch them end up more or less on the same planet given how far afield they are from the supposed target. Either one taken on its own is a puzzling through-the-looking-glass version of Doctor Who. But for two separate companies to come up with the same bizarre take on Doctor Who suggests something else at work.

Given the fondness of this project for the idea that there is some intrinsic alchemical logic underlying Doctor Who, it's tempting to allude to some vague sense of a proper order of things in Doctor Who here—the occasional and uncanny sense we've had before that this ship is not as rudderless as it should be. But in this case, it seems to me there's a much more prosaic option—given what British comics were, there was only one way the strip could have been, and sure enough, both World Distributors and Polystyle did it that way.

For the average American comic-book fan, there is a lot about the British comics industry that is puzzling. But the thing that should be noted first is that virtually nobody talks about British comic books. It's not that there aren't any. It's just that there aren't very many, and fewer still that actually matter. Instead, the primary form for British comics is the anthology magazine. The most famous of these are probably, in terms of children's comics, *The Beano* and *The Dandy*, and in terms of science fiction, *Eagle* and *2000 AD*. (Though some would make a case for *Eclipse*, those people are inevitably Americans who forget that the British comics scene extended beyond Alan Moore. Or, more depressingly, it's the Brits who forget that.) The format of these was generally simple—a couple strips of maybe four to eight pages each, published weekly. And that was the format of Polystyle's *TV Comic*, which was a cheap publication devoted to the comic adventures of various TV concepts, including Doctor Who.

I could—and really should someday—write a book about how this format shaped British comics and, in turn, American comics following the massive influx of British writers in the late '80s/early '90s. But one of the big things is that it meant that comics often had a bit of a house style. A magazine still had to feel coherent, after all. Furthermore, there's a fairly tight structure to these strips. With eight pages, fitting a cliffhanger, resolution of last week's cliffhanger, advancement of the plot, and some exposition to catch people up who have forgotten since last week is a challenge even with the larger page size of British comics. And so the pace of any action-based strip had to be fairly frenetic in order to function at all.

Even in a setting like the World Distributors Annuals, which doesn't serialize stories, the structure this implies is prevalent simply because it's the structure people expect action comics to be in, much as American graphic novels, even those made wholly outside the mainstream superhero comics industry, frequently break into individual chapters of roughly the same size as a single issue comic book. And so it's not a huge surprise that World Distributors' Annuals and Polystyle's *TV Comic* ended up with similar-seeming Doctor Who comics—that was just how comics were.

How are they, by the way? Well, let's grab a random strip— a serial called "The Witches" from when the comic was a two-pager to assess. Here's a summary of a strip: the annual universe-wide reunion of witches is going on at the planet Vargo. Two late arrivals talk animatedly about the Grand Witch talking, and eagerly await her sharing new spells. Instead she offers a demonstration of her power, turning a tree into stone. Immediately thereafter the TARDIS arrives, with the witches speculating that it might be the Grand Witch's doing, but she denies it. Inside the TARDIS, the Doctor tells his grandchildren John and Gillian (Oh yes, them ... I should maybe have mentioned these two strange characters) to hide while he investigates. He puts on his utility belt, then proclaims himself the Wizard of Omega. The Grand Witch declares she will test his power, and summons a giant monster to attack him.

Characterizing all of this is a lot of spoken exposition—not just technobabble, but characters loudly explaining what they are doing while they are doing it—and a lot of scenes that almost connect together, but end up falling just short of actual sense. But it's pretty standard as British comics go—not a highlight of the medium by any stretch of the imagination, but not unusually bad, and certainly with its charms.

The larger question might be why Doctor Who would take such a strange shape. A utility belt? The Wizard of Omega? John and Gillian? What the heck is this? Certainly the comic exists in a sort of orthogonal reality to the television series. Jamie takes ages to appear, and is the only companion other than John and Gillian that the Doctor has. Ben, Polly, Victoria, and Zoe simply don't appear in the comics. The Doctor also never really develops, being pictured with the stovepipe hat that Troughton in practice abandoned in *The Underwater Menace* for years after that story had aired. He's hardly the only one to be behind the times, though—the Cybermen stay stuck in *The Tenth Planet* form, for instance.

There are a couple of reasons for this. First, the comics were done fast and on the cheap. The Cybermen were probably drawn by someone who hadn't seen the show, or at least hadn't paid much attention to it, who had photo references that happened to be from *The Tenth Planet*. Second, we're lucky they had Cybermen at all, since generally the strip avoided the actual TV characters because they would require royalty payments to use. Which also explains John and Gillian, who are the strip's original companions, and amount to a vague and royalty-free conflation of Susan and the Ian/Barbara pair aspect.

Stranger are things like the utility belt. Or, for that matter, the witches themselves. Who are, a perusal of the rest of the story suggests, actually witches and not a sci-fi concept pretending to be witches, with the Doctor having to find a proper spellbook to defeat them. But on the other hand, these strips were vetted by the production office (including, apparently, Terrence Dicks for a while), and occasionally went out of their way to engage with the series. This meant that occasionally the strip would even tuck nicely into continuity—at one point in the Hartnell era the Zarbi made an appearance in the strip almost immediately after *The Web Planet*. More strangely, late in the Troughton era, after *The War Games* had aired but before Pertwee was announced as the Third Doctor, the strip managed to come up with the bizarre conceit that the Doctor had adventures between his trial and his actual regeneration, an idea that will prove relevant in a few essays' time. (In truth, apparently, his regeneration was at the hands of a bunch of scarecrows. Really.)

Which suggests again that what's going on is simply that the sorts of comics being written simply nudged the show in particular ways. After all, it's not like the Doctor behaves completely wrong in the strips. Yes, he's more violent than the Doctor should be, but if you look at the things he actually does, they're still somewhat Doctorish—he's still an unpredictable, chaotic figure who is in constant action—which is very much like the character Troughton plays. They even have him correctly being good at chemistry and the like. The problem isn't quite that they don't get the Doctor. It's that they don't seem to get what a Doctor Who story is. In fact, they seem almost hell-bent on not doing Doctor Who stories.

No, really. The logic behind the comics seems often to specifically be that they should do what the TV show can't. Not just in terms of budget, although they are happy to enjoy their lack of one. But also in terms of approach—hence, for instance, a story that seems to involve real witches instead of being a science fiction show. But even when the strips are firmly science fiction they're often based around action sequences with giant robot or reptile monsters in a way that the series never was, in no small part because Doctor Who is a low-budget television show that requires that the Doctor usually defeat a menace by talking to it or by touching some wires together.

But look at what that requires. If the plot is going to involve more action—and both to distinguish itself from the series and to fit in with the expectations for a British comic strip of its genre, the plot of the *TV Comic* strips was always going to have to involve more action—the way the Doctor interacts with it will have to change too. The comics aren't so much mischaracterizing the Doctor as accurately characterizing what would happen if the Doctor were in action hero plots all the time. (And if we're being honest, the Venusian karate of the Pertwee era is just a different way of approaching the same problem.)

Perhaps most significantly, we should note that the comics retain a certain degree of Doctor Who logic. Remember what I said earlier about the way in which the comics don't quite fit together correctly? The way events do not necessarily seem like rational responses to one another, and that exposition is shouted out at random because there's nothing else that would make it clear? Right. But think about it for a moment—much of what is effective in Doctor Who comes from the careful and memorable use of set pieces. Robert Holmes, in particular, is going to master this someday. But even this season, look at something like *The Seeds of Death*, which chains together its space-travel set pieces and foam-machine set pieces with a perfectly pleasant but not particularly logical plot that involves Ice Warriors with really dumb invasion plans that rapidly multiply to incorporate new elements that appear out of nowhere, often for no other reason than that a cliffhanger is due. This is how Doctor Who works—it smashes together some odd ideas (Pirates, cowboys, and space travel! Martians, teleporters, and rockets! Cybermen, London, and the military!) and then works its way through the implications, stringing the cool bits together with some basic plotting. The comics are the same way, only with a completely different pool of set pieces because of their action tropes. But the basic logic—that a series of interesting and memorable impressions is more important than a coherent plot—is familiar to Doctor Who viewers.

The Polystyle comics, in other words, don't so much get Doctor Who wrong as get Doctor Who right through the strange looking glass of comics. Which is, perhaps, why people care enough about the comics that an essay like this is more than just an odd historical side note. Because for all their freakish wrongness, there's something oddly appealing about these comics. Indeed, Gareth Roberts has twice nicked plot concepts from Troughton-era issues of *TV Comic* for his Doctor Who episodes. They are unmistakably Doctor Who, and unmistakably part of Doctor Who history. A very weird and oddly fascinating part, in fact.

Tied to One Planet (*The War Games*)

It's April 19, 1969. Desmond Dekker and the Aces are at number one with "The Israelites," the first reggae song to hit number one in the UK. One week later The Beatles take number one with "Get Back," their second to last number one single in the UK. It stays at number one for six weeks. Also in the charts over this time are The Who, Fleetwood Mac, Herman's Hermits, Dean Martin, Frank Sinatra, The Isley Brothers, Simon and Garfunkel, Tom Jones, and The Fifth Dimension. Of these luminaries, it is of course Tommy Roe who unseats The Beatles with "Dizzy," before he himself is unseated by "The Ballad of John and Yoko," which is the last time The Beatles ever hit number one. This happens the same week that the ninth episode of *The War Games* airs, and remains through the rest of Patrick Troughton's tenure as the Doctor, a final instance of the odd parallelism between The Beatles and 1960s Doctor Who.

While in the news, British troops arrive in Northern Ireland to provide support for the Royal Ulster Constabulary, Robin Knox-Johnston completes a solo circumnavigation, and Charles de Gaulle steps down. In the US, the first death from AIDS occurs, although it will be years before the nature of this event is understood. Apollo 10 launches. This is worth highlighting, if only because it's a question almost everyone would get wrong if asked—the first American death from AIDS predated the moon landing? And, to grab a quick bit of intercontinental spirit, John Lennon and Yoko Ono do their Bed-In in Montreal.

But let's actually take one historical event in this time period and unpack it, because it was truly something special, and forms a vital metaphor for *The War Games*. In Berkeley, California, People's Park was opened. Those of you with particular love of grammar fascism will note my use of the passive voice there. It is deliberate. It is difficult to say that People's Park opened. That implies some degree of planning and design. In practice, People's Park was a plot of land seized by Berkeley University via eminent domain and then abandoned when proper construction stalled. Community members, irritated at this, proposed developing a portion of the plot as a park. And then, in the classic California guerilla-theater style, which had been out of date since 1967, they occupied the area and developed it into a park. The original version of this essay predated the Occupy movement. Going over it to revise it, the grotesque inevitability of what follows is crushing.

Governor Ronald Reagan, who had run on a platform that included accusing California's colleges of breeding "communist sympathizers, protesters, and sex deviants," overrode the University's promise not to begin developing the property without warning and to consult with the protesters, constructed an eight-foot fence around the unused lot to keep people from planting flowers there. A small riot erupted over this with protesters attempting to re-enter the park. Edwin Meese III, Reagan's chief of staff and future attorney general, took charge of the response, authorizing police to use whatever means they wanted. Clad in riot gear with their badges obscured to prevent identification, the police stormed in, beating protesters and, in an egregious case, fired shotguns loaded with buckshot far more dangerous and lethal than normally accepted for crowd control. A student was killed and a carpenter blinded in the process. Hundreds of others were injured. Reagan followed this by establishing what amounted to martial law in Berkeley, imposing a strict curfew and lining the streets with barbed wire.

Reagan defended his actions by saying "If it takes a bloodbath, let's get it over with. No more appeasement."

The conflict over the park would continue for decades.

While on TV... *The War Games* is not an easy work to approach. For one thing, it's the second longest Doctor Who story ever, and unlike the longest, it does not divide logically into smaller pieces. This is an actual (honest to God) ten-part story. On top of that, we get two companion departures, a regeneration, and, oh yes, the introduction of the Time Lords. I mean, where do we even start here? Miles and Wood make an excellent case that the answer to this is generally "the wrong place," arguing that the bit of this everyone makes a fuss over—the appearance of the Time Lords—is basically an irrelevant epilogue. As they put it, there's a vast cosmic crime over the first eight-and-a-half episodes, at which point the police are called, and fandom, inexplicably, only cares about the police.

But how can you call this unfair? I mean, it's true—the thing we've been stressing over and over again for two Doctors now is the fact that the Doctor is not yet a Time Lord and thus the show continually implies things that don't gel with its future. After this story it becomes a lot harder to make counterfactual readings of stories. The weight of a single and unitary text imposes an increasingly rigid vision on the future. But as much as this story looms over the 1970s and beyond, it looms even larger over the 1960s, making the stories from this era feel as though they're from a different show than everything after this. Miles and Wood ask, with reason, whether the nature of this shift at the end is sufficient to say that Doctor Who ended in 1969. And they argue, unsurprisingly given that they asked the question, that there's a fair case it did. But the flip side of this, which they ignore, is that you can equally well argue that Doctor Who finally debuts here—that this is where the proper and understood mythos of the series kicks in.

It's a little staggering, actually. I've watched the whole Troughton era now and immersed myself in 1960s Doctor Who and 1960s culture, and even still, watching *The War Games*, it's easier to slide into the counter-historical reading in which the Time Lords stand revealed and Doctor Who as we know it really gets started, than it is to read this as a conclusion to the Troughton era that we've actually been talking about all book. So massive is the gravity of this final sequence. If one is to treat *The War Games* in its entirety at all then it's still tempting to treat it as a two-story hybrid in which the story about humans and war comprises eight episodes followed by an epilogue about Time Lords.

But we know enough, by this point, to know this must be the wrong way around—that reading this story as the start of the Time Lord era cannot possibly be correct and that there must be some story that actually aired in mid-1969 and was experienced by people for whom the revelation that the Doctor is a Time Lord from an unnamed planet is in some sense a surprise and not the completion of a lore they knew going into Totters Lane forty-nine stories earlier.

Though we should perhaps note that this supposed original audience is, in fact, unusually small and obscure. This story got brutalized in the ratings, coming in dead last among Troughton stories and with the second lowest average viewing figures in all of Doctor Who. (Only *The Smugglers* did worse.) The eighth episode was watched by only 3.5 million people—a feat that three of the four episodes of *Battlefield*, the worst-rated story of the season that got the show cancelled, managed to top. As many people watched the last episode of *Survival* in 1989 as saw Troughton's regeneration. This is perhaps part of why this story is so distorted in the memory—its supposedly key scenes were not widely seen. For all its classic status and influence, the fact remains that this story could not have been widely remembered on its own merits.

Still, we have to figure this out. This story is a vital transition point in Doctor Who, and that means we need to see what's going on here, as opposed to what we imagined to be going on years after the fact. So let's start at the very beginning of the story. We open with the TARDIS arriving in the midst of World War I. What's perhaps most worth remarking on here is how unusual this is. The last time the TARDIS appeared in Earth history at all was nearly two seasons ago with *The Abominable Snowmen*, and that was an appearance in exotic Tibet. The last time it appeared in a known point in time and in the midst of a real historical event that would be relatively familiar to the audience was *The Highlanders*. The entire format of this story, in other words, is odd for Troughton. In a very real sense, this story is dragging him back to the absolute beginning of his tenure, and in doing so extending its reach implicitly to the Hartnell era, where history was a real thing that the series visited. In fact, the beginnings of *The War Games* and *The Highlanders* are markedly similar. One of the big character points for Troughton in *The Highlanders* was the scene in which he flatly told Polly he was fine with running away if he was avoiding cannonballs. Likewise, here, once he figures out that he's in the midst of World War I, he wants nothing more than to get out of there immediately.

We should also stop and look at what World War I was. World War II's reputation as "the good war" may be an endlessly contested point (especially in the UK, where the restraint/military action debate between Chamberlain and Churchill is viewed as a fundamental and continually rehashed debate about the nature of military power in the modern world), the fact that World War I was the bad war is almost, at this point, beyond all doubt. It happened, essentially, because of a pile of century old alliances required particular actions in response to the assassination of an Austrian archduke. All parties involved expected a brief military conflict that would clean up some of the alliances and allow everybody to get on with their lives.

Instead they got the wholesale massacre of a generation of European men in the most brutal war in recent memory. As was explained memorably in the novelization of *The War Games* (which I remember with some fondness), World War I fell in an unfortunate midpoint in the development of military technology between the invention of the machine gun and the invention of the tank. The result, combined with the grisly horrors of poison gas, was an absolutely gruesome war that required catastrophic death tolls for even the minutest of tactical gains. It was World War I that brought to popular awareness the concept of post-traumatic stress, or, as it was known at the time, shell shock.

In other words, if restaging the Chamberlain/Churchill debate endlessly in things like *The Abominable Snowmen*, *The Dominators*, and *The Krotons* was a serious debate about moral responsibility and war, restaging World War I was something completely different. A depiction of World War I is almost necessarily anti-war, and, in 1969, that meant specifically anti-Vietnam. World War I was the crowning example of military folly—the point where it became obvious that being a soldier wasn't a fun game played in the name of patriotism. This was a point with real and immediate social relevance.

So when the Doctor shows up in World War I, we're supposed to view him as landing somewhere truly awful—something that hasn't happened, again, since about *The Highlanders*. Which is actually a bit strange if you think about it. The anarchist Doctor was always most interesting as a figure of social justice—as the force that tears down unacceptable structures and would not stand for evil. And yet the show has mostly squandered this, dropping him into safe, banal situations. Mostly it's only been David Whitaker who has managed to come up with ways to push the Doctor in interesting directions, although Robert Holmes has made a late bid for brilliance. The rest of the regular writing stable has been a mess of generic bases under siege that at times just seem like a waste of Troughton's prodigious talent.

In a sense, then, *The War Games* opens by rerunning the structure of the Troughton era at high speed. Its first episode doesn't quite look like a World War I historical, but it appears closer to that than to anything else that Doctor Who has, in six years, set us up for save perhaps for *The Time Meddler*, where there is a constant sense that there might be something wrong with history. But slowly, from there, the story grows. What initially seems like a story about soldiers being hypnotized and meddling with time grows inexorably, the stakes becoming more and more alarmingly high.

This is where the single-story aspect of *The War Games* proves most significant. Unlike *The Daleks' Master Plan*, *The War Games* is a story where a single situation gets worse and worse. There are places where *The War Games* drags, certainly, but for the most part it's a steady escalation of problems. What starts seeming to be a story about mind-controlled soldiers becomes a story about a war across timelines that becomes a cruel game run by evil overlords seemingly for their own amusement. This, in turn, finally becomes a story about a massive, galactic war crime.

There is, in this process, only one brief moment that doesn't seem like an escalation. The revelation, that (what we thought were) the grimy horrors of World War I are actually just a game being played by aliens, comes mostly as a relief. The cliffhanger to the second episode, in which the Doctor and company the mists in World War I and are attacked (by Romans of all things), is far more interesting and exciting than the Doctor getting swept away by a machine that will obviously take him to the central command of all of this stuff at the end of the next episode. The second episode's cliffhanger throws everything we think we know out the window. The third episode's cliffhanger is little more than "and then the Doctor gets to the place where he can advance the plot." Once we get to the third episode, well, it's just aliens! The Doctor can handle a fake World War I run by aliens! I mean, it's a pity they're not Cybermen or something really easy, but still. Aliens are the things the Doctor beats all the time.

But wait a moment. Look at the sheer strangeness of that. It's a letdown when it turns out the Doctor isn't stuck in something real but is instead in the midst of a completely over-the-top and mildly illogical alien scheme. That may be how the suspense swings, but it's a huge problem in terms of the psychedelic transformation that sparked the Second Doctor's tenure. The point of that transformation was that the Doctor realizes there are monsters in the world—terrible darknesses that have to be fought. But what we see, as we breathe a sigh of relief that it's only psychotic aliens, is that these monsters have been paper tigers. The Doctor has been hiding behind them. He can't handle the truly scary things. Never mind the corners of the universe that have bred the most terrible things. What about Earth?

Except that the show is cleverer than that. Of course it is—this is written by Terrance Dicks and Malcolm Hulke. Dicks will never get called a genius by enough people, due in no small part to the ruthless narrative efficiency of his genius, but the fact of the matter is that he's very, very good at stitching bits of a story together. Hulke is probably recognized as the better writer, with his specialty, as we've already seen in his previous effort, being that he creates situations with far more depth to them than they initially appear. They are the exact two writers this story needs. Because once the lens zooms out and we see the aliens, we assume that's it—that's where the real story is. We think we understand this story.

We're wrong, and Dicks and Hulke (I suspect mainly Hulke in this case) pull off a brilliant end-run on our expectations. Sure, defeating the aliens is relatively easy. But that's not what the Doctor is actually trying to do. Just because it turns out that the Doctor didn't land in World War I does not, after all, mean that he isn't dealing with real humans. This point is reiterated over and over again. The cliffhanger to the fourth episode, in which Carstairs holds a gun on Zoe, is horrifying precisely because he's been an ally that we've grown to trust and now has had his identity taken away. The bulk of what is moving about the sixth episode is watching Moor's struggle with his conditioning. Over and over again we are told, both implicitly and explicitly, that the real problem isn't these aliens but with fixing the horrible abuse they've put the humans through.

This is flagged to us perhaps most clearly by the fact that the aliens, although, you know, alien, do not actually act like traditional monsters. In fact, the basic setup of a squabbling War Chief and Security Chief who are both under the command of a War Lord who tries to administer between them is actually extremely familiar. In fact, look at it this way—the War Chief is trying to ally, on his own terms, with the resistance and the alien outsiders, even though such an alliance is doomed because they'll betray him in the end, and the Security Chief is trying to stop him but is stymied by his superiors. Where have we seen this before?

Only in every base under siege story of the last three years. Which is brilliant. In its middle section, *The War Games* is a base under siege story in which the TARDIS crew are the monsters and the villains are the base. They flit around the edges of the base, gathering an army, picking away at its defenses, and steadily close in while the base descends helplessly into internal squabbling. It's hard not to view this as an overt critique of most of the Troughton era. (And note that since Dicks took over as script editor, there's been exactly one straight-up base under siege story, and Dicks rewrote most of it because he was unsatisfied with Hayles's original script. One senses that the traditional base under siege model was never much to his liking.) The Doctor, this suggests, has perhaps been on the wrong side in his endless fighting with monsters. The point of his regeneration, after all, was a dark mirror to humanity. The point of Mondas was never "fear monsters." It was "fear a part of yourself." And this has always been the problem with the bases under siege: that they ignore people in favor of a set of rigid and predefined roles.

Which is ultimately where the sting in the trap is. The Doctor doesn't have any real trouble stopping the War Lord. That's easy. What he can't manage is the people. He has no way of getting all the kidnapped soldiers home. And so he has to call in the Time Lords.

What does this mean? Here we must be very careful. As I said, one cannot walk anywhere near this part of the episode without confronting the future. But we've done this dance of finding alternate paths the series could have taken before. And it's important here, because the Time Lords remain mysterious in this story. They're consciously left ambiguous and unexplained. Their planet is never named. The nature of their civilization is never really shown. And there are clear differences here with future stories. In the future it's implied that stealing the TARDIS was the Doctor's big crime, but here he's tried for interference. Indeed, the Time Lords don't seem to have TARDISes here—their time machines are identical to the SIDRAT machines used by the War Chief.

The second thing to note about the Time Lords is that in this story, contrary to assumptions, they are not defined primarily in terms of the Doctor. Yes, the fact that they are the Doctor's people is absolutely crucial to why we care about them, but in a story in which the primary villain is called the War Lord, introducing the Time Lords as another faction has to be understood largely in terms of this, and surely would have been to anybody unaware of the next twenty-six seasons. But who exactly is the War Lord? It's never particularly explained in the story. His entire planet is apparently villainous, and he's its leader. They've got a bit of a galaxy conquering obsession. And that's about what we have.

But we can make at least some inferences. First of all, *The War Games*, while clearly a story with real concerns about the nature of war, is not a pacifist story. The Doctor is all in favor of armed resistance against the games, after all. It's not that war is bad. It's that war for its own sake is bad. That is the primary crime of the War Lord: he forces people to fight wars for no purpose other than the glory of war. His sin is allowing war to get out of control.

Likewise, the Time Lords seem extremely detached rulers. Their fundamental law, after all, is non-intervention. But they are not wholly detached. The Doctor has no doubt that they'll intervene to deal with the War Lord. In other words, it is clearly not that they oppose intervention so much as that they oppose, and this is a word that is familiar in talking about the Doctor's own people, meddling. This is made all the clearer when the Time Lords make a great show of accepting the Doctor's plea that there is evil that has to be fought.

So what is it about the Doctor's actions that they find objectionable? Narrative logic dictates that it must be the same thing about the Doctor's actions that failed him in the rest of the story. After all, this has been a coherent ten-parter by and large, and so one assumes it's not just going to jettison its themes at the last second. The Doctor failed and had to call in the Time Lords because, at the end of the day, he was incapable of dealing with the problems of humans beyond fighting monsters for them. Because, in the end, he was as out of his depth as the villains—stuck defending against crises with no real skill anywhere else. The Doctor's crime is that he was only ever really good for bases under siege. That he might throw himself into a crisis, but he'd never throw himself into the aftermath.

Which is the thing that almost everybody misses about *The War Games*. The story is a blistering condemnation of the Doctor. It firmly sides with the Time Lords. Part of this condemnation comes from how thoroughly the Doctor is beaten. His companions are taken away, he's forced to regenerate, he's exiled, and, on top of all of that, he meets his final end gurning helplessly on a TV screen. This is a particular insult—for his entire tenure, Troughton peered knowledgeably out of video screens, seeming to have a genuine level of control over the technology he existed in. Here, in his final seconds, he's beaten by one. This is a humiliating defeat by any measures.

But frankly, even the Doctor seems to side with his accusers. He makes a show of running, yes, but in something we've never really seen before, he seems to give up. Not just in the sense of knowing he's beaten, but in the sense of feeling as though he deserves it. Oddly, it's Troughton who is most responsible for this final selling out of his own character, infusing lines like "I had every right to leave," (his goodbye to Jamie) or the story's best line, shortly after Jamie and Zoe promise always to remember him, in which he turns to his Time Lord captor and says, "They'll forget me, won't they?" with a weary sadness that suggests that he has, on some level, always known this was coming for him.

And yet there's more than that. Troughton, in his final scene, goes out of his way to make his character look bad. Given some last banter and badgering with authority—the sort of thing the audience's love for the character is based on—he gleefully overplays it, filling the Doctor with sudden pomposity and outright irritation (look at how much of a brat he is over picking a face). Whereas the Time Lords act relatively friendly, exchanging bemused smiles with each other at the Doctor's antics, and generally seeming like benevolent adults trying to lightly punish a misbehaving child so he'll improve his ways. So when the Time Lords finally get irritated at him and stick him into a monitor, it feels like he deserves it. By the time he regenerates the audience nearly wants him gone too.

But in another sense, this is the real endpoint of the 1960s. The revolution failed. However much we may have liked it—and for my part, I loved it, especially in the Doctor Who sense in which the psychedelic revolution is literally embodied in Patrick Troughton's Doctor—it failed. It's time to break up the band. It's time to face the reality that the bad guys aren't external monsters, but the people who want to send riot police to crush the sex deviants planting flowers. It's time, in other words, to face reality. This is the message every sane and useful mystic in the world will tell you. It's all well and good to journey among the interiors of the mind and at the furthest fringes of consciousness and reality. It's all well and good to face gods and demons and encounter the fundamental truth of the universe. But the real test is what you can bring back from those mystical realms to reality. The real test is how you can live as a mystic in the real world.

The Doctor, like psychedelia, failed. Now it's time to come back down to Earth.

Time Can Be Rewritten: *World Game*

It's October of 2005. This means, in practice, that we're between the Christopher Eccleston and David Tennant years. We've already talked about this time period a bit in the previous volume's essay on *The Time Travelers*, so I'll just refer you there for the general time, but suffice it to say that these are the dying embers of the BBC Books line, coming out after the series has conclusively moved on to other things. Which is oddly fitting, as here we are, hanging around in the Patrick Troughton era long after it's moved on with a story written nearly twenty years after Troughton's death.

The simplest question is why there are even stories being covered after *The War Games*. Well, see, it turns out that for plot related reasons, the reunion stories of the 1980s opened up some seemingly massive continuity errors, mostly in the form of having Troughton's Doctor interacting with the Time Lords and knowing about the outcome of his trial despite the fact that neither of these things happen until seemingly a short period before his regeneration. This bothered people for a while, until the Paul Cornell, Martin Day, and Keith Topping proposed something called "Season Six-B" in *The Discontinuity Guide*. And this novel is Terrance Dicks mucking around with that concept.

I'd explain the idea of Season Six-B, but it's one of those absolutely ludicrous moments of Doctor Who that is probably best approached experientially instead of from a distance. And anyway, the point of doing this as a Time Can Be Rewritten entry is that we're approaching Season Six-B in part as if it were actually meant to slot into 1960s Doctor Who. For now, never mind the '80s continuity errors this fixes. After all, why should the 1980s get to come and unambiguously muck up our 1960s when the 1960s don't get the right to sneak into the 1980s and wreck havoc with them?

Of course, this approach acquires an interesting relationship with the rails that is not entirely based on having any contact with them, and the problems begin more or less on the first page. Dicks's novel begins with "the genuine and original summary record of the trial of the Doctor," noting that the version "with which we were, until now, familiar was substantially re-edited for the public record." We then get a differing version of the trial from the one we saw on television in 1969. One in which the Doctor's plea about fighting evil is not, as in the original, "accepted," but is merely said to be "not without merit," after which, rather surprisingly, the Doctor is sentenced to death.

Dicks is making a very bizarre claim here—one that is not merely a retcon, but something with far wider-reaching implications. It's not just that what we saw on television is here said to be wrong (which is already a bit of a strange claim for the novels to make, given that in almost every fan's assessment they are given a less privileged place in Doctor Who than the televised stories), it's that it's said to be wrong because the Time Lords have been censoring material that could be viewed as damaging to them. In other words, this doesn't just make a huge change to the television show, it tells us that the television show has been vetted by its own fictional characters and reshaped into a piece of propaganda to serve their needs. This is bewildering in its implications, in no small part because, if we're being honest, it renders the show massively less interesting. I mean, I don't want to watch the adventures of the Doctor as censored by a bunch of fictional characters. That doesn't sound fun at all.

Stranger is that the overall goal of Season Six-B doesn't require this at all. Basically, where Dicks is going with this is that the CIA (that's the Celestial Intervention Agency—a facet of Time Lord society devised by Robert Holmes in the mid-'70s) use the Doctor's imminent execution to get him to act as a CIA agent doing their dirty work, and that he goes from that into the exile depicted at the end of *The War Games*/start of *Spearhead from Space*.

But if that's all Dicks wants, he's gone for spectacular overkill in achieving it. All of Season Six-B could be accomplished by having the Doctor fade off the monitor and end up somewhere different where he's told that, actually, he'll be working for the Time Lords now. You don't need to overtly contradict anything seen on screen to get to the desired goal of a late-career Second Doctor as a Time Lord agent. Which makes the scale of Dicks's retcon stick out oddly. Why retcon, essentially, the entirety of Doctor Who by rendering it all unreliable narration?

Part of the answer, at least, is an overt playfulness. The bulk of the new account of the Doctor's trial would be recognizable to people familiar with Dicks's oeuvre as a very lightly rewritten version of his prologue to *Doctor Who and the Auton Invasion*, i.e. his novelization of *Spearhead from Space*. These books, as we've talked about, form a huge part of the collective memory of Doctor Who, and the sequence in question is one of the better remembered of the line. So what's being played with isn't just Doctor Who continuity but the specific textual material of an iconic part of Doctor Who.

More broadly, *World Game* represents a massive unshackling of fandom's id with regards to the 1960s. We talked in the last Time Can Be Rewritten entry about how writers of books set in 1960s-era Doctor Who are oddly reluctant to import too many major concepts from later in the series. The big one is that the words "Time Lord" virtually never appear in a pre-*War Games* story.

But here, suddenly, there's no real restrictions on it. This is the one place you can put the Second Doctor in frame with the full continuity of the Time Lords. And so Dicks runs with it, working in the CIA, the 1985 story *The Two Doctors*, psychic paper from the 2005 series (despite an edict against references to the new series—Dicks apparently correctly bet that he could get away with it), the High Council (who become the people trying the Doctor, as opposed to "just some guys"), etc.

But the problem with this is something we already hit on in the entry on *The War Games*—the Time Lords of *The War Games* are not the Time Lords of *The Deadly Assassin* and other stories from the '70s and beyond. As tempting as it is to treat *The War Games* as if it established the series' entire mythos, it didn't. In fact, it established relatively little—basically just the name of the Doctor's people and a glimpse of what their planet was like. For all the talk of the story spoiling the mystery of the Doctor, it's actually a vanishingly slender revelation.

And yet Dicks, from that, begins to spin far bigger implications, dropping in lines like "The deviousness and corruption of Gallifreyan politics had been one of the Doctor's primary motives for leaving the Time Lords in the first place" that go far beyond the relatively modest exposition of *The War Games* and into something far more wide-ranging in its ambitions and, perhaps more damningly, far less wide-ranging in its implications.

But beyond that, Dicks seems to misunderstand bits of the Gallifrey that followed *The War Games* (or, more sympathetically, disregard the nature of them in favor of the fan consensus of them). The CIA, for instance, was clearly never meant to be taken entirely seriously. The clue, and this should go without saying, is in the name. To anyone outside of the US, there is a certain comedy value to the actual CIA. They are, after all, the organization that cooked up, apparently in all seriousness, absurd plans like trying to assassinate Castro with an exploding cigar. But more broadly than that, the CIA has a reputation as almost pantomime villains—selfish spymasters obsessed with their own power and willing to work with all manner of dictators, war criminals, common criminals, thugs, and murderers if it advanced their goals, which seemed to not quite be equivalent to advancing their country's goals. The CIA, in other words, is that great combination—vaguely malevolent, hugely corrupt, and massively incompetent.

So when Holmes—a master of bleak humor, after all—created a CIA for Gallifrey, the implication is clear. And when he suggests that the Doctor's past missions were on behalf of the CIA, the implication is not that the Doctor is a super-cool secret agent. It's that the Doctor has, thus far, been clowning around with the dunce Time Lords. The CIA isn't supposed to be a powerful, feared organization. They're supposed to be a bit rubbish. They're Americans, for crying out loud.

What's strange is that despite the faint absurdity of the premise, there's a pretty good story under here. Well, OK, perhaps that's not that strange. This is Terrance Dicks. Aside from the fact that any Doctor Who fan who grew up with the Target novelizations (that'd be me, for one) has an almost Pavlovian response to Dicks's prose, the fact of the matter is, and I've alluded to this before, he's an extremely good writer, at least at the sort of thing he attempts. He has a strong grasp of crisp, clear, functional, and exciting prose. As a result, he's also good at one type of book: children's literature.

That's not an insult at all. Writing quality children's literature is hard. The ruthless clarity of prose Dicks cultivates is something a vanishingly small number of writers are actually good at. Perhaps the best thing that can be said about Dicks's writing is that there is virtually nothing he has ever written that is confusing. This might sound like damning with faint praise, but given the fact that Dicks is usually writing Doctor Who, a series with plots that actually make no sense if you look at them for too long, this should be admitted as the accomplishment that it is. Dicks can structure a traditional and entertaining adventure story, stock it with quality set pieces, and drop in some engaging descriptions, characters, and dialogue with the best of them. Frankly, J.K. Rowling made her career off of writing Terrance Dicks-style novels—it wasn't until *Order of the Phoenix* that the Harry Potter books stopped sounding like his work.

So yes, the book itself is surprisingly fun. The Doctor and his one-off companion Serena run about French and British history of the eighteenth century trying to keep the timeline on track while bored immortals try to mess with history. It's perfect—Dicks gets to write a greatest hits collection of eighteenth-century European history and the Napoleonic wars, dropping in action set pieces to keep it moving. This is exactly what Terrance Dicks is good at, and the mere fact that the premise he's working from is cataclysmically flawed is in no way capable of keeping Dicks from making good with a plot that was made for him. Dicks effortlessly writes clear and engaging prose. It's tough to overstate how much of an advantage that is.

But it doesn't change the fact that, as a Second Doctor novel, this is profoundly misconceived. Its most grotesque feature may be the decision to equate the Second Doctor explicitly with Talleyrand, a French diplomat who notably changed sides at least six separate times over the course of his career becoming more or less the only person to successfully serve in every single regime that came to power from Louis XVI to his death in 1838. This comparison is made repeatedly—Serena makes it explicitly, and the Doctor describes himself by saying "I do what I can, and what seems best to me at the time," and, earlier, explicitly is willing to throw some ethical qualms out the window for the sole reason that his life is on the line.

There are, of course, versions of the Doctor this might describe. The most obvious, of course, is the one who should be taking over by now: the Third Doctor, who willingly and happily got in line as a military employee. The Third Doctor is also the Doctor Dicks is most associated with, having script edited his entire tenure. (Although to be fair, Dicks wrote multiple Fourth Doctor stories, script-edited the tail end of Troughton's tenure, and, perhaps most importantly, has written for the first ten Doctors in book form.) And, of course, one of the things that virtually everybody points out about the transition from *The War Games* to *Spearhead from Space* is that it's just about the sharpest stylistic change in the history of the series. And it's probably also worth pointing out that the

Pertwee era had been in something of a critical freefall for the last fifteen years when *World Game* came out.

What I'm getting at is that part of what this book accomplishes is the creation of a transitional Second Doctor—one who is himself becoming more like the Third Doctor, and thus makes the controversial decision of the Third Doctor to just join up with UNIT more understandable. Of course, it's tough to see this as much of a defense … after all, as much as Doctor-as-Talleyrand is an absurd description of Troughton's Doctor, it's not exactly flattering to any Doctor. If this is Troughton on his way to becoming Pertwee, then what he appears to be becoming is an amoral opportunist of the worst sort.

But even if we were to take the novel's eventual rehabilitation of Talleyrand as being meant to apply to the Doctor as well, there's a larger problem here. At best *World Game* can be said to soften the transition to *Spearhead from Space* (although as we'll see when we finally do get there, that transition is less abrupt than its reputation would suggest). But this isn't a Third Doctor novel. It's a Second Doctor novel, and one that contradicts televised episodes starring Troughton, and, more to the point, erases the entire point of *The War Games*, which concludes with the Time Lords issuing a blistering critique of the Doctor's own methods that Dicks's retcon completely undoes. And replaces it with the Doctor adopting even more morally bankrupt methods, turning the psychedelic anarchist of Troughton's Doctor into a company man.

But all of this amounts to meta-commentary on the memory of Troughton's era. It makes sense in 2005, but placed alongside the Doctor Who that existed in 1969 it's jarring. There's very few ways to look at this story that make it look like a good Patrick Troughton story. And this highlights an important thing about *The War Games*. For all that its revelations are treated as explaining the past of Doctor Who, they represent in many more ways a decisive break with that past. In practice all *The War Games* explains is the Doctor's future. For all of Dicks's genuinely entertaining play with the continuity and mythology of Doctor Who here, the one thing he fails to ever quite engage with is the era he's supposedly writing for.

Time Can Be Rewritten: *The Two Doctors*

It's February 16, 1985, which is, if we are being honest, yet another odd time for it to be on the road from June of 1969 to January of 1970, but hey, there was still an awful lot of acid going around in 1969, and who are we to question it. Perhaps Doctor Who just nipped off to Woodstock and lost track of things like everyone else. We'll be here again later, so we may as well skip the music and news and get on to the meat of things, namely the latest adventure of Patrick Troughton, a story called *The Two Doctors*.

Starting off, it's shocking how much has changed in this six month gap between Seasons Six and Seven. I mean, look at the new opening credits. The starfield opening is certainly lush, and it's hard to imagine how it was done with 1970s technology, but what the heck is with this awful theme music? This isn't going to stay around for the whole decade, is it? Still, things pick up immediately after. And you get to see the switch to color live! They turn the switch right in the middle of the episode, with the opening scene fading from black-and-white to color! That's cool!

Much as it's tempting to just continue to review this trying to maintain the conceit that it is a Patrick Troughton story, I think we have to admit, this approach is not even remotely maintainable through the full two-and-a-half hours of *The Two Doctors*. So let's back up and take this more honestly. In the previous essay we looked at the slightly bewildering Season Six-B idea on its own, as a follow-up to the Troughton era, and found it wanting. Today, in the second and final part of our tour of a fictional season of Doctor Who, we look at the story most responsible for this idea. It's fair, before we get too deep into this, to ask why we're even monkeying around here in the first place instead of bringing the book to a more dignified conclusion.

The answer, roughly, is that this whole idea is too self-evidently ludicrous to take seriously, making it enormously fun to take seriously. It is obvious watching *The War Games* that there is no Season Six-B. Or, actually, no. It's not obvious, because *The War Games* is so far from supporting a Season Six-B that in and of itself, nobody would have come up with such a silly idea. (Except, apparently, Polystyle.) Season Six-B, in terms of *The War Games*, isn't even wrong. It has no relationship whatsoever with *The War Games*. And yet multiple writers have opted to set stories in this obvious anachronism. It's a paradox within Doctor Who—something that clearly does exist from one perspective, and clearly doesn't from another.

I should also, I suppose, briefly disclaim regarding the Colin Baker era, given that it is possibly the most contentious era of Doctor Who there is. Actually, it's not even particularly contentious—almost everybody finds massive fault with it. It's more that there's an elaborate blame game, with all of the primary sources having massive axes to grind with the other primary sources and generally suggesting that the era would have been great if it weren't for X. (Generally X is either John Nathan-Turner or Eric Saward.) I tend to agree with the assessment that the Colin Baker years are deeply, deeply flawed. I think the problems are far, far deeper than what can be laid at the feet of one or even two particular creative forces. All of which said, I actually enjoy the era, with this story being one of the high points. It's just that, more than any other era of Doctor Who, it is one I often have to enjoy in spite of itself.

So yes. To get up to speed, in 1985, while Colin Baker was the incumbent Doctor, Robert Holmes was commissioned to write a story pairing him with the Second Doctor. The result is *The Two Doctors*. But for reasons obscured by the mists of 1985 (which will turn out to be a very misty year, with almost nobody involved in the series having an account of it that is entirely compatible with anyone else's), he did so in a way that wrecked havoc with continuity. Specifically, he has the Second Doctor and Jamie traveling alone together (Victoria is said to be "studying graphology") in an apparently accurately steerable TARDIS doing missions for the Time Lords. All parts of this, including, frankly, Victoria the graphologist, seem patently ludicrous in terms of the Troughton era, where the Doctor clearly could not steer the TARDIS and where Jamie has clearly not heard of the Time Lords (since he asks about them in *The War Games*).

The resulting continuity problems are why the Season Six-B idea was cooked up. Mind you, Holmes seemed to know what he was doing at the time. Which isn't surprising—we shouldn't forget that Holmes wrote the stories immediately before and after *The War Games*. In an interview he states his view that the Time Lords were in partial control of the TARDIS throughout Troughton's tenure and that the trial was a hypocritical sham—certainly a view consistent with his later interpretations of Gallifrey, though equally clearly not intended by Terrance Dicks and Malcolm Hulke in 1969. I've my own theories on why he tortured continuity so viciously, but we'll do this story again in Volume Five, so I should leave something in the tank for that reading. (One clue—it has to do with *Attack of the Cybermen*.) Tat Wood, in *About Time*, also makes a strong argument based on the fact that there is a continually advancing "present" for Time Lords and that Troughton was working not for the Time Lords of *The War Games*, but rather for Time Lords from the Colin Baker era who were looking for someone they could send subtly.

All of which said, Season Six-B still feels like a better explanation than Holmes's, if only to account for Troughton's behavior in this story. Some fans opt to get hung up on the fact that the Doctor and Jamie are visibly older in this story than they were in the 1960s. This strikes me as a strange thing to complain about for anyone who is generally OK with pretending that men in rubber suits are monsters, especially given the difficulties of casting a fifteen-years-younger Patrick Troughton in 1985. But that's not the only issue here. At one point in the first episode the Doctor lays into Jamie for speaking in a "mongrel" tongue. This would be alarmingly cruel coming from the Sixth Doctor's mouth. To hear it out of Troughton's is jaw-dropping. There is no point anywhere in Seasons Four through Six where Troughton's Doctor would ever say anything like that to Jamie. If nothing else, Season Six-B makes more sense than fouling the actual televised Doctor with that.

But that's hardly the only problem here. Watched immediately after *The War Games* or, as I ended up watching it, interleaved with episodes of *Spearhead from Space*, *The Two Doctors* is jarring in its extremity. It's not just the anger of the Second Doctor. It's not even the violence of it—the lion's share of *The War Games*, after all, is set in a reenactment of World War I. Rather, it's the way the series here revels in the violence and treat it as a source of active pleasure.

It's not just a problem with the Doctors, although they certainly are out of sorts. Troughton is less upset about watching his dinner companion coldly murder someone, or, earlier, about being an accomplice to another murder than one might hope. Baker, on the other hand, is almost unrecognizable as "the Doctor" at times when compared to the character as understood in 1969. It's not just that he dispatches one of the main villains by smothering him with cyanide—something that is not quite unreasonable in and of itself given that the villain is a murderous sociopath who wants to eat him and his companions. Also, it should be noted that the Doctor is actively wounded and being hunted by said villain prior to this. Rather, it's that, after killing him, Baker's Doctor stands over his corpse and makes wisecracks at him. This is the problem— it's not difficult to imagine Troughton killing things—he basically ran around with a gun shooting Ice Warriors in *The Seeds of Death*. But the sheer physical, visceral nature of this death is difficult, and it's downright impossible to imagine him reveling in it and gloating about it.

But it's not just the Doctors reveling in death here. It's the entire production. Every inch of this story seems to fetishize death, whether it be in discussions of it or, in the end, in grotesque shots of Sontarans with their (alarmingly bright green) viscera spewing about the place. This is Doctor Who that does not just use violence to resolve plot threads here and there, it seems to love violence and see violence as central to the show's pleasure.

Admittedly, the story has a point to make about that. Not just in the way that it ends with the Doctor committing himself to vegetarianism (a commitment that actually seems hard to justify for Baker's Doctor, who has been far less confronted with the horrors of the Androgum diet than any of the other leads), but also, as Rob Shearman points out in his quite brilliant guest-defense in *About Time*, in the entire treatment of the Androgums. Shearman makes the compelling case that the central cleverness of the Androgums is that they act and are treated like generic Doctor Who monsters, but they look basically human only with red eyebrows and some warts. Thus, Shearman argues, the Androgums become a critique of typical Doctor Who monsters. The Doctor standing over Shockeye's body and gloating is supposed to be uncomfortable. And this is a controversy that doesn't just apply to the Colin Baker era—the problems highlighted by having everyone treat the Androgums as though they're generic monsters when they look and act so recognizably human apply equally well to the monster-obsessed Troughton era.

Shearman also argues that Troughton's Doctor is made deliberately unlikable through the whole thing, with his only turn at clowning around in the manner the fans wanted being when he himself has been turned into an Androgum, arguing that this is the sort of crowning glory of Holmes's by then famous sense of black humor (which has not been on full display in either of the Holmes stories we've covered). It's a fair argument—Holmes is certainly that clever. And, of course, the idea of Troughton's Doctor as a clown is largely something that post-dates his era. He's much darker and moodier in the 1960s than people remember. But there's something we can't quite get around in all of this: even in its more redemptive reading this story remains incredibly cynical and, at times, downright mean-spirited.

Yes, there's a brilliant black humor in tweaking fan expectations and parodying the normal treatment of aliens by having excessively human monsters. After all, I ended the Troughton era by observing that the problem the show was running into was, basically, that it had a psychedelic trickster god, an eighteenth-century Scotsman, and a futuristic walking computer ambling about and in no way intervening in any real human dramas. It was, in other words, all monsters and no heart.

Certainly *The Two Doctors* can't be accused of having nothing to say about people. But I'm not sure it can be credited as having anything good to say about people, especially in comparison with the Troughton era. The lack of connection with human concerns is certainly alleviated, though notably only in Baker's Doctor. Holmes, in playing Troughton fairly unsympathetically through this, actually never really has him interact meaningfully with human concerns. Indeed, Holmes doesn't really have Troughton interact meaningfully with much of anything in this story—he's shorted any real moments of triumph or accomplishment in the entire plot. After about the twenty-minute mark he spends the bulk of the story either tied to a table or turned into an Androgum, and he's largely uninvolved in the resolution.

But here we come back to the first problem we noticed with Troughton's Doctor in this story—his laying into Jamie for his "mongrel" tongue. Yeah, the Doctor has human concerns in this story. But his concern with humanity seems largely to be disdain. Look at the interaction between Baker's Doctor and Peri throughout the story, especially coming off of the effortless camaraderie of the Troughton/Hines/Padbury team. Look in particular as Peri appears to mouth "asshole" at him after a particularly bruising bit of "banter." (Although apparently the canonical epithet is "I know" in response to the Doctor saying something snide about humans, I'd point out that the mouth motions are virtually identical.) And this is a story where he and Peri are getting along relatively well. Troughton's Doctor may have been blind to humanity at times, but again, he at least always seemed to like people. Baker's Doctor seems to understand them, yes, but he also seems to hate them.

It's not that this story is, as Tat Wood suggests in his review of it, hopelessly cynical (even if I do disagree with Wood on where the cynicism is located). Troughton's Doctor was fundamentally a utopian character. In the end, it can be argued, misguidedly so, but utopian all the same. This is worth something—indeed, it's worth a great deal. Baker's Doctor isn't at all. Baker's show isn't at all. It's not that the show has nothing to say, nor that what it has to say is wrong. It's just that it doesn't seem to have anything good to say about the world. It is an ugly, cynical, and vicious show, at least when compared to the Troughton era. Admittedly, 1985 was an ugly, cynical, and vicious year compared to 1966–1969, but the degree to which it shows is painful.

Which is basically where it seems to me that the entire Season Six-B debate ends up. Yes, in terms of what happens on screen up to 1985, this season is probably the easiest and simplest explanation for the continuity errors involved in *The Two Doctors*. It only involves retconning a single episode of the Troughton era, unlike Holmes's apparent intentions, which muck up most of the era. Tat Wood's explanation is attractive, but fails to account for Jamie not knowing who the Time Lords were in *The War Games*, which is still a significant hole. Watching *The Two Doctors*, at least, Season Six-B is probably the easiest way to account for this.

But from the perspective of the Troughton era? It's not just that, as we saw last time, Season Six-B is ludicrous in terms of the 1960s. It's something more than that. It's not that this season is a bad way of reconciling 1985 Doctor Who with 1969

Doctor Who. It's that, for someone who loves the Doctor Who of 1969 in all its psychedelic and utopian glory ... why would you want to reconcile it to this wretched, violent show from 1985?

Now My Doctor: Patrick Troughton

If the version of this essay in the Hartnell volume was one of the hardest versions to write, this version is by far one of the easiest. There are relatively few points within Doctor Who fandom more agreed upon than the fact that Patrick Troughton is absolutely magnificent. An essay about why Troughton is such a good Doctor is positively straightforward. Actually, the real problem is that one is spoiled for choice. The problem isn't explaining what about Troughton is so good, it's managing to bring it all together into an explanation.

At the heart of it, perhaps the simplest and most obvious thing to point out is that almost everything we think of as "Doctorish" today is Troughton's invention. Hartnell's contribution to the series is enormous, but the idea of the Doctor as a figure that is continually fun to watch comes from Troughton. The idea of the Doctor as a figure who says and does funny things regularly comes from Troughton. The idea of playing the Doctor as a brilliant buffoon flying by the seat of his pants comes from Troughton.

Except this isn't *quite* true. Hartnell has scads of comedic material and is frequently an absolute joy to watch. He's similarly making things up as he goes along on a regular basis, and he's just as prone to flitting between genius and pure idiocy. But if you showed anybody a chunk of a Hartnell story and a chunk of a Troughton story and asked them which actor's performance was the closest to that of Eccleston, Tennant, or Smith they'd pick Troughton every time. But it's very difficult to nail down why without making a statement that just isn't true about Hartnell.

All of which said, most of the stuff we've already said is stuff that would come up if you asked someone. Which is to say that it's not quite that Troughton adds those characteristics but that his Doctor is defined by those characteristics while they were incidental to Hartnell's. Hartnell's Doctor was, at times, charming and clownish and funny, but that wasn't what his character was about. Hartnell's Doctor was, in the end, defined as an, at times, outright off-putting old man who, at least in his first appearances, was actively untrustworthy. Whereas after a consciously off-putting first story Troughton's Doctor rapidly beds in as a charming, genial figure. Formulated simply, in Hartnell's era traveling with the Doctor was scary—only Vicki meaningfully chose it. In Troughton's era, traveling with the Doctor was fun—it's just the monsters that are scary. And the only two companions who weren't there voluntarily—Ben and Polly—were quickly deemed surplus to requirements.

It's this aspect of the character—the fact that how fun Troughton is to watch is one of the fundamental pleasures of the show—that is why Troughton appears to be the model for all future Doctors. Even when the comedic aspects are reeled back considerably for Pertwee, this aspect remains. And because of this Troughton, especially in his three post-'60s appearances, was very much pigeonholed as "the clown" and written as a pleasantly doddering old fool.

But this is a misrepresentation of what Troughton actually did with the part. Yes, he was frequently charming, but that's only a part of his character. If one actually watches the stories one is struck by how often he takes a very different tact. There are as many scenes of Troughton yelling at people and berating them as there are scenes of him being charming and funny. And while there aren't really any stories after *The Power of the Daleks* where he's actively made to be untrustworthy and suspicious, there's always a glint of, if not menace, at least the sense that the charm and kindness could turn cold and ruthless if need be. His jovial nature isn't a front as such—that would imply that it's not genuine—but it is one of a number of faces that he can show.

This gets at the real heart of Troughton's take on the character, and the one that has been a recurring theme throughout this volume—the degree to which he is mercurial. This is, as readers of this project both astute and casual have probably noticed, a crucial concept in my take on Doctor Who. But here I mean it not only in the mystical sense I normally deal with, but in the most mundane and straightforward sense of the word. Troughton's Doctor is immensely changeable. More than any other take on the Doctor, he's defined by his ability to react in seemingly endless new and unpredictable ways.

As I've noted in the preceding pages, Troughton is an astonishingly active actor. He plays the Doctor so that every single line consists of him visibly and consciously doing something. This is something that good drama writers set up— one of the basic maxims you get taught when learning scriptwriting is that every line should have a clear verb behind it—something a character is actively trying to accomplish in saying the line. Doctor Who is often lax in this— understandable, given that it so often has to have characters delivering lengthy stretches of exposition, which is death to that sort of drama writing.

And yet Troughton is capable of picking up all of this slack. He's capable of making the Doctor into a character who is constantly animated and thinking. This is the heart of his charm—the fact that he's always, in every scene, delivering a compelling and arresting performance. And on top of this, he does it without stealing scenes or hamming things up. He compels in every scene in a way that elevates everyone else around him, giving them more material to work with and more opportunities to shine. They don't always—there are stories in which he's clearly just too good for this show. But more often Troughton drags a story, kicking and screaming, to glory.

In this regard, then, it's absolutely heartbreaking that his tenure is the one most ravaged by missing episodes. There's an essay earlier in the book in which I suggest what the most glaring and painful omissions from the archive are. But frankly, every frame of Troughton that's missing is a body blow. The episodes of his tenure that exist show just how much detail goes into his performance, and for all of that to be missing is absolutely gutting.

But worse are the ways in which the absence of so much of his tenure has made it far too easy for a default fan memory of the era to take hold. Because so much of the era is missing it's easy to focus on some of the louder aspects of the era—most infamously the various monsters. But to turn Troughton's tenure into a recitation of monsters is to overlook Troughton himself, just as the later caricature of him as the goofy professor in the reunion stories overlooks Troughton's actual portrayal of the character.

Troughton inherited, at the start of his tenure, what is very possibly the hardest job that anyone has done on Doctor Who in terms of acting. Troughton had to reinvent a defined part with no map for what that meant. If Troughton failed—if Troughton was anything less than absolutely spectacular—that would have been it for Doctor Who. And instead Troughton played the part with such panache, charm, and variety as to expand the concept of what "The Doctor" could be to something that could have nine more successors to him and counting. And yet we're infuriatingly prone to pretend that his era is more important for introducing the Yeti.

But in another sense this is the perfect image of Troughton. His Doctor always flitted around the edges of scenes. He's not an invisible presence by any measure, but he is a subtle one. He controls the events around him, but his control is almost imperceptible. He's a constantly whirring, shifting presence, corralling people into doing what he wants without ever making it obvious what he's doing. It would be a bridge too far to say that this works better on audio and in reconstructions— it manifestly doesn't—but there's a bitter and appropriate irony to the way in which so much of this is permanently erased and rendered invisible.

Still, one wishes that the chunk of Troughton we had the most of was a different one. It's not that Season Six, from which only seven episodes are missing, is bad. Much of it is great. But *The Dominators*, the second complete Troughton story we have, is very visibly the story where Troughton gives up on the part and starts establishing a "default" version of the Doctor that he can just phone in. That's not to say that there aren't great moments after that, and Troughton is particularly engaged in *The Mind Robber*, but it marks the start of a decline. Yes, the Trougthon/Jamie/Zoe TARDIS crew is delightful, but so are all of Troughton's crews.

Equally, though, I find it hard to miss the bulk of Season Five which, as I've noted, consists of dreadfully formulaic stories. The worst thing about its absence, to be honest, is that it's allowed people to perpetuate the absurd myth that *The Web of Fear* is the pinnacle of Patrick Troughton's tenure. No, for me the high-water mark of Troughton's Doctor—the points where he really shines—are across Season Four. While the missing episodes I think are the greatest losses mostly fall elsewhere, the truth of the matter is that the stories I most wish I could watch are the stretch from *The Power of the Daleks* to *The Evil of the Daleks*.

These are the stories where Troughton takes on the impossible acting job and figures it out. They're ones made under some of the most ludicrous time pressures imaginable— the production difficulties on *The Underwater Menace* meant that the remainder of Season Four was being shot with only a week's lead time before transmission. But as a result they're the ones where his Doctor is the most unpredictable. Even Troughton hadn't quite figured out what he was doing with the role in them. And yet his conviction never wavers in them. He remains utterly convincing across all of the facets we see. And so we get to see things we'd never seen before in the Doctor, and some things we wouldn't get to see again for decades, most obviously the actual menace behind the character in *The Macra Terror* and the two Dalek stories.

But what's really astonishing is that this is introduced alongside the prospect of an overtly humorous, clowning Doctor. We go from the downright dangerous Doctor of *The Power of the Daleks* to the silliest we've ever seen him in *The Highlanders*. Then we get Troughton brilliantly deciding not to compete with Joseph Furst's festival of ham, revealing yet another facet in *The Underwater Menace*. Then we get the "corners of the universe" speech in *The Moonbase*, which is altogether different again. And so on and so forth, showing entirely new perspectives on the character in story after story. And unlike the repetitiveness of Season Five or the running out of the clock in Season Six, virtually every story in Season Four is distinct from the ones on either side of it.

Even the trio of bases under siege are markedly different, with *The Moonbase* being the most straightforwardly "traditional" of them (indeed, so much so that it established the tradition), *The Macra Terror* being the most surreal (as giant crabs in a holiday camp will manage), and *The Faceless Ones* disguising its base under siege as a clever techno-thriller with an impressive late game twist. And Troughton finds new things to do in each one. Eventually it turns out that Troughton has more ideas for the program than the people writing it, and slowly but surely the swirling haze of mercury he entered with turns into the same post-psychedelia hangover that blighted the rest of the culture of the late 1960s.

But there, in the beginning, was one of the real wonders of Doctor Who. A show that, for a brief moment, was so much in flux that it seemed as though it could be anything. It's something the show could only be then, in that moment, and it was Patrick Troughton, one of the greatest actors of British television, who made it possible.

My Doctor.

About the Author

Elizabeth Sandifer lives in Ithaca, New York and writes about Doctor Who, British comics, and whatever else happens to be obsessing her at any given moment.

She blogs at eruditorumpress.com.

Made in the USA
Columbia, SC
13 August 2020